FLASH MOBILE

FLASH MOBILE
DEVELOPING ANDROID AND iOS APPLICATIONS

MATTHEW DAVID

ELSEVIER

AMSTERDAM • BOSTON • HEIDELBERG • LONDON • NEW YORK • OXFORD
PARIS • SAN DIEGO • SAN FRANCISCO • SINGAPORE • SYDNEY • TOKYO
Focal Press is an imprint of Elsevier

Focal Press is an imprint of Elsevier
30 Corporate Drive, Suite 400, Burlington, MA 01803, USA
The Boulevard, Langford Lane, Kidlington, Oxford, OX5 1GB, UK

Notices

Knowledge and best practice in this field are constantly changing. As new research and experience broaden our understanding, changes in research methods, professional practices, or medical treatment may become necessary.

Practitioners and researchers must always rely on their own experience and knowledge in evaluating and using any information, methods, compounds, or experiments described herein. In using such information or methods they should be mindful of their own safety and the safety of others, including parties for whom they have a professional responsibility.

To the fullest extent of the law, neither the Publisher nor the authors, contributors, or editors, assume any liability for any injury and/or damage to persons or property as a matter of products liability, negligence or otherwise, or from any use or operation of any methods, products, instructions, or ideas contained in the material herein.

ISBN: 978-0-240-81568-8

For information on all Focal Press publications
visit our website at www.elsevierdirect.com

11   12   13   14   15   5   4   3   2   1
Printed in the United States of America

Working together to grow
libraries in developing countries

www.elsevier.com | www.bookaid.org | www.sabre.org

ELSEVIER   BOOK AID
International   Sabre Foundation

Dedication

Life is comprised of moments. It is what is said and done in these "moments" that defines our lives. My family is forever blessed that the following people shared moments from their lives with us:

Dick and Anne: You both ran the gauntlet with us and we all made it through! We treasure your friendship in ways that words will never be enough.

Marcia, my "mom-in-law": You are always there, and you are always supporting us. We love you deeply.

Arthur: At the hardest time, you were there. I will never forget.

My deepest thanks I give to my wife and children. I love you, hon.

CONTENTS

Section 6

Companion website: www.visualizetheweb.com/flashmobile

AUTHOR'S NOTE

When I first used Flash, back in 1996 (it was called FutureSplash back then), the only place you saw Flash was in a web page. Today, Flash is in apps (thank you AIR), on phones (iPhones and Android), tablets (iPad and BlackBerry PlayBook), and even in your TV (hello Google TV!). It has come a long way and it feels like it is just getting started.

This book was a blast to write. The technology is fun, and developing for Android and iOS just feels right with Flash Professional.

There are a lot of great people I need to thank who helped in the creation of this book: first and foremost, Paul Temme, the guy who trusted my idea and saw that the book got the breath of life it needed; Carlin Reagan for pushing me to deliver on time; the good folks at Focal who laid out the content; and all the readers who sent e-mails and offered support. Thanks!

Always feel free to contact me with any questions: matthewadavid@gmail.com

Cheers,
Matthew David
November 5, 2010

FOREWORD

Change: It's what we expect from technology, from the PC to the web, through to HD TV. But nothing has been as disruptive as the change the iPhone and Android phones have brought. For the first time the power of a computer will fit in your hand, you are always connected to the Internet, and these devices are loaded with hardware such as video cameras, microphones, GPS chips, and accelerometers.

As a designer, the last few years have been both exciting and frustrating. Adapting to new technologies has come at a significant cost. For iOS development you need a Mac and a solid understanding of Objective-C; Android requires learning Java; and let's not even get started with this mobile web thing.

Then a funny thing happened on the way to the AT&T store to pick up an iPhone. Adobe had this teen-crazy idea: let's put Flash in your pocket. Unfortunately Apple was not going to have anything to do with it. No Flash on the iPhone for you! So, undaunted, Adobe did an end-around on Apple. If you could not play a Flash movie on the iPhone, why not create an app (containing a modified version of AIR) and stick the Flash content in that way?

Crazy idea? Yes. Did it work? You betcha!

The problem was Steve Jobs. He did not like this idea at all. In what has now become a famous open letter, Steve Jobs publicly decried Flash as a "yesteryear" technology and banished Flash apps from the iTunes App Store.

Undaunted by Mr. Jobs' comments, Adobe changed direction and brought Adobe Integrated Runtime to the Android, BlackBerry, and PalmOS operating systems. What must mean a lot of gnashing teeth over at Apple, Flash content performs very well on mobile devices. It is not slow, as Apple was making the world believe. In fact, it is a designer's dream. Now you can take the content you develop for the web and desktops and port it to an ever-increasing number of mobile devices. No need to learn Java, Objective-C, or any other language. You can just leverage your knowledge of Flash and ActionScript.

Android is fast catching up with Apple's early lead. In addition, other technologies such as Windows Phone 7 are proving to be compelling alternatives to iOS. The thumbscrews are being tightened on Apple.

And then Apple blinked. In a shocking turn of face, Apple changed its position on allowing Flash Professional built iOS apps in the iTunes App Store. I guess Flash is good enough after all.

The opportunity this presents you, as a designer, is unprecedented. Today's handheld phones are extremely powerful. You have to take care as you convert your content from the web to Android or iOS, but you can do it. In the future, as systems become more powerful, you will be able to directly port desktop AIR apps to your phone.

The focus of this book is to step you through what you need to know in order to be a successful iOS and Android app developer. You will learn how to build applications without using any code, how to add deep complexity with ActionScript, how to build games, and how to package your solutions for delivery in Apple's App Store and Google's Android Market.

Now is the time to learn and apply mobile development skills. Your computer is now resting in your hands.

SETTING UP FLASH CS5 FOR ANDROID DEVELOPMENT

Today, there are 5 billion people around the world using mobile phones. It is a staggering figure. No other technology is advancing at the rapid speed the mobile industry is experiencing. As a frame of reference, there are only 1.7 billion PCs being used around the world.

A new category of mobile phone is rapidly growing: the smart phone (Figure 1.1). Three years ago, a smart phone allowed you to send e-mail. Today, when you think smart phone, you think e-mail, web, games, MMS, video conferencing—you think of a computer in your pocket.

There are a number of companies leading the next wave of smart phone market. Google, Apple, RIM, Nokia, Microsoft, and HP (with Palm) all have their own operating systems and hardware. It seems almost every three to six months these companies leapfrog each other. Consider this—at the end of 2009, a mobile phone running at 500 MHz with a 3 MB camera was considered screaming fast. Now, you can pick up those same phones for less than $100. It you want

Figure 1.1 A small selection of smart phones.

something faster you go for 1 GHz with a 1 GB of RAM, an 8 MP camera, front and rear facing cameras, proximity devices up the wazoo, and sophisticated operating systems (OS) that rival, and in some cases exceed, what you can accomplish on your desktop. And in 2011, companies that make the ultra-efficient system-on-chip designs used in mobile phones such as Qualcomm's Snapdragon are headed to 2 GHz with multicore infrastructures housing accelerated GPUs, CPUs, and a ton of RAM.

This is not a mobile phone in your pocket. It is a screamingly fast computer.

With this all said, the smart phone market is still very small. You can take all the iPhones, Android phones (Figure 1.2), and BlackBerrys and you will have less than 300 million devices worldwide. With a global figure of 5 billion mobile users, it is clear that the smart phone market has massive potential for growth.

So, what does it mean to develop for a smart phone? At the end of the day, there are essentially two ways you can develop for a smart phone:

- Develop directly to the software development kit (SDK)
- Develop using an intermediate technology

Each mobile device comes with an SDK that you can use for development. An SDK comes with the development tools, bundling tools, and emulators you need to test your code. When you need access to the latest and greatest technology, you need to use an SDK.

Figure 1.2 A Samsung Android phone.

The challenge you have with using core SDKs is that you need to use the native development language. This is different for each SDK. For instance, Apple prefers you use Objective-C whereas Google prefers you use Java.

The second way to develop mobile devices is to use an intermediate technology that allows you to build for multiple devices using only one language. An example of this is the 3D game development technology called Unity 3D. Unity uses JavaScript to let you to script your games and then converts the JavaScript into code that will allow you to build iPhone, Android, and Windows Desktop applications. The downside to using intermediate technologies is that you are dependent on the development company to update their tools to the latest SDKs and technologies. This can be hard work as the SDKs are frequently updated. For instance, Apple has updated its iOS operating system four times in three years, and Google's Android has been updated five times in less than two years.

With that said, it is much easier to develop using intermediate languages. You can leverage skills you already have without having to go through the learning curve of adopting a new language.

In May 2010 at the Google I/O conference, Adobe announced that it would be bringing both the Flash Player and AIR (Adobe Integrated Runtime) to Google's Android 2.2. This is really big news for Flash developers for several reasons:

1. The version of Flash coming to the Android is the latest 10.1 version, not some crippled alternative.

Figure 1.3 Here you can see a collection of Android phones from different providers that are all capable of running Flash and AIR.

2. AIR gives you an immediate in-road into mobile device development, leveraging the tools and knowledge you already have.
3. Flash is coming to 19 other mobile device companies.
4. Android runs on tablets and TVs as well as phones.

The Flash Player that is now available for all Android 2.2 users, shown in Figure 1.3, is very efficient. There has been a lot of noise from companies such as Apple stating that Flash is a battery hog and will kill your phone's CPU. Is this true? The reality is that it is not. Tests have been conducted showing that the Flash Player on mobile devices is highly efficient and does not cause the CPU-crippling results Apple is stating. The Flash Player works inside the browser in Android. You trigger the use of the Flash Player by tapping on the Flash content in the web page. For instance, you can view a Hulu.com video by tapping on the content in the page.

Adobe's modification of AIR for mobile devices was the really big story at Google's I/O. AIR is a very powerful, mobile technology. It reaches for the same goals that Java set in the 1990s: write once, run anywhere. Unlike Java, AIR really achieves its goal. AIR apps are built in the Flash Professional development environment using Flash technologies you are already used to, such as ActionScript to program your solutions, MPEG video for video, and the same animation techniques you have been using for years.

Adobe's support for Flash on mobile devices will be coming to 19 other mobile development companies. This means that the techniques you learn in this book will be applicable beyond just Android. Other entities that will be adopting Adobe's technologies include RIM's BlackBerry, Nokia, HP/Palm WebOS, and Microsoft's Windows Phones Series 7. Notably absent is Apple, Inc. The year 2010 will go down as the year that Apple drew a line in the sand and said very publicly, "We will not support Adobe's Flash." It is a shame that Apple has made this stance, since Apple's iOS is a very important part of the mobile market. Let's hope it changes its mind.

Earlier I mentioned how rapidly the mobile market is growing. Today, that market is predominantly composed of phones; but there are additional tools joining this market. During 2010, Apple released the massively popular iPad, a tablet computer that is very mobile and very light. Not to be outdone, rival companies, such as Nvidia, Samsung, Dell, and Cisco, are also coming out with their own tablets. The devices range in size from 5 inches all the way up to 11 inches and beyond. What they all share is that they are running Android as their OS. They come prepackaged with support for Flash.

Another device that is coming out of the mobile world is Google TV. At its essence, Google TV is really a modified version

Figure 1.4 The Archos Android tablet runs Flash and AIR.

of Android that runs directly on your TV. And, yes, your Flash apps will run here, too. Last year you could run your Flash applications only on Windows and Mac computers. Today you can add smart phones, tablets, and TVs. Your Flash can literally go with you wherever you want to go.

It is not all roses, of course. To get your Flash apps running in AIR on all these new devices, Adobe did choose to make one big change: You must develop your solutions using ActionScript 3.0 (AS3). AS3 has been around since 2006. If you have not made the jump to AS3, then I will help you as we step through this book. You can no longer leverage the older AS1 and AS2 scripts that you have been using for years. Time to start fresh.

The first section of the book explains how a Flash designer can set up a Flash CS5 environment to publish Android apps. Later you will step through the process of downloading, installing, and running the Android SDK, necessary for your development. By the end of this section you will have created your first Android application using Flash CS5. At the end of this book you will have the knowledge to build almost any type of Flash-based application for the Android OS 2.2 and greater. How cool is that?

So, let's get started.

Designing and Developing for Android Hardware

Before we get involved with setting up your design and development environment, let's take a little time to review how you should approach developing applications that run on an Android device.

There are a number of design considerations you always want to keep in the back of your mind as you work on your apps. They are:
- Different hardware
- Hardware acceleration
- Touch interaction

An Android phone is simply very different than a desktop, and you need to develop your app to take advantage of these differences.

Working with Android Hardware

The Android platform has been available for less than two years. In that time it has gone from being available on a few phones to being installed on dozens of different phones available on almost every mobile carrier. Today there are over 50 different mobile phones running Android OS 1.5 and greater. Flash is supported on all phones that run Android 2.2. Table 1.1 gives you a list of the Android phones that currently support Flash and AIR. The table is broken down by manufacturer, name of the phone, screen display (where available), and additional notes about the phone.

You can see from the devices listed in Table 1.1 that there is a broad range of hardware specifications for Android phones.

The number one hardware difference you will need to keep in mind is screen size. The default screen size for Android development is 320 × 480 ppi (points per inch) but, as you can see from the list, this is not always the case. Screen resolutions range from 240 × 320 for the HTC Wildfire all the way up to 854 × 480 for the Motorola Droid X. How do you design apps for this broad range? The trick comes in how you use Flash to do the work for you. We will be getting into that in more detail as you work your way through the book. Just keep in mind that not all Android phones are created equal.

In addition to screen size, the second feature that you will find different from one device to another is RAM and CPU. The more RAM you have determines how much data can be crunched with active apps. The multitasking feature in Android allows for six core apps to be running simultaneously. But you may have many more utilities running. To run more applications will require more RAM. Current smart phones have 256 MB of RAM, with others having as much as 1 GB of RAM. Future devices will have RAM levels that rival desktop computers. For now, however, develop applications that carefully manage the amount of RAM you use.

The CPU listed earlier is slightly misleading. Almost all smart phones are developed with a system-on-chip design (SOC). An SOC merges the CPU, GPU, RAM, and other systems into one chip. This architecture is typically built on ARM CPUs. The ARM architecture is highly energy efficient, allowing mobile phone batteries to last longer. Intel, Nvidia, and AMD are also starting to join the ultra-efficient mobile chip market. At first, the original

Table 1.1 Android Phones That Support Flash and AIR

Manufacturer	Name	Display	Notes
Acer Inc	Liquid E	320 × 480	Smart phone with underclocked 768 MHz Snapdragon processor.
Acer Inc	Liquid E Ferrari	320 × 480	A customized version of Liquid E with Ferrari visual styling.
Acer Inc	beTouch E400	320 × 480	SIM-free smart phone with a 600 MHz CPU, 3.2″ resistive touch screen, and a 3.1 MP camera.
Acer Inc	Liquid Stream (S110)	320 × 480	1 GHz SnapDragon CPU, 3.7″ AMOLED WVGA capacitive touch screen, 5 MP camera.
Dell	Thunder	320 × 480	4.1″ WVGA OLED screen, and an 8 MP camera.
Dell	Flash	320 × 480	3.5″ WVGA LCD screen, 5 MP autofocus cam, 512 MB of RAM and ROM with microSD expansion up to 64 GB, WiFi, TV-out, an 800 MHz Qualcomm MSM7230 processor.
Dell	Smoke	320 × 480	2.8″ QVGA touch screen, 5 MP autofocus cam, microSD expansion to 32 GB, WiFi, Bluetooth, and an 800 MHz Qualcomm MSM7230 processor.
HTC Corporation	HTC Aria	480 × 320 (HVGA) 3.2″	A mid-range AT&T exclusive, running on Android 2.1 with HTC Sense; uses 600 MHz MSM 7227 processor, 5 MP camera; similar to HTC Legend.
HTC Corporation	HTC Desire	480 × 800 (WVGA) 3.7″	Similar to Nexus One but adds HTC's Sense UI Optical trackpad and Hard buttons, but does not have dual microphones as the Nexus One.
HTC Corporation	HTC Hero, HTC Droid Eris, T-Mobile G2 Touch in Ireland, the UK, Hungary, The Netherlands, and Germany	320 × 480 3.2″ 180 ppi	The Hero has two design versions. The original design is similar form factor to the Magic; the U.S. release design is more curved at the edges and has the controversial "chin" removed. Both use HTC's customized UI called HTC Sense, which looks considerably different compared to HTC Dream and Magic phones.
HTC Corporation	Droid Incredible	800 × 480 3.7″ AMOLED	Successor to the HTC Droid Eris; sports an 8.0 MP camera with dual-flash LED, FM radio tuner, and 8 GB onboard flash memory, 3.7″ AMOLED screen, native resolution of 480 × 800 px.

Continued

Table 1.1 Android Phones That Support Flash and AIR—continued

Manufacturer	Name	Display	Notes
HTC Corporation	HTC Legend	480 × 320 (HVGA) 3.2" AMOLED	Announced at Mobile World Congress 2010 in Barcelona.
HTC Corporation	HTC Evo 4G (formerly HTC Supersonic)	480 × 800 4.3" 217 ppi	A high-end Android phone, includes the HTC Sense UI, similar form factor to the Droid Incredible and HTC HD2. Contains many advanced phone features, including an 8 MP rear-facing camera along with a 1.3 MP front-facing camera. The Evo 4G is currently (as of 5/22/10) the only phone to offer 4G Internet access (currently using Clearwire WiMAX).
HTC Corporation	Google Nexus One, Codenamed HTC Dragon, HTC Passion	480 × 800 (WVGA) 3.7" 252 ppi	The first phone to be sold directly by Google, the Nexus One was initially available exclusively online, unlocked. It can now be bought on subsidized contract with various networks.
HTC Corporation	myTouch 3G Slide	320 × 480 (HVGA) 3.4"	5 MP camera, QWERTY four-row keyboard, and a Swype on-screen keyboard.
HTC Corporation	HTC Wildfire	240 × 320 (QVGA) 3.2"	5 MP autofocus camera with LED flash, 802.11b/g WiFi, GPS/AGPS, Bluetooth 2.1+EDR, 512 MB Flash and 384 MB of RAM, microSD expansion.
Motorola	Motorola Droid, Motorola Milestone worldwide GSM version	854 × 480 3.7" 265 ppi	
Motorola	Motorola Droid X	854 × 480 4.3"	
Motorola	MOTO XT720, Motoroi, Motorola Milestone XT720	320 × 480	8 MP camera(Flash), HDMI, FM radio, T-DMB, available only in Korea.
Pantech	Sirius Sky	480 × 800 (WVGA) 3.7"	1 GHz Snapdragon processor, 3.7" (WVGA 480 × 800, AMOLED), 5 MP camera, WiFi, Bluetooth, GPS, and microSD expansion.
Pantech	Sirius Izar	480 × 800 (WVGA) 3.7"	Qualcomm MSM7227(600 MHz), 3.2" (WVGA 480 × 800, LCD), 5 MP camera (AF), WiFi, Bluetooth T-DMB and microSD expansion.

Table 1.1 Android Phones That Support Flash and AIR—continued

Manufacturer	Name	Display	Notes
Pantech	Sirius Alpha	480 × 800 (WVGA) 3.7"	Minor upgrade of Sirius Sky.
Samsung Group	Galaxy A	3.7" AMOLED	5 MP camera, T-DMB, GPS, Bluetooth, 802.11n Wi-Fi, and video calling. Will be available only in South Korea.
Samsung Group	i9200	320 × 480	4.3" AMOLED 1280 × 720, 2 GHz CPU, 1 GB RAM, 4 GB ROM, 32 GB flash, microSD oraz 8 MP primary camera + 2.0 secondary camera
Samsung Group	Galaxy S	480 × 800 (WVGA) 4.0" Super AMOLED	1 GHz processor

SOCs in the 2007/2008 smart phone market were very slow compared to a PC. Today, however, it is common to have a 1 GHz CPU/SOC with 2 GHz multicore SOCs shipping 2011. For a good Flash/AIR experience you need to be running a 1 GHz CPU/SOC architecture. The Motorola Droid runs at 500 MHz, and can run Flash, but you are better off testing with an HT Evo, Nexus One, or Motorola Droid X, all of which run at 1 GHz or faster.

Android Hardware Acceleration

Phones come loaded with technology in the hardware. This is awesome for you as a developer. Following are some key hardware technologies that you will want to keep in mind as you develop for the Android OS:

* Touch-sensitive screen
* Sound/microphone
* Vibration
* Camera
* GPS
* Accelerometer/compass

The touch-sensitive screen seems like an obvious hardware feature, but it is your main input to your device and you use your finger. More on that in a moment.

Every Android phone supports audio, both to listen through speakers and to record with a microphone. We will cover audio in more detail later in the book, but you will want to keep your audio files in MP3 and WAV format. Unlike desktop computers, where you cannot guarantee if there is a microphone installed by the manufacturer, you can guarantee that there is a mic on every Android device. Why? It's a phone! You need one to speak through when you make calls.

Haptic feedback is the method by which you can provide vibrations to the end user through the phone. This is good for situations where the audio is turned off; the app is designed for the deaf or hard of hearing. You can also add vibration to games to add to the overall sensory experience.

All Android phones come with a camera, with many of them supporting video and LED flash.

A Global Positioning System (GPS) allows you to create solutions that are dependent on location. Want to develop an app that shows you the movie theater nearest to your current location? Use GPS to do the location work for you.

Accelerometers and compass hardware detect when the phone is being moved and in which direction along three distinct axes (X, Y, and Z). Expect newer phones to start shipping with gyroscopes to add three more axes (pitch, yaw, and roll). These three hardware features give you pinpoint control over your game development. Think Wii Remote, but for phones.

These hardware features highlight the main tools you use from the Android hardware. Adobe's Flash will interact with all of these special hardware features.

Touching Your Application

In the previous section we talked about using touch as the way you interact with Android. This is a very important concept as you look to develop solutions for the Android OS. No matter what Steve Jobs will tell you, a finger is simply not as accurate as a stylus. It is, however, much more convenient to use.

In addition to the actual size of the input area you develop in your solutions, you will also want to bear in mind that not all touch screens are created the same. The apps you will create in this book are designed to work on all touch screens, no matter what the device. If, however, your application requires very accurate touches and gestures, such as swipe, then you will want to test on several of the devices listed earlier. This is because vendors use different touch screens. Some are more accurate than others.

Configuring the Android SDK Publish Setting

The core of your development completed in this book requires only the use of Flash CS5. To test your applications you will need to have the Android SDK installed on your computer. The SDK will allow you to complete the following:

- Run command line Flash build tools
- Test your Android App in an emulator
- Install your Android onto a physical device

Installing the Android SDK is not something to fear; you just need to follow the steps. For the most part, Google has made this a rather painless experience. This section will take you through what you need to do to install Android onto your development computer.

The first thing you need to do is see if your development environment will support the Android SDK. The minimum requirements are:

- Windows XP (32-bit) or Vista (32- or 64-bit)
- Mac OS X 10.5.8 or later (x86 only)
- Linux (tested on Linux Ubuntu Hardy Heron)

You will want to also ensure that your computer is fairly fast. I run my development on an iMac with 4 GB of RAM and 2.2 core duo CPU. This works great for me. If your computer is new within the last three years, then you should be fine. In addition, you will need about 300 MB of hard drive space to install all the software.

The next step before you even get to installation is to ensure that you have the latest Java Developer Kit (JDK). Version 5 or 6 will work. You can download the latest JDK at *http://java.sun.com/ javase/downloads/index.jsp*. The Android SDK will not install if you do not have the JDK installed.

Now, to download and install the Android SDK:

1. Start by going to *http://developer.android.com/sdk/index. html* and downloading the latest SDK release (a ZIP file; Figure 1.5).
2. Save the SDK to your hard drive.
3. From the root of your computer, create a folder called Developer. Unzip the files from the Android SDK to this folder. There will be a lot of files.
4. Open the Developer folder. Click the subfolder called Android and then the folder called Tools.
5. Double-click the file called Android to access the Android SDK and AVD manager. The role of the Android SDK manager is to allow you to download and install Android SDK releases (Figure 1.6).
6. When the Android SDK and AVD Manager opens, select Available Packages on the left screen. You should see a link to an XML file with a check mark to the left of it. If you do not see anything, choose the Refresh button.
7. Select the check mark.

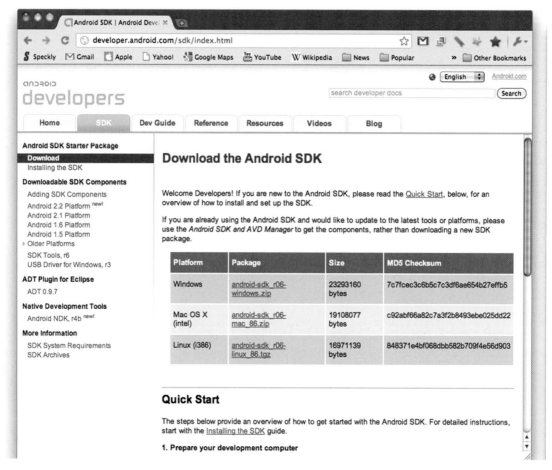

Figure 1.5 Google's Android SDK site.

8. The Android SDK will check which SDKs are available for testing. You will see SDKs for Android Platforms 1.5, 1.6, 2.1, and 2.2.

9. Select the check marks alongside the Android 2.2 SDK. Choose the Install Selected button.

10. The files will download and install onto your computer. This may take some time depending on the speed of your Internet connection.

When you have completed the installation you will have all the files and tools needed to test your Flash applications in Android simulators or on a physical Android device.

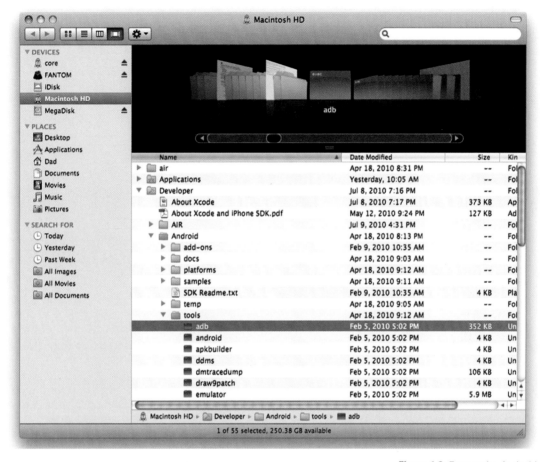

Figure 1.6 Extract the Android SDK to your hard drive.

Setting up Flash CS5 for Android Development

Adobe is going to great lengths to make is very easy for you to develop Android applications. To this end, you can now develop Android applications with either Flex or Flash CS5 Professional. Flex development requires the use of a command line utility to make the final Android application.

I hate command lines. So, to make life easier, you can stick with Flash CS5 Professional. This is how we will be building applications for Android throughout this book.

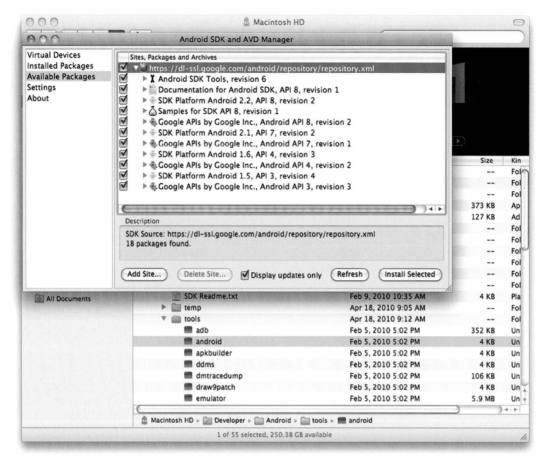

Figure 1.7 You only need to download Android 2.2.

Flash CS5 does not ship with native support for Android. Ironically, it does ship with support for iPhone development—but you cannot publish to the Apple iTunes Store. Trust me, I have tried and failed.

You will need to install the tools needed for Flash CS5 to create files for Android. Follow these steps to install the Android tools you need:

1. You must be running the latest release version of Flash CS5 Professional. Run Adobe update tool to ensure that you have the latest patches and updates.
2. If you have Flash CS5 running you will want to close it.
3. Go to Adobe's AIR for Android web page at *http://labs.adobe.com/technologies/air2/android/* and download the MXI file.
4. Open the Adobe Extension Manager installed on your computer. Open the MXI file and choose install (Figure 1.8).

Figure 1.8 Extract the Android SDK to your hard drive.

That's it. You now have all the tools needed to build your first Android application with Flash CS5 Professional.

Installing Your AIR Application onto an Android OS

Flash uses AIR to create your applications for Android. By default, AIR is not installed on the Android phone. This does not stop you from installing your new app, it will simply stop you from running it.

Fortunately, AIR is freely available in the Google Marketplace. If your phone does not have AIR installed you will be prompted to download and install it from the Marketplace. There are no complex hoops to jump through. If you have installed one app, then you know how to install AIR and enjoy all the Flash apps in the Marketplace.

Building Your First Application for Android Using Flash CS5

The goal for your first Android application is a simple one: to get a basic Flash movie running successfully on your Android phone. The following steps will take you through the whole process, at the end of which you will have your first native Android application created using Flash tools. The next section explains how to install the Android Application onto your device.

1. Begin by opening Flash CS5. Select File → New to open the new file window.
2. Select Template from the top button of the new file window (Figure 1.9).

Figure 1.9 Flash CS5 has a template for Android applications.

3. Choose AIR for Android from the left category window. On the right hand side you will see 480x800Android. Select OK (Figure 1.10).
4. To keep things simple, we are going to create all we need for a simple test. Save your file to your hard drive. Name the file FirstApp.fla.
5. On the Stage use the text tool to draw a text region. Android does not support the new TLF text. Change the text format to Classic Text (Figure 1.11).
6. Set the font Family to _sans.
7. Change the font size to 20.
8. With the text field still selected, change the text type to Dynamic Text.
9. Give the text field an ID of txt.
10. Open the Actions window and add the following ActionScript. The goal for this is to show you that the ActionScript you have

Figure 1.10 Currently there is only the AIR for Android template, but you can create your own for tablet devices.

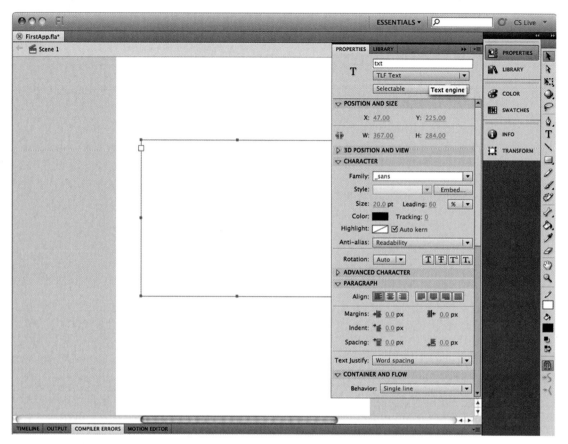

Figure 1.11 Use text tools that you are already familiar with in Flash.

been using all along will work. Enter the following ActionScript (Figure 1.12):

txt.text = "hello, world";

11. At this point you can test your Flash movie by pressing CTRL+ENTER. The movie should show you the text "hello, world" on your screen.

12. The next steps are to convert the Flash movie into an Android application.

13. Select the Stage and choose the Properties panel. In the Profile section you will see AIR for Android Settings. Select the Edit… button (Figure 1.13).

14. The Application and Installer options window will open. Across the top of the window you will see three buttons, General, Deployment, and Icons, that toggle three different settings windows (Figure 1.14).

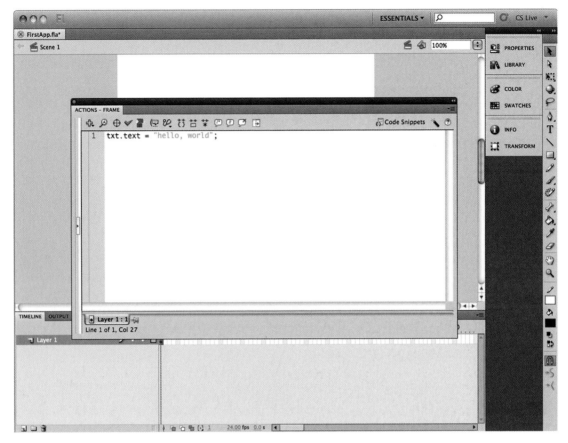

Figure 1.12 Add dynamic content using ActionScript.

15. The General button shows you the following settings:
    - Output file
    - App name
    - App ID
    - Version
    - Aspect ratio
    - Full screen
    - Auto orientation
    - Included files
16. The Output file is the location of the final file that will be installed on your Android device. The file format for Android apps is APK. For this example you can keep the default filename. It should be called FirstApp.apk, and will save to the same folder as your Flash FLA file.
17. The App name is the name of the app as it will appear on the Android phone. The default is to use the name of the FLA file. Change the name to My First App.

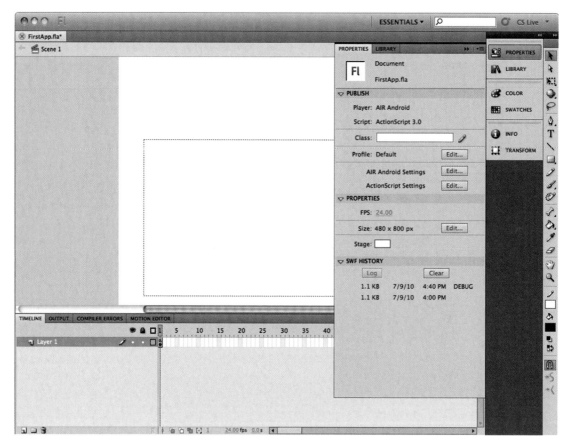

Figure 1.13 The Android application is created using special publish settings.

18. The App ID is used when you publish your app to the Marketplace. For now you can keep the default, FirstApp.
19. The version number allows you to add a version number to your Android app. It is up to you how you want to number your versions.
20. The Aspect ratio forces the default presentation of your Android app into either Landscape or Portrait. For now, keep the Aspect ratio as Portrait. Later, when you develop your first games, you will learn how to design for Landscape aspect ratio.
21. Select the checkbox for Full screen. The Full screen setting forces the application to use up the whole screen and hide the status bar on the Android phone.
22. Do not select the Auto orientation checkbox. Auto orientation will allow the app to rotate as you rotate your phone.

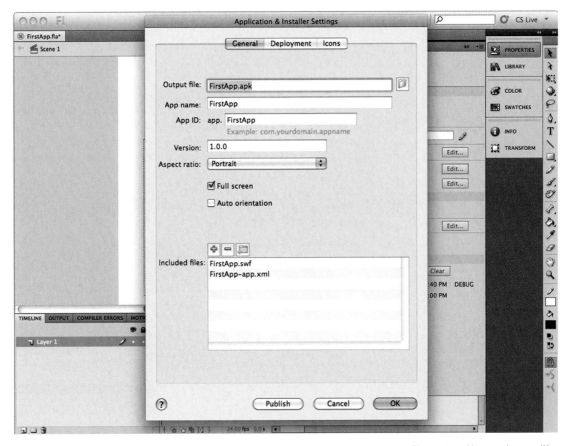

Figure 1.14 You need to modify three screens to create your Android apps.

23. The Included files section allows you to add additional files into your final APK package. This can include files such as video, audio, and other SWF movies. You do not need to worry about that at this time.

24. Now, select the Deployment button to go to Deployment screen (Figure 1.15).

Each AIR app you build for Android requires a certificate. For development purposes you can use the same certificate over and over. Let's create a Developer certificate.

25. Select the Create button. A new screen will open, asking you for additional information for the certificate.

26. For Publisher Name, Organization Unit, and Organization Name, insert Self. This is not a magical term, you can really enter anything you want.

27. Select the country from the drop-down menu.

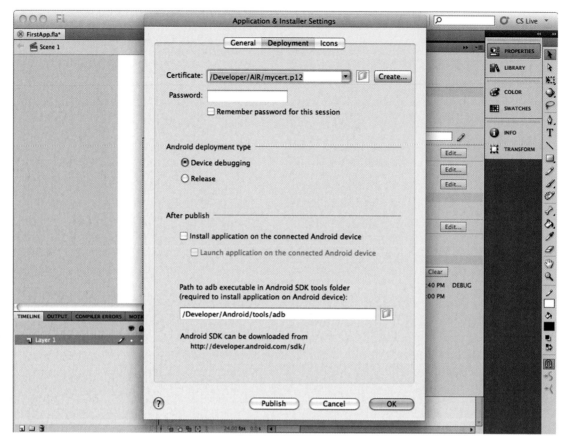

Figure 1.15 The Deployment tab controls how you build your application for Android.

28. Enter a password. Make sure you remember the password because you will need to use it for future applications.

29. You can use the default 1024-RSA certificate strength.

30. The default validity period is 25 years (Figure 1.16). That should be good enough for what we are doing.

31. Select the folder where you would like to store the certificate. The certificate will default to the file name mycert.p12.

32. Select OK. A window will pop up stating that a "Self signed certificate has been generated." Select OK.

33. You will go back to the Deployment window. Enter your password. Choose the Remember password for this session checkbox. While you have this FLA file open, you will not need to keep re-adding the password each time you compile the file.

34. The Android deployment type option allows you to choose Device debugging or Release. For now, select the Device debugging option.

35. Flash can install the final APK file directly onto your Android device for you. This where you need to have the downloaded

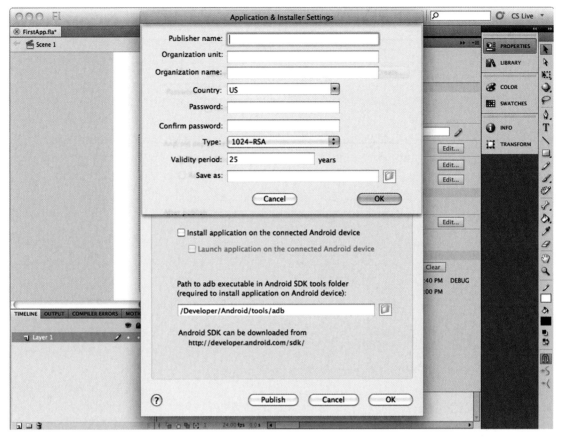

Figure 1.16 A certificate is valid for 25 years.

Android SDK. The After publish section will install the Application on your device but you need to have the Android SDK ADB tools. You can find the ADP tools within the Android SDK's Tools folder.

36. Don't worry about icons at this time.

37. Select the Publish button.

38. The app is small and should take only about 15 seconds to publish. You have now created an APK file and, if you selected the install options, you now have your first Android app running on your phone. How cool is that? Knuckle punch!

At this point you have your first application running on your Android phone. The good news is, now that you have one application running you do not need to go through the hard work of installing JRE, Android SDK, AIR for Android, or a Developer's certificate again. You have done the hard work. Now you can focus on creating great AIR solutions with Flash CS5 for the Android platform.

PROJECT: CREATING YOUR FIRST APP USING FLASH CS5

In the first section of the book we looked at setting up your Flash environment to work with Android. You also looked at design considerations you should bear in mind when developing Android apps. The goal of this project is to bring these two things together.

During this project you will apply the following:
- Set up a default AIR for Android file
- Develop background image details for the Android app
- Work with embedded text
- Create icons for your project
- Test your application on your Android device

The goal of this section is to validate how easily you can build your Android applications. There should be no heartaches when it comes to Android development and I think you are going to be very pleased with how fast you pick it up.

Setting up Your Development Environment

Throughout this book you will go through the steps needed to create a new Android application. Following this project, I am going to make an assumption that you know enough about the default setup, and will not need me to run through this process each time. Phew, you won't need to keep hearing me say, "Download the Android SDK...." We can just focus on the fun stuff.

For now, let's step through the whole process.

Before you get started you will need a physical Android device to test with. This is essential for your development in this book. You can either buy an unlocked phone that is not connected to a carrier or drop the pennies to buy your own Android phone from any of the many mobile carriers. Remember, your phone must be

27

running Android 2.2. There are a lot of cheap Android phones on the market that are running Android 1.6. AIR and Flash are supported only on Android 2.2 and later (Figure 1.1Proj).

Your development environment also needs to be either Windows or Macintosh OS X 10.5+.

Figure 1.1Proj Android 2.2, codename Froyo, is Flash friendly.

With your Android 2.2 device in hand, let's set up your development environment.

1. Start by going to the Android development site at *http://developer.android.com/index.html*, as shown in Figure 1.2Proj.
2. Select the SDK tab along the top of the page.

Figure 1.2Proj All the Android code you need is at developer.android.com.

3. You will need to download either Windows or Mac OS X (Intel) versions of the SDK. At this time, there is not a Linux version of Flash that allows you to develop AIR for Android apps. (Figure 1.3Proj).

4. The Android SDK will download in a ZIP file. Save this to your computer.

Figure 1.3Proj The latest Android SDKs can be downloaded for Windows, Mac, and Linux.

5. Create a new folder in the root of your main hard drive and name the file Developer.
6. Open and extract the files in the Android SDK to the Developer folder you just created (Figure 1.4Proj).

At this point you have all the files you need from Google. Let's direct our attention to Flash CS5. To get started with AIR for

Figure 1.4Proj Extract the files for the Android SDK to your local hard drive.

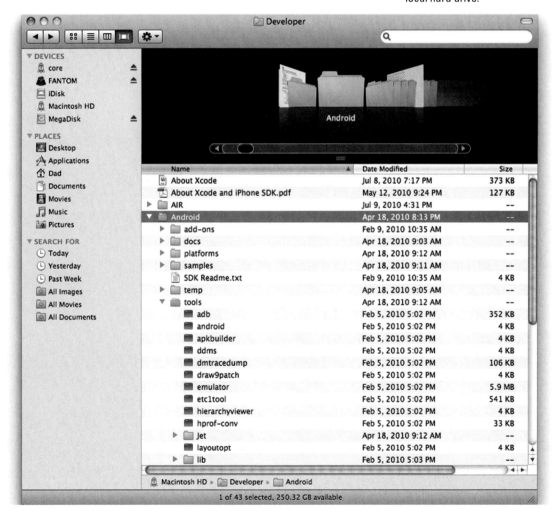

Android you will need the latest version of Flash CS5. When you have Flash CS5 installed, jump over to *http://labs.adobe.com/technologies/air2/android/* to download and install the Android MXI extensions for Flash CS5 (Figure 1.5Proj).

Figure 1.5Proj Adobe's AIR for Android files can be downloaded from its labs site.

Close Flash CS5 before starting your first AIR for an Android project. Follow these steps to get up and running:

1. Open Flash CS5.
2. From Create from Template, open the splash screen and select AIR for Android (Figure 1.6Proj).
3. Choose the default AIR for Android template from the New from Template window (Figure 1.7Proj).
4. Select the OK button. Your default, blank Android file is ready for you. At this point you now work on the fun bit of creating your Flash content (Figure 1.8Proj).
5. Save your file as AndroidWelcomeMessage.xfl.

Figure 1.6Proj The AIR for Android template has all the settings you need for your Android app.

Figure 1.7Proj Android templates you can choose from.

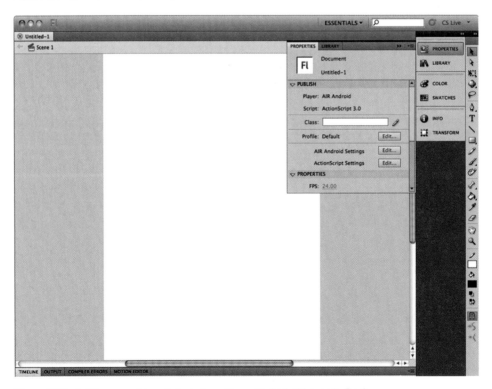

Figure 1.8Proj All you need to get started working with Android apps in Flash.

Creating the Graphics

Let's get started on the graphics you need for your Flash movie. As mentioned in the previous chapter, the best format for creating graphics in Android apps is the PNG bitmap format. Luckily for you, one of the best PNG image editors is Adobe's Fireworks. Fireworks is packaged with the CS5 Web Suite of tools. This means you already have all the tools you need installed on your computer.

If you do not have Fireworks installed you can download a 30-day evaluation copy from Adobe.com. The project you are going to build is very simple: You will create an icon of the Android logo that you can select.

Go to the accompanying website for this book, www.visualizetheweb.com/flashmobile, to download the files used in this book. Project 1 will have a graphics file labeled google_android.png. You can open this image with Fireworks.

The image is fine as is (Figure 1.9Proj). You will, however, need three icons for your final app. Let's go ahead and create those now.

Figure 1.9Proj A PNG graphic of the Android logo in Adobe's Fireworks.

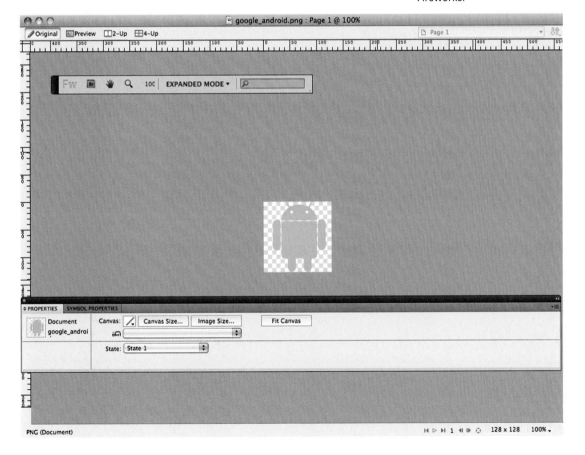

1. The three icons you need to create are 72 × 72, 48 × 48, and 36 × 36 pixels.
2. Select the Android logo. Open the properties panel. Change the X and Y properties to 0.
3. Change the size of the logo to width 52 and height 72 pixels.
4. Select Modify → Canvas Size. The Canvas Size screen opens. Change the width and height to 72 × 72 pixels (Figure 1.10Proj).
5. Save your file as Android_logo_72.png.
6. Repeat this process for 48 × 48 and 36 × 36 pixel icons, and name the files Android_logo_48.png and Android_logo_36.png, respectively. There is no magic to how the files are numbered. This is just an easier way to remember what each file does.

At this point you have all of the graphics you need for your first application.

Figure 1.10Proj Use Fireworks to create the image icons for the final application.

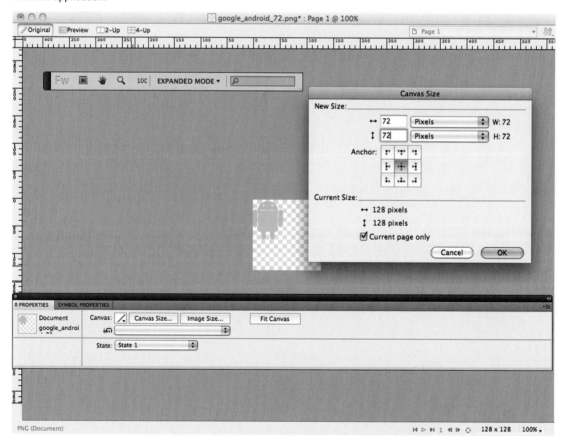

Building an Application

Now, let's get down to the fun part: building applications.

1. Open Flash CS5, if you do not still have it open, and open the AndroidWelcomeMessage.xfl Flash movie.
2. Select File → Import → Important to Stage…
3. The Import window will open. Navigate to the folder containing your images. Select google_android.png, as shown in Figure 1.11Proj.
4. The Import Fireworks Document window opens. Select Import as a single flattened bitmap. Choose OK (Figure 1.12Proj).

Figure 1.11Proj Import the PNG file you need for the application.

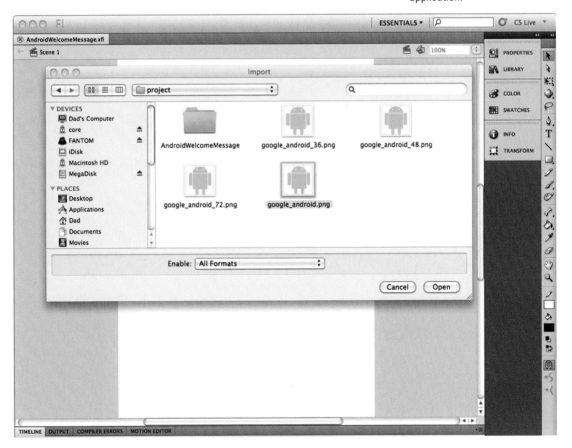

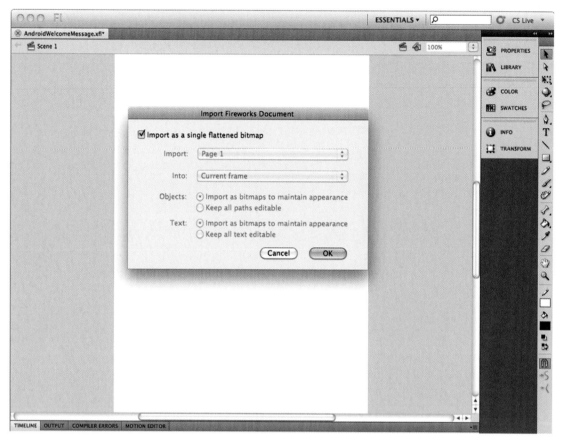

Figure 1.12Proj Flatten the imported Fireworks PNG image.

5. Select CTRL+K (Windows) or CMD+K (Mac) to open the Align panel. Select Align to stage and center the imported image (Figure 1.13Proj).
6. Change the pointer tool to the text tool.
7. On the Stage, below the Android image, draw a rectangular text region. Open the properties panel and change the text type to TLF, read only, set the color to black and the font size to 40. Don't forget to change the line setting to multiline.
8. Name the new text field myText (Figure 1.14Proj).

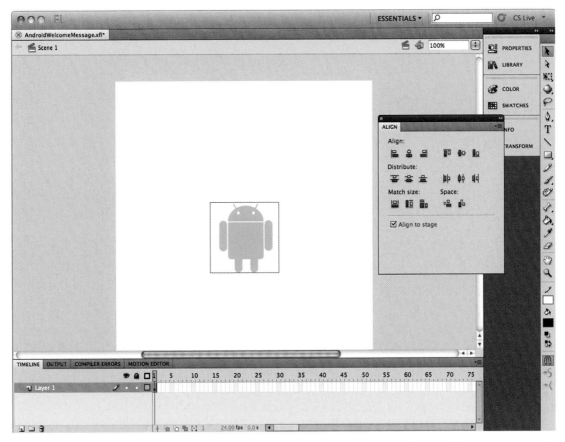

Figure 1.13Proj You can use all the image manipulation tools in Flash, such as Align, in your Android apps.

9. Right-click the Android image on the Stage. Select Convert to Symbol.
10. Name the new symbol android_image as shown in Figure 1.15Proj.
11. The image is now a movie clip. With the Android movie clip still selected, open the Properties panel. Name the movie clip android_Btn (Figure 1.16Proj).
12. Open the Actions panel.

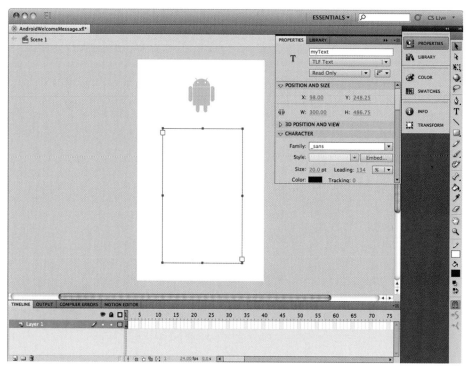

Figure 1.14Proj You can use the new TLF text on Android phones.

Figure 1.15Proj As you might expect, you can use Flash symbols in your Android apps.

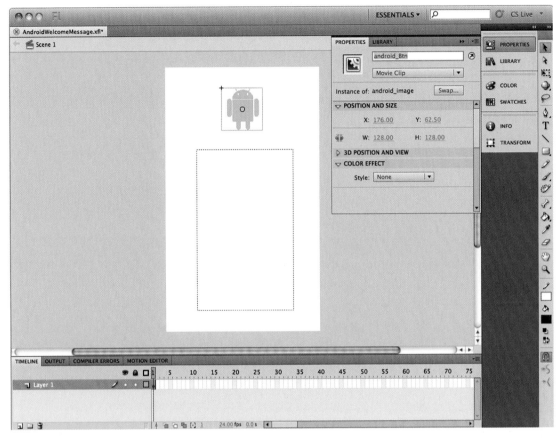

13. Select Frame one from the timeline. In the Actions panel add the following ActionScript (Figure 1.17Proj):

```
var theDate:Date = new Date( );
var day = theDate.toLocaleDateString();
android_Btn.addEventListener(MouseEvent.CLICK, onClick);
function onClick(event:MouseEvent):void
{
myText.text = "Welcome to Android App development using
Flash CS5. \n \nThe date of your first app is: " + day;
}
```

Figure 1.16Proj A named movie clip can be referenced in ActionScript.

14. The first line of this script defines a date object; the second line captures the date as a string object.

15. Line three associates a mouse click event with the android_btn object on the stage. A single tap is treated the same as a single click on the mouse.

16. Line 6 generates a message that is posted to the text object when you press the Android icon.

17. Press CTRL+ENTER (Windows) or CMD+ENTER (Mac) to test the application. Click on the Android icon to reveal a message, as shown in Figure 1.18Proj.

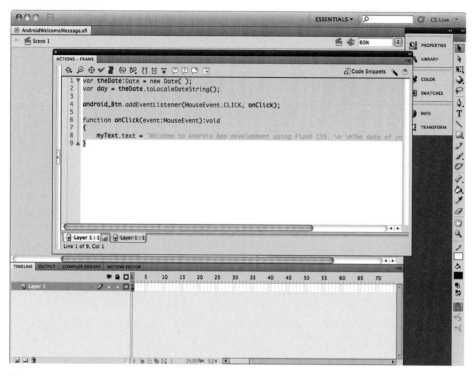

Figure 1.17Proj You will use a little ActionScript to test that AS3 will work on your Android phone.

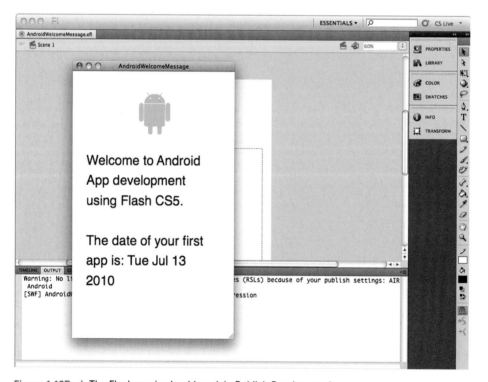

Figure 1.18Proj The Flash movie should work in Publish Preview mode.

The Flash movie you have created is simple, but it contains all the elements of any large and complex movie: you have ActionScript and images, and you use the timeline. Now you need to publish your app as an Android solution.

Running Your App on Your Android Phone

The final step is to publish your Flash movie as an Android application.

1. Select the Stage and open the Properties panel.
2. In the Publish section, select AIR Android Settings (Figure 1.19Proj).
3. The Application & Installer Settings window opens. For now, keep the default settings on the General tab (Figure 1.20Proj).

Figure 1.19Proj The AIR Android Settings control how you build your Android app.

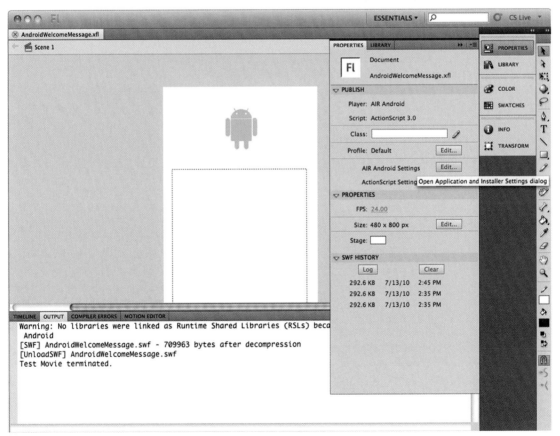

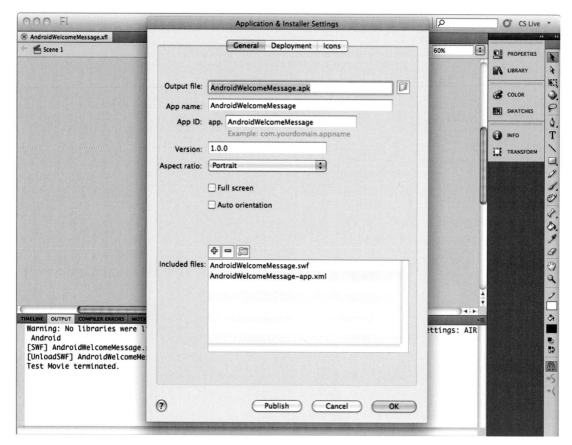

Figure 1.20Proj The name of your app and the filename are two of the settings on the General tab.

4. Select the Deployment tab, as shown in Figure 1.21Proj. The Certificate setting should be the same setting you created during the first chapter of the book.

5. Enter your password and check the Remember password for this session checkbox.

6. Connect your Android device to your computer. Select Install application on the connected Android device.

7. Check Launch application on the connected Android device.

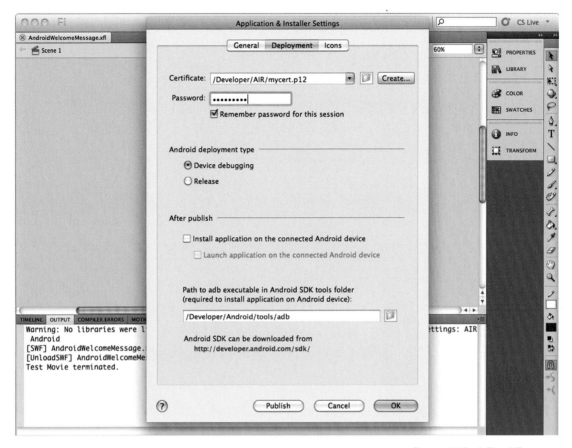

Figure 1.21Proj The AIR Android Settings control how you build your Android app.

8. Select the Icons tab. Select each icon in the list. Use the folder button to find and connect each icon you created earlier (Figure 1.22Proj).

9. Select the Publish button. The publishing process will take a couple of minutes depending on the speed of your computer. The final results will be a running app on your Android phone. Click the icon to bring up the message.

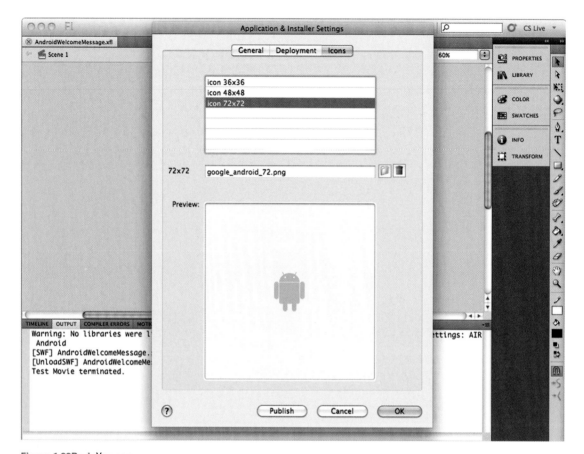

Figure 1.22Proj You can
associate three different
sized icons for your Android
applications.

You have created your first complete Android application
using Adobe's Flash CS5. In this chapter you learned how to
install the Android SDK, update Flash CS5 with AIR for Android,
and you created your first application that is now running on
your Android phone. Well done!

In the next section you will expand on what can be accomplished in AIR for Android by leveraging animation, video, audio,
and components.

RAPID ANDROID DEVELOPMENT IN FLASH CS5

Android apps place a focus on delivering specific content in your hand. For instance, you want an app to play a card game, another app to read news headlines, and more apps to show you your horoscope, weather, and driving conditions. All specialized, bite-sized apps.

The result is that you can develop Android apps faster. In this section you will learn how to rapidly prototype and build Android apps with little or no code.

Creating Content for Your Android Phone That Does Not Require Programming

Flash CS5 allows you to build solutions that will run on the Android OS that require no programming. In this chapter you will learn how to build solutions without using ActionScript. Well, maybe I throw in a little ActionScript, but not much (promise!). You will see how rich animation and video can be used very easily to create Android solutions.

The core to the success of Adobe's Flash is its broad range of sophisticated rich media. The goal of this chapter is to show how to use the following rich media techniques in Flash CS5 effectively for Android development:
- Creating animation
- Playing back sound
- Presenting video
- Working with 3D

Many of these rich media techniques will be familiar to you if you have already worked in Flash CS3 or CS4. The Android OS, however, gives you challenges that you would not expect to encounter if you are developing Flash for websites running on desktop computers. The Android OS is typically running on a much slower CPU with limited graphical enhancements. With that said, you are going to be very surprised at what Adobe has done to make sure your Flash development experience is a good one.

Using Images in Your Animation

Every animation requires at least an image. As mentioned in the previous section, you will want to keep your animation images in a bitmap format such as PNG. Vector-based drawings will chew up the graphics processor on your Android phone, resulting in slow animation and shorter battery life. Not much fun there.

The Secret to Fast Frame Rate for Your Animations

The key to success with consistent high quality animation on the Android phone is simplicity. Keep the number of animating objects on the screen down to less than 20. More than 20 and you will see frame rates dropping as the GPU on the phone struggles to keep up.

Animation Techniques You Should Use on Mobile Devices

Flash provides you with a wealth of animation techniques you can use. From simple frame-by-frame animations to Classic Tween and Motion Tween techniques, you have lots of choices when it comes to animation in Flash CS5. Throw in the many third-party animation tools and there is very little you cannot accomplish.

The goal of this section is to show you animation techniques you can apply without having to add ActionScript. Each technique will be assessed for its performance on Android devices.

There are three basic animation techniques we are going to look at:

- Frame-based animation
- Classic Tween
- Motion Tween

Each of these techniques can be tweaked to run on the Android phone. The good news is that you do not need to do too much tweaking.

Frame-by-Frame Animation

The first animation style you will likely ever use in Flash is frame-based animation. This is an old technique from the classic days of animation started in the late nineteenth century with the infamous Zoetrope. The premise is this:

1. Create a drawing, such as a motorbike.
2. Copy the drawing, and modify the drawing very slightly (the bike wheels might be turning).
3. Copy the second drawing and modify it slightly.
4. Rinse and repeat.
5. Add all the frames in sequence to film. Voila! You have your frame-based animation.

The goal is to keep modifying the illustration frame by frame to reflect changes to your overall animation. By the time you reach your final frame and play back all the frames, you will have your overall animation.

Frame-based animation is the oldest animation type supported in Flash. The history of the technique goes back to 1997 when Flash was called FutureSplash. To this end, there are a number of great tools in Flash that allow you to easily create frame-based animation movies. Let's get started with adding frame-based animation to Flash.

1. Start by opening Flash CS5 and selecting the AIR for Android template. Choose the default template and save your file as FrameAni.xfl, using the new uncompressed file format in Flash CS5.
2. For this example, you will be using the Android.png file in the support document. Select File → Import → Import to Stage…
3. Select Android.png and import it onto your stage. You will have two layers as shown in Figure 2.1. The top layer is the Android logo and the second layer is text.

Figure 2.1 The start of the Android frame-based animation.

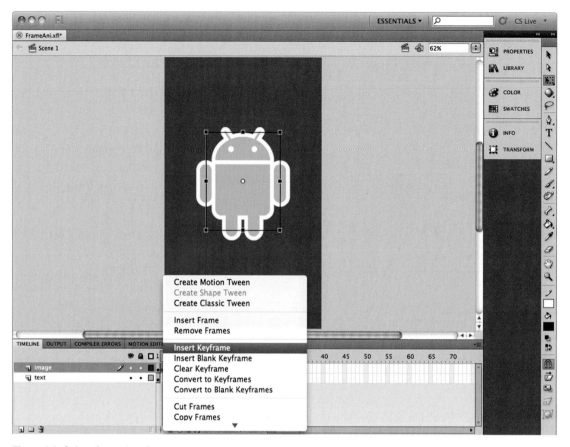

Figure 2.2 Select frame 2 and press **F6** to start the keyframe process.

4. The goal of the animation is to rotate the Android logo. Start by selecting frame 2 in the Image layer in the Timeline panel (Figure 2.2).

5. Right-click on your mouse and select the Keyframe option. A keyframe is a special frame that copies the content of the previous frame and adds it to a new frame. When in the new frame you can apply changes to the frame. In this instance, let's add a slight rotation to the drawing.

6. The Android logo should be selected on the Stage. Press Q to change the cursor to the Free Transformation cursor. With the freeform cursor active you can rotate the logo by selecting the top right-hand corner of the image.

Figure 2.3 The Free Transform tool allows you to rotate and resize an object.

7. Select the icon and rotate it very slightly, as shown in Figure 2.3.
8. Select frame 3 in the Image timeline and choose the Insert Keyframe command. The image will be copied from the previous frame. Select the image and rotate it some more.
9. Keep repeating this process until your Android icon completes a full rotation. It should take about 32 frames.
10. Select CTRL+ENTER (PC) or CMD+ENTER (Mac) to test the movie. You should see a spinning logo. You will also see the Android name blinking on and off—this can be fixed easily.

Building Solutions Using the XFL File Format

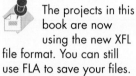 The projects in this book are now using the new XFL file format. You can still use FLA to save your files. The XFL format is an uncompressed format that allows you to view all the files in your project easily. It makes it easier to manage very large and complex solutions.

11. Select the layer named text. Choose the final frame Image layer and select F5 to quickly add a frame. The frame you add is not a keyframe but a frame that will extend how long the text is on the screen (Figure 2.4).

12. Test your movie again. You will see the animation and the text on the screen. Go ahead and publish the movie to your Android Phone to see how the animation performs.

Android OS likes frame-based animation when you are using PNG images. The reason for this is that frame-based animation is the most basic animation type in Flash. There are no calculations that need to be created to define the animation.

As you have probably realized as you stepped through this exercise, frame-based animation can be tedious and complex. Any slight mistake can cause hours of rework. This is why, in Flash, you can also leverage Tween animation.

Figure 2.4 A standard frame is used to keep the text on the screen.

A Tween is technique where animation is added by Flash between two points. Flash supports two different Tween techniques: Classic and Motion.

Leveraging Classic Tween Techniques

As the name indicates, Classic Tween is a technique that has been included with Flash since its first release, and is a "classic" animation technique in Flash. A Classic Tween requires two keyframes in a layer on the timeline. Let's step through the process.

1. Start by creating a new AIR for an Android movie. Save the file and name it classicTween.xfl.
2. Import the Android logo and text.
3. Name the layer the logo is in "logo."
4. Select the Android logo. Right-click and choose, Convert to Symbol. Name the new symbol "android." The Classic Tween requires that you use either a Graphic or Movie Clip symbol in the animation sequence (Figure 2.5).

Figure 2.5 A Classic Tween can be accomplished only with a Graphic or Movie Clip.

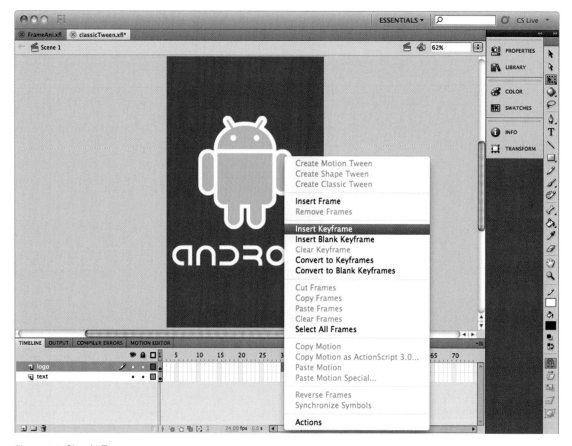

Figure 2.6 Classic Tween
requires two keyframes.

5. Select Frame 30 on the logo layer in the Timeline panel.
6. Right-click and select Insert Keyframe (Figure 2.6).
7. You have now defined two points in time: the first frame and frame 30.
8. Let's set up the animation sequence to fade out the logo. Select frame 30 of the logo layer.
9. Open the Properties panel. In the Color Effect section, choose Alpha from the Style drop-down menu (Figure 2.7).
10. Change the Alpha level to zero. This will make your animation invisible.
11. At this time, if you play the animation all you will see is the logo on the screen for most of the animation and then blinking out at the end. This is not what we want. Let's add a Classic Tween to control the animation.
12. Select frame 1 of the logo layer in the timeline.

Figure 2.7 Changing the alpha property.

13. Right-click and select Create Classic Tween (Figure 2.8).
14. You will now see shading in frame 1 and 30 with an arrow in it. Play back your animation. You will now see your Android logo fading over the duration of the animation (Figure 2.9).
15. Select the layer named text. Choose the final frame Image layer and select F5 to quickly add a frame. The frame you add is not a keyframe but a frame that will extend how long the text is on the screen.

As you can see, this is a basic animation Tween. What you will find, as you work with the Classic Tween technique, is that it becomes increasingly difficult to perform complex animation sequences over time.

This is where the new Motion Tween comes to your rescue.

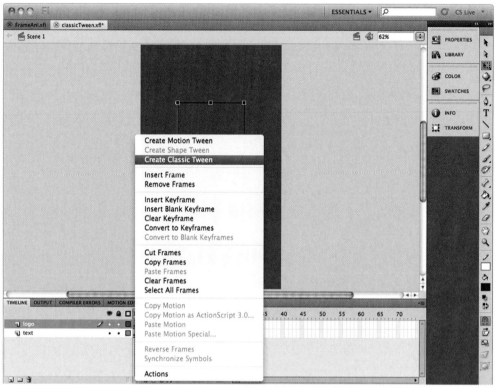

Figure 2.8 Insert a Classic Tween to the first frame of your animation.

Figure 2.9 Purple shading and an arrow indicate that this is a Classic Tween.

Using Motion Tween

The Motion Tween technique was added as part of Flash CS4. It is very new and is the biggest leap for animators since the first version of Flash. It is a whole new way of creating and managing animation in Flash.

The new Motion Tween is also very easy to use. You can recreate animation effects in fewer steps than the Classic Tween. To demonstrate this, we will recreate the animation sequence developed in the Classic Tween.

1. Start by creating a new AIR for Android template in Flash CS5 and save the template as motionTween.xfl.
2. Copy the Android logo into the new motionTween.xfl file.
3. Right-click on the Android logo. Remember, at this time, the logo is still an illustration and has not been converted into a Library symbol. Convert the Android logo into a symbol.
4. Right-click the Android logo symbol on the stage and select the Create Motion Tween option (Figure 2.10).

Figure 2.10 The Motion Tween option can be applied to Library symbols on the stage.

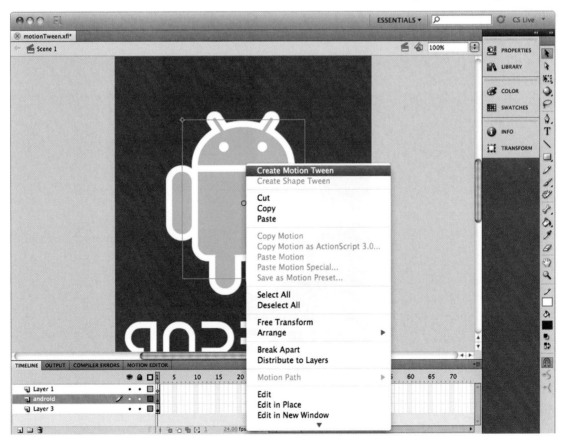

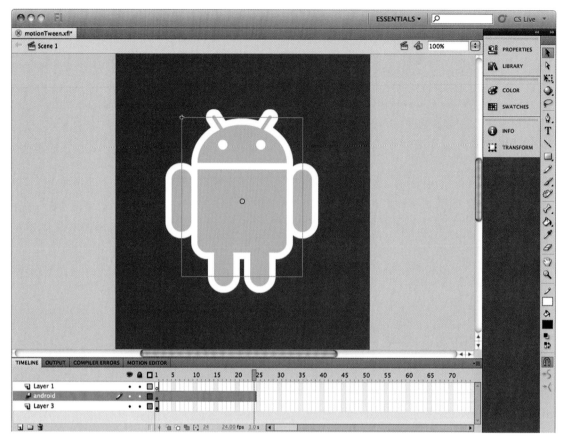

Figure 2.11 By default, a Motion Tween will run for one second, or 24 frames.

5. A 24-frame-long blue line appears in the same layer as the logo. This is the time your animation will run. The 24 frames reflect one second of animation (Figure 2.11).

6. Select the final frame in the blue line. Do *not* insert a keyframe. With the final frame selected, open the Properties panel and change the Alpha levels for the image to 0.

7. That's it—test your new animation.

The Motion Tween animation technique now in Flash CS5 makes it much easier to create new and complex animation sequences. Let's go ahead and modify the new Motion Tween on the logo so you can see how much more control you now have.

1. Select frame 12 of the logo timeline. This should be the middle of your Motion Tween. Drag the Android logo to the bottom left corner.

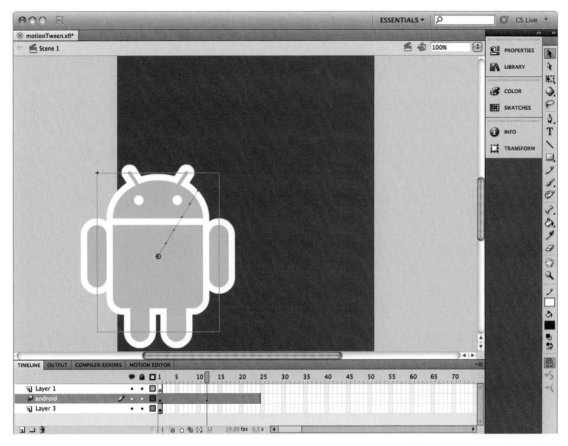

Figure 2.12 The purple line is the Animation Spline.

2. As you drag the logo you will see a line appear on the screen showing the animation path you are creating. This new path is called the Animation Spline (Figure 2.12). It is a mathematical path that lets you see what is happening with animation. In addition, you will see a small, black diamond appear on the frame. This is a visual indicator that you have done something on this frame.

3. Test your movie. The logo will now bounce up and down along the Animation Spline. This is great, but what if you want to add more animation? The old Classic Tween method requires adding more key frames; the new Motion Tween does not.

4. Select frame 6. Drag the logo to the top left-hand corner of the stage. Notice the Animation Spline is automatically updating to reflect your new, modified animation path (Figure 2.13).

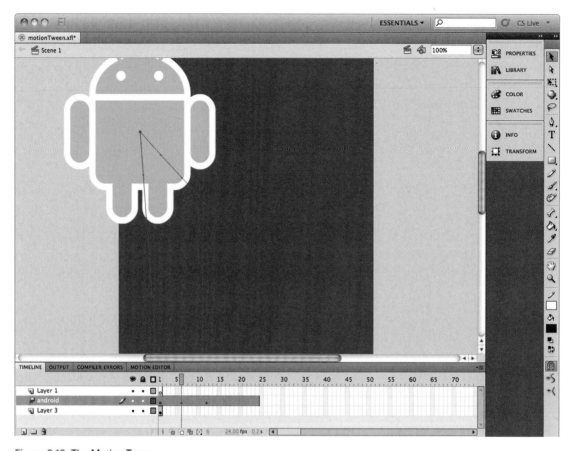

Figure 2.13 The Motion Tween automatically updates the Animation Spline without requiring new keyframes.

5. Select frame 18. Drag the logo to the top right of the stage. Again, the Animation Spline updates without you having to add any additional keyframes (Figure 2.14).

6. Play your movie. Voila! Instant animation.

OK, so you have seen how you can add new points in the Motion Tween timeline where something happens. In this case, the "something" is simply moving the logo around the screen. But the Motion Tween does not stop there. What if you want to lengthen the time of your animation sequence or change the placement of the animation on the screen? You've now got the tools to do that.

Currently the animation on the screen lasts for one second. This is defined by two values: the overall frame rate of a default AIR for Android movie is 24 frames per second (fps), and the Motion Tween in the timeline is exactly 24 frames long.

1. The length of time the animation is on the screen can be modified by selecting the far right frame of the Motion Tween in the logo layer and dragging it out. Drag the last frame of the Motion Tween to frame 96 (Figure 2.15).

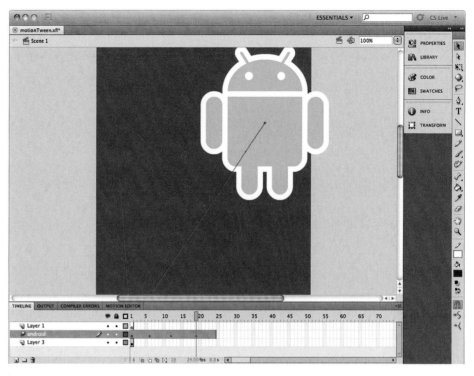

Figure 2.14 Keep updating the Motion Tween by selecting frames and moving your objects on the stage.

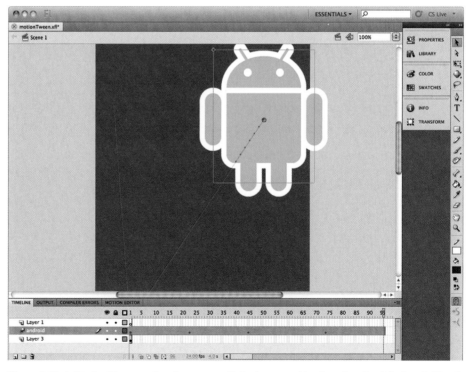

Figure 2.15 A Motion Tween animation can easily be increased by dragging the right-hand side of the selected Motion Tween on the stage.

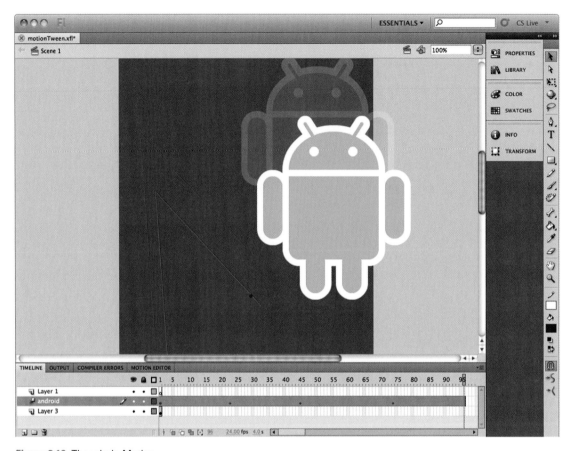

Figure 2.16 The whole Motion Tween animation sequence can be moved by selecting the Animation Spline.

2. Next, let's move the whole animation from the current position on the screen to a different position. To do this, select the green Animation Spline and drag it. You will see that the whole animation path moves as you move the Animation Spline (Figure 2.16).
3. Play back the animation.

The animation sequence now takes 4 seconds to play. You will notice that the animation is smooth. All you have done is extend the period of time for the animation. You have not reduced the frame rate. In addition, while the logo is still following the same animation path as you had originally set, the whole path has been moved and the new animation point has also been included.

These two simple steps (changing the overall time of the animation sequence and changing the position of the whole animation) could be done in the Classic Tween technique but would have required many additional steps. You certainly could not have accomplished these changes with three steps.

The Subselection tool and Free Transform tool can also be used to add more detail to your animation path.

The Subselection tool allows you to select vector points in your animation. Each vector that can be modified is highlighted with a green dot in the Animation Spline. With a vector point selected you can push out and modify the curve of the animation.

The Free Transform tool allows you to select the whole Animation Spline and stretch, skew, and rotate the Spline as if it were a single object.

Move through these steps to use the Subselection tool and Free Transform tool on your Motion Tween Animation Spline path.

1. Let's use the animation created with the Motion Tween. Right now, as you play the animation, the movement is very angular.
2. From the Tools panel select the Subselection tool (press A for the keyboard shortcut) (Figure 2.17).
3. With the Subselection tool active, select and hold a green dot in the Animation Spline. Pull back slightly to show the subselection handles.
4. Click, hold, and drag the subselection handles to modify the shape of the curve. At this point you are modifying the arc of the curve.
5. Select a second point on the Animation Spline and change the arc of the animation.
6. Now select the Free Transform tool from the Tools panel (or press the Q button for the keyboard shortcut) (Figure 2.18).
7. Select any point in the animation. The whole Animation Spline will be highlighted with resize and rotate handles.
8. Move your cursor over the top right-hand corner until the cursor changes to a rotate icon. Rotate the animation path. Notice that the whole Animation Spline rotates, not just the one frame you are working on (Figure 2.19).
9. With the Free Transform tool still selected, click and drag the center top resize handle to increase the size of the object.
10. Play back the animation. You will see that the whole animation sequence has been changed by the controls of the Free Transform tool.

But there is more. The Motion Tween comes with its own editor that allows you to modify still further the animation sequence you are creating.

Working with the Motion Editor

The Motion Editor is a tool that Adobe had designed to fine-tune your Animation Spline. Figure 2.20 shows the Motion Editor.

Working with Frame Rates

Not all Android phones are created equally. Some are faster than others. Some are slower. To compensate for the difference you will want to program your applications for the lowest common denominator. Frame rate is a great way to control user expectation from your application. Complex first-person shooter (FPS) games require rapid frame rate changes that exceed 60 fps. But not all solutions are FPS games. The human eye will see fluid motion at speeds as low as 21 fps. The default 24 fps in Flash should be more than fast enough for even complex animation sequences. By keeping the frame rate at 24 you are reducing the frame rate refresh speed on the phone's graphics chip. Slower frame rates mean that slow hardware will give the same experience as fast hardware.

Forcing Horizontal or Vertical Movement of an Animated Object

Sometimes you just want an object on the stage to move either vertically or horizontally. It can be hard to control this with the freeform movement of the Selection tool. However, you can fix the movement of an object to either a vertical or horizontal axis by holding down the SHIFT key. With the SHIFT key selected, you can move a selected object only left/right or up/down.

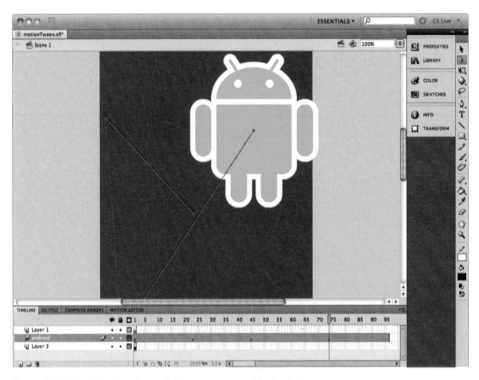

Figure 2.17 The Subselection tool allows you to modify the Animation curve.

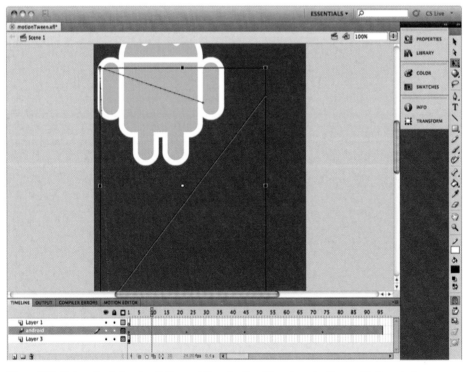

Figure 2.18 Select the Animation Spline and then the Free Transform tool to modify the whole animation path.

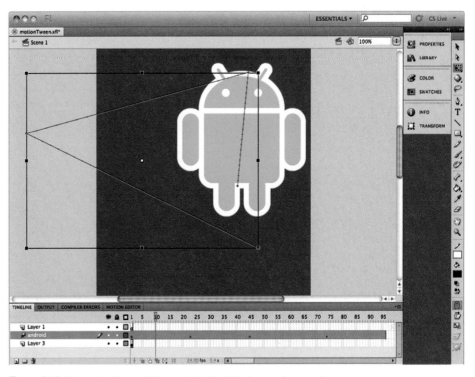

Figure 2.19 The animation path has rotated but the images have not.

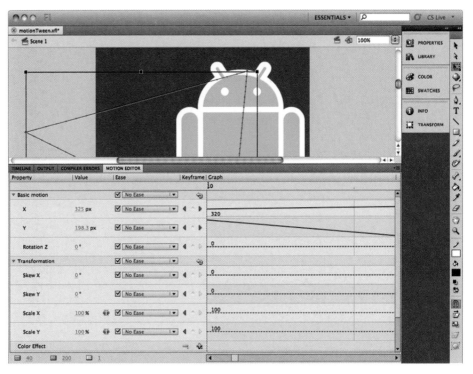

Figure 2.20 The Motion Editor gives you additional pixel level control over your animation.

The Motion Editor has main sections:
- Modifying property values for a Tween (left-hand side)
- Adding and removing keyframes (center gutter)
- Playhead to preview your changes (right-hand side)

Select any point in the Motion Tween on the stage and the settings will update in the Motion Editor.

The Motion tool is split into five main areas:
- Basic Motion controls X, Y, and Rotation Z-based animation.
- Transformation controls that skew and scale along the X and Y axis.
- Color Effect allows you to add color transformations such as Alpha.
- Filters allow you to apply any of the core six filter types (Drop Shadow, Blur, Glow, Bevel, Gradient Glow, Gradient Bevel, Adjust Color).
- Eases are the prebuilt and custom animation types.

As you can see from the list of controls, the Motion Tween comes with a lot of controls you simply do not have when using the Classic Tween.

Converting Motion Tween to ActionScript

The single difference between a Classic Tween and a Motion Tween is how the animation is constructed. With a Classic Tween the animation is dictated by the timeline. With a Motion Tween, the animation is created mathematically. In many ways comparing a Classic Tween to a Motion Tween is like comparing a bitmap image to a vector image: one is built by frames and the other is built by math.

Indeed, a Motion Tween is all controlled through the first frame of the Motion Tween sequence. The number of frames controls only how long the animation plays but does not necessarily control the transformation in the animation.

To demonstrate this, Adobe has included a Copy Motion as ActionScript 3.0 feature that allows you to copy out any Motion Tween on the stage into ActionScript.

Having the Motion Tween in ActionScript allows you to extend the functionality of the animation sequence beyond what is capable with the Timeline and Motion Editor tools. For instance, you may want to trigger a sound clip to play when the animation has completed.

Copying the ActionScript requires only that you have a Motion Tween on the stage. In the following example there is a simple shape that is moving from one location to another.

Right-click on the Animation Spline and you will see an option called Copy Motion as ActionScript 3.0. Select this option.

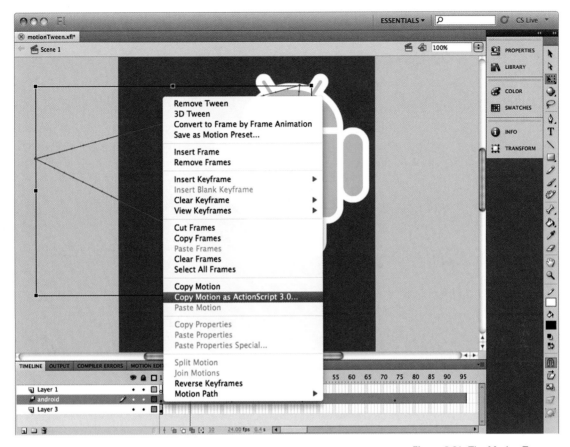

Figure 2.21 The Motion Tween is constructed of ActionScript.

Open up a text editor and paste the ActionScript into it (Figure 2.21). You should see something very similar to the following:

```
import fl.motion.AnimatorFactory;
import fl.motion.MotionBase;
import fl.motion.Motion;
import flash.filters.*;
import flash.geom.Point;
var __motion_myMovie:MotionBase;
if(__motion_myMovie == null) {
    __motion_myMovie = new Motion();
    __motion_myMovie.duration = 24;
    // Call overrideTargetTransform to prevent the
scale, skew,
    // or rotation values from being made relative to
the target
    // object's original transform.
    // __motion_myMovie.overrideTargetTransform();
```

```
        // The following calls to addPropertyArray assign
data values
        // for each tweened property. There is one value in
the Array
        // for every frame in the tween, or fewer if the
last value
        // remains the same for the rest of the frames.
        __motion_myMovie.addPropertyArray("x", [0,13.0435,
26.087,39.1304,52.1739,65.2174,78.2609,91.3043,104.348,
117.391,130.435,143.478,156.522,169.565,182.609,195.652,
208.696,221.739,234.783,247.826,260.87,273.913,286.957,
300]);
        __motion_myMovie.addPropertyArray("y", [0,2.73913,
5.47826,8.21739,10.9565,13.6957,16.4348,19.1739,21.913,
24.6522,27.3913,30.1304,32.8696,35.6087,38.3478,41.087,
43.8261,46.5652,49.3043,52.0435,54.7826,57.5217,60.2609,
63]);
        __motion_myMovie.addPropertyArray("scaleX",
[1.000000]);
        __motion_myMovie.addPropertyArray("scaleY",
[1.000000]);
        __motion_myMovie.addPropertyArray("skewX", [0]);
        __motion_myMovie.addPropertyArray("skewY", [0]);
        __motion_myMovie.addPropertyArray("rotationConcat",
[0]);
        __motion_myMovie.addPropertyArray("blendMode",
["normal"]);
        __motion_myMovie.addPropertyArray("cacheAsBitmap",
[false]);
        // Create an AnimatorFactory instance, which will
manage
        // targets for its corresponding Motion.
        var __animFactory_myMovie:AnimatorFactory = new
AnimatorFactory(__motion_myMovie);
        __animFactory_myMovie.transformationPoint = new
Point(0.499826, 0.500000);
        // Call the addTarget function on the AnimatorFactory
        // instance to target a DisplayObject with this
Motion.
        // The second parameter is the number of times the
animation
        // will play - the default value of 0 means it will
loop.
        // __animFactory_myMovie.addTarget(<instance name
goes here>, 0);
}
```

If the animated object on the Stage does not have an ID, one will be automatically generated for it. The ActionScript is constructed of three main sections:

- Lines 1–5 import additional animation classes that are developed by Adobe for animation. This reduces the amount of work you need to do in your animation.
- The IF statement starting at line 7 describes the animation for an object called myMovie on the stage.
- Following this is a description of the key movements of the object. For this example the animation is very simple—only the X and Y properties are being modified. A more complex animation would see additional properties described.

Working with the Motion Tween, Motion Editor, and ActionScript gives you exact control over your animation. However, Motion Tween animation requires more graphics processing by the Android phone. To manage the experience and expectations of your client, keep fewer than 20 Motion Tween animation sequences on the screen at the same time. With more than 20 animation sequences running simultaneously you will likely see a drop in the frame rate and the ability for the Android phone to keep up with your creativity.

Controlling Sound

Sound is an area where the Android OS excels. There are three good reasons why sound is so good:

- The Android OS has an MP3 player built in
- Every Android comes with speakers
- Audio out (headphones)

Android leverages a separate media class to handle audio. This media class can be tapped by Flash to allow playback of content.

There are no big surprises when it comes to audio files supported on the Android OS. Table 2.1 breaks down the different file formats and codecs supported on your Android phone. If you have been working with Flash for a while you will see familiar file types such as MP3, WAV, and MP4 (and a mobile version of MPEG4 called 3GP). Additionally, you will see the open source Vorbis audio format. Vorbis is *not* supported in your Flash movies. Although Android OS does support the format, the AIR for Android player does not.

Flash gives you several ways to connect to audio in your movies:

- Directly importing audio into the library
- Controlling audio with media components
- Leveraging ActionScript to control audio

Through the use of these techniques you can employ exact control over audio in Flash.

Table 2.1 Supported Formats and Codecs

Format	Encoder	Decoder	Details	File Type(s) Supported
AAC LC/LTP HE-AACv1 (AAC+) HE-AACv2 (enhanced AAC+)		X X X	Mono/stereo content in any combination of standard bit rates up to 160 kbps and sampling rates from 8 to 48 kHz	3GPP (.3gp) and MPEG-4 (.mp4, .m4a); no support for raw AAC (.aac)
AMR-NB	X	X	4.75 to 12.2 kbps sampled @ 8 kHz	3GPP (.3gp)
AMR-WB		X	9 rates from 6.6 kbps to 23.85 kbps sampled @ 16 kHz	3GPP (.3gp)
MP3		X	Mono/stereo 8-320 kbps constant (CBR) or variable bit-rate (VBR)	MP3 (.mp3)
MIDI		X	MIDI Type 0 and 1 DLS Version 1 and 2. XMF and Mobile XMF; support for ringtone formats RTTTL/RTX, OTA, and iMelody	Type 0 and 1 (.mid, .xmf, .mxmf); also RTTTL/RTX (.rtttl, .rtx), OTA (.ota), and iMelody (.imy)
Ogg Vorbis		X		Ogg (.ogg)
PCM/WAVE		X	8- and 16-bit linear PCM (rates up to limit of hardware)	WAVE (.wav)

Adding Sound to Flash

Adding sound files to Flash has not changed too much over the years. If you have added files to the Library then you have already completed the steps needed to link to a sound clip.

You can import sound files into Flash by select File → Import → Import to Library… and selecting a sound file. The following file formats are supported in Flash (Figure 2.22):

- ASND (Windows or Macintosh), the native sound format of Adobe® Soundbooth™
- WAV (Windows only)
- AIFF (Macintosh only)
- mp3 (Windows or Macintosh)

If you have QuickTime® 4 or later installed on your system, you can import these additional sound file formats:

- AIFF (Windows or Macintosh)
- Sound Designer® II (Macintosh only)
- Sound Only QuickTime Movies (Windows or Macintosh)
- Sun AU (Windows or Macintosh)

Figure 2.22 Flash support for the most popular sound formats.

- System 7 Sounds (Macintosh only)
- WAV (Windows or Macintosh)

When you select a sound in one of these audio formats you will see it appear in your Library. A small speaker icon will be associated with the file. You can select and play back the audio clip directly in the Library (Figure 2.23).

By default, the name for the sound file in the Library will be the same name as the file you imported. Double-clicking the name in the Library will allow you to change the name to one that is more meaningful.

Follow these steps to update the sound file you have imported:

1. In Flash, open the Library. Select the sound you want to modify. Select the Play button in the preview window to test the sound clip.
2. Right-click on the sound clip. You have three options that are of particular importance: Edit with…, Edit with Soundbooth, Update… (Figure 2.24).

Figure 2.23 Sound files in the Library can be played by selecting the speaker icon.

Sound Editors You Can Use

There are a lot of tools on the market that you can use. One of the most popular is the Open Source solution called Audacity (*http:// audacity.sourceforge.net/*; Figures 2.25, 2.26). Audacity will run on all the popular operating systems and the price is great. It is free!

3. If you have Adobe Soundbooth installed on your computer you can select Edit with Soundbooth. This will open Soundbooth on your computer with the sound file from your Flash Library. You can now edit the file. Selecting the Save option saves the updated file directly to Flash.

4. If you do not have Soundbooth installed then you can select any other audio editing tool. Using the Edit with… option allows you to use any third-party tool to update your sound clips. The file will be saved directly back to Flash.

5. In addition, you can change the original file on your hard drive and update your file in Flash. The imported audio file in the Library does not lose its link with the original audio file on your hard drive. This is very useful when you know there will be changes to the original sound file but need a placeholder sound until you have the final version. After you have made updates to the original file, select Update… in Flash. The Update Library Items window will open. Select OK.

Figure 2.24 Right-click on the sound clip in the Library to edit the chip in sound editing software.

Figure 2.25 Audacity is a free piece of software you can use to edit your sound clips.

Now that you have a file in your library, you can start to use it in your applications. The first place where you can see your sound files working in Flash is in the timeline.

1. Open the Timeline panel.
2. Select frame 1 of the default timeline.
3. In the Properties panel, expand the Sound section. The first option is a drop-down menu called Name. Select this drop-down to see the different sound files in the library.
4. Choose a file.
5. To see the sound file in the timeline more easily, add additional frames to the layer you are working in (press the F5 button for a keyboard shortcut).
6. A visual copy of the sound file wave pattern is now inserted into the timeline.
7. Test the movie and you will hear the sound clip.

Figure 2.26 Here you can see the sound clip being edited in Audacity.

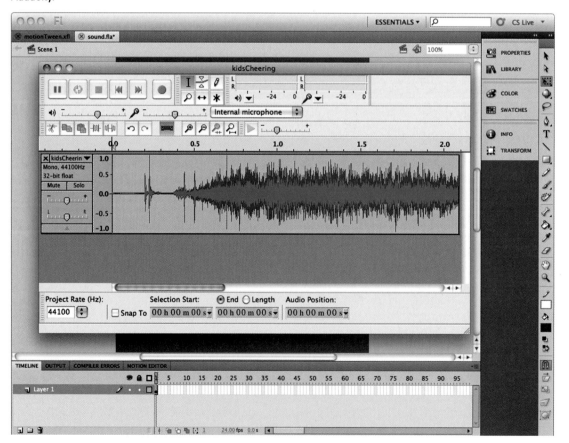

You may notice that the audio file does not sound the same as the original file when you test the movie. This is due to the publish settings in Flash. Flash will convert the audio file into 16 kbps MP3 format when it is published. You can change this.

1. Select File → Publish Settings…
2. The Publish Settings window opens.
3. Select the Flash tab.
4. In the Images and Sounds section of the Flash Publish Settings, choose the Audio Stream and Audio Event Setting buttons (Figure 2.27). This will open the Sound Settings window.
5. Change the bitrate to 128 kbps (Figure 2.28). This is the equivalent of CD quality sound.
6. Select OK and publish your movie. You will hear that the audio now sounds much better.

Play around with sound in your timeline. It is a great way to get comfortable with the sound tools.

Figure 2.27 The Publish Settings control how audio is played.

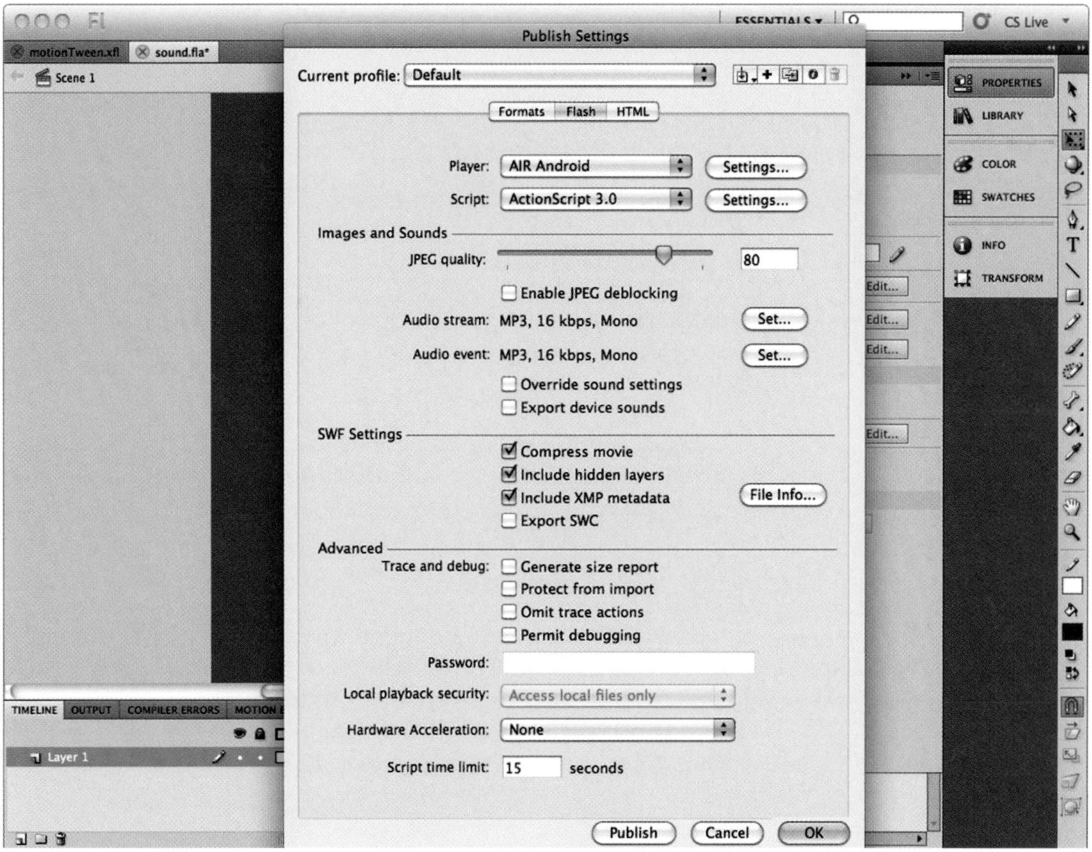

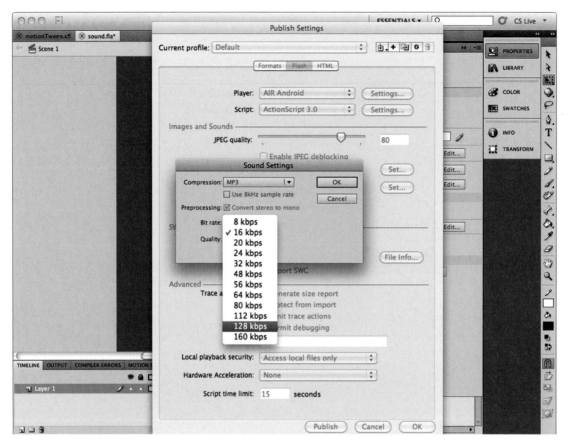

Figure 2.28 Both the Audio Stream and Events playback settings can be modified.

Working with ActionScript

As you might imagine, you can use ActionScript to control audio files. We will not get too deep into this here since we will be covering ActionScript in more detail later in the book. *But,* I really like ActionScript and I want to show you something you can do with ActionScript right now without having to do too much work.

In this example you are going to use the Code Snippets panel to do the heavy lifting for you. The Code Snippets panel is a place where you can access commonly used codes in ActionScript. The great news is that Adobe has prepopulated the Code Snippet panel with a bunch of very useful scripts that make things easy for you.

Let's take a look at how you add MP3 playback using ActionScript without having to write too much ActionScript.

1. Start by creating a new AIR for Android file.
2. On the stage, import the Android logo. Right-click the Android logo and convert it into a Movie Clip symbol.
3. The code snippets require that a symbol has a name. Select the logo symbol on the stage. Open the Properties panel and give the symbol the name playSound.
4. With the playSound symbol selected, open the Code Snippets panel (Figure 2.29).
5. Expand the Audio and Video collection.
6. Double-click Click to Play/Stop Sound.
7. Test your movie. You will see that when you click on the play-Sound movie clip that a sound file starts to play. Press the movie clip again and the sound stops playing.

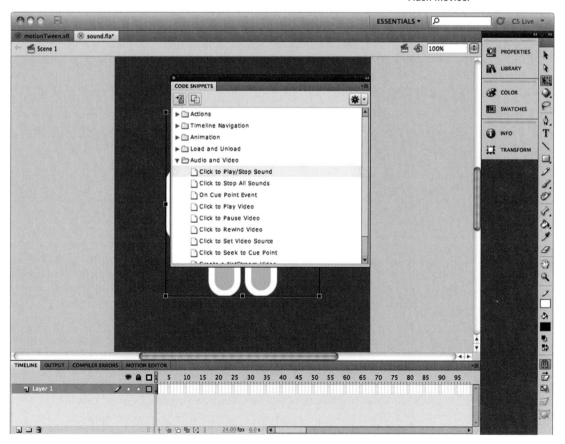

Figure 2.29 Code snippets provide a way to quickly add complex interactivity into your Flash movies.

You probably noticed that the Actions window opened when you added the code snippet. The following ActionScript was added:

```
playSound.addEventListener(MouseEvent.CLICK,
fl_ClickToPlayStopSound);
    var fl_SC:SoundChannel;
    var fl_ToPlay:Boolean = true;
    function fl_ClickToPlayStopSound(evt:MouseEvent):void
    {
        if(fl_ToPlay)
        {
        var s:Sound = new Sound(new URLRequest("http://
www.helpexamples.com/flash/sound/song1.mp3"));
        fl_SC = s.play();
        }
        else
        {
        fl_SC.stop();
        }
        fl_ToPlay = !fl_ToPlay;
    }
```

At the top of the code snippet is a set of instructions explaining how you can modify the code. For instance, you can change the URLRequest to point to a different MP3 file.

We will get into what the ActionScript is doing later in the book. I have added it here so you can see how easily you can control audio files in your Android apps without knowing how to write ActionScript.

Controlling Video

Video is huge on the web. Just look at sites such as YouTube, Hulu, and Vimeo. The sites broadcast billions of hours of video.

What is the technology driving these sites? Yeah, it's Flash.

You will hear a lot of talk about HTML5 video standards; however the reality is that Flash has the following when it comes to video:
• Consistent playback experience
• Broad support for media standards
• Sophisticated controls

For the most part, Flash is a tool you use to connect to video files and play back through the Flash SWF player. Video on the web is driven by CODEC licenses. CODEC (Compression/Decompression) is the technology that is used to contain audio and video files. The most popular audio CODEC you will know is MP3. Video comes in dozens of different CODECs. Currently, the AIR for Android player will allow you to play back the following video formats:
• Flash Video VP 6
• MPEG-4

Recording Sound on Your Android Phone

All Android phones ship with another hardware feature used for sound: a microphone. You can use the microphone to build audio recording applications. The audio recording features can be incorporated into AIR for Android apps but we will not cover it here. The technique to add audio requires detailed ActionScript. You will dig deep into that later in the book.

Flash VP6 is a legacy format released with Flash Player 8. The format only plays in Flash.

The Motion Pictures Experts Group is the leader of standardized video CODECs. MPEG-4 is the current standardized release of its video format. Companies such as Apple, Microsoft, and Adobe support tools to edit and playback MPEG-4 video.

There is also an additional format that is being experimented with called WebM. The new WebM video format is an Open Source CODEC released by Google following its acquisition of On2. WebM is now a video standard being supported by Flash, Google Chrome, and Mozilla FireFox 4.0+. Microsoft has stated that if you have WebM installed then IE9 will also support the standard.

OK, here is a very interesting piece of news. On2, the company that wrote the format for WebM, is the same company that developed the video format for Flash Video VP6. In other words, Adobe has a long history with On2, which is now part of Google. Although WebM is not currently supported in AIR for Android it is clear that is a case of "when" not "if" the support will come.

AIR for Android does support both Flash Video VP6 and MPEG-4 video. MPEG-4 video in AIR for Android benefits from the video acceleration built into the core Android OS.

Adding Video to Your Flash Movie

There is a lot you can do with video in Flash. To this end, a lot of what you can accomplish with video in Flash is through ActionScript.

The ActionScript method gets complicated very fast. Fortunately, Adobe has included a set of components that allow you to quickly insert a video player into your Flash movie.

Flash components are tools you can use to add rich functionality quickly to your movie without having to create the tool from scratch. An example is a drop-down menu control.

The components are located in the Component panel, as shown in Figure 2.30. You will see in the Component panel that there are three groups of components. The one you are interested in right now is a group called Video.

Select the FLVPlayBack 2.5 component and drag it onto the stage (Figure 2.31). You will see that the FLVPlayBack component looks like a video playback control. It is important to remember that components are just Flash elements (Flash Movie Clips, ActionScript Classes, etc.) that you can modify. This separates Flash from other development environments that make it difficult to modify their core controls.

Creating Video for Android Phones

There are dozens of great tools you can use to create video: from simple solutions such as Windows Movie Maker all the way up to professional solutions such as Sony Vegas and Apple's Final Cut Pro. When you export your videos from these tools you will want to ensure you select MPEG-4. If you do not have MPEG-4 as an export feature then you can use tools such as PavTube to convert the video files into MPEG-4.

Working with Components

Custom controls, such as components, are commonly found in most development environments such as Apple's Xcode and Microsoft's Visual Studio. There are functional tools you can use to rapidly enhance your applications.

Expanding the Video components reveals a long list of components. You are interested in the FLVPlayBack 2.5 component.

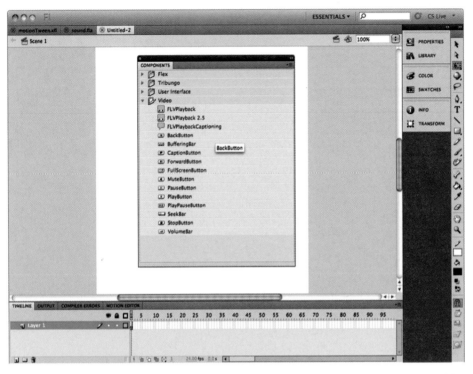

Figure 2.30 The Video Controls allow you to quickly add audio and video content to your Android apps.

Figure 2.31 The Flash Video Player component on the stage.

Select the FLVPlayBack on the stage and open the Properties panel to access the component properties. The FLVPlayBack video component comes with a large number of properties you can modify. Common features you will use include:

- Autoplay
- Cue points
- Preview
- Scale mode
- Skin
- Source
- Volume

Autoplay is a feature that will start the video playing automatically when the Flash movie loads.

Cue points are points in your video file that you can add with a video editor or through ActionScript. You can use cue points to trigger events to happen. For instance, a training video can be tied to an interactive quiz, playing when the question is answered correctly.

Scale mode allows you to have the video file you are playing scale to the size of the FLVPlayBack component on the stage.

The skin is a generic theme for the video player. There are more than three dozen basic skin types. Each skin can then have a custom color theme applied to it. This leads to the potential of thousands of varieties.

The source property allows you to link directly to the video file you want to load. This can be an FLV, 3GP, or a DRM free MP4 video file.

The final setting is Volume. Here you can define the default volume setting for your video file.

Working in the Third Dimension

The Holy Grail for game development is rich, immersive 3D. You can see this in any first-person shooter that has been developed since Castle Wolfenstein in the early 1990s.

You can create 3D in Flash several ways:

- Directly in Flash CS5
- Working with 3D third-party design tools
- Leveraging open source classes

With all of these great choices for using 3D, you might be wondering why this section is being covered last. There is a good reason: 3D can get programmatically complicated and will dramatically drop the performance of your Android solution.

3D is the Holy Grail for a reason—it is complicated and difficult for computers to process. Unlike animation or video, 3D adds a whole new level of complexity with the Z axis for depth.

Adding Files to Your Android App

 The FLVPlayBack is set to have you link to an external video file. When you select this option you must remember to include the video file in your Android Packaging process. If you do not, then your video files will not be included in the final Android APK file and you will not see the video playback on your Android device.

Working Full Screen Mode

 Flash supports the feature of letting your video use the whole screen to play back the video. This is true of AIR for Android. The Flash FLVPlayBack component supports a default full screen button. There is no need for additional ActionScript.

3D models are constructed in triangular polygons. The more polygons you have the more realistic the image you are creating in 3D.

The Android phone can handle 3D models, but millions of polygons will bring your 3D animation to a crashing stop. To keep an optimal performance for 3D on higher end Android phones you will want to keep your 3D models simple.

Leveraging Flash Tools for 3D

Two simple tools you can use for creating 3D in Flash are the 3D Rotation and Translation tools added in Flash CS4. These two tools are very basic 3D tools that allow you to add a simple 3D effect to a 2D object. For instance, a video player can spin in 3D across the screen.

Let's step through the process of adding the 3D rotation to an object on the stage.

1. Start by creating a new AIR for Android Flash file. Name the file Flash3D.xfl.
2. On the stage add the Android logo. Convert the logo into a Movie Clip symbol.
3. Select frame 1 in the timeline containing the Android logo. Right-click and insert a Motion Tween.
4. Select the final frame of the Motion Tween.
5. Select the 3D Transform tool in the Tools panel (Figure 2.32).
6. Click the Android logo. You will see a target-shaped icon with a cross hair appear on the logo.
7. Select the top vertical cross hair. Click and drag your mouse down. You will see that the logo changes perspective over a vertical 3D space.
8. Select the left side horizontal cross hair. Click and drag your mouse across the screen. You will see that the logo changes perspective over a horizontal 3D space.
9. The changes you have made are on the final frame of the Motion Tween. Test the movie. You will see the Android logo spin in 3D space.

This is the most basic type of 3D you can apply to objects in Flash.

"Real" 3D in Flash on Mobile Devices

There are two ways you can add complete 3D models to your Flash movies. This is important for times when you need a little 3D to lift up your presentation.

A tool you can use to create 3D models is Electric Rain's Swift 3D. The tool has been around for years and has gained a very loyal following for a simple reason: it is arguably the easiest 3D modeling tool you will ever use.

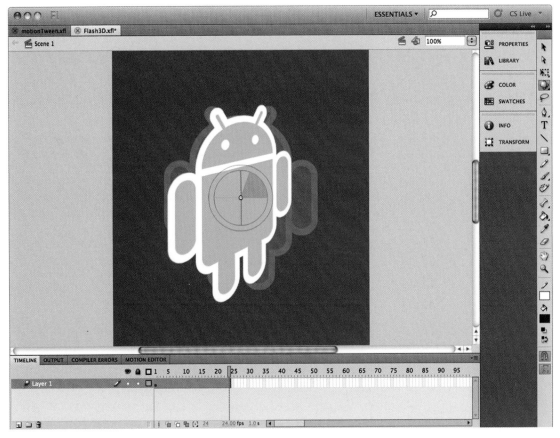

Figure 2.32 The 3D Transform tool allows you to control your 2D objects in 3D space.

The power of Swift 3D comes in the many ways you can export your 3D models. There are many times when you only need a 3D object to enhance a point in your Flash project. To this end, Swift 3D allows you to export your 3D design as a 2D Flash movie. The movie is constructed of many frames of 2D images. When you play it back, it will look like a 3D model. This is a fake 3D approach, but it is one that will work for a lot of scenarios.

If you need a fully interactive 3D model, Swift 3D is there to help you, too. Currently, Adobe's Flash does not natively support real 3D. However, the power of ActionScript allows 3D to be added through an open source project called PaperVision3D. PaperVision3D is a framework of classes you can add to your Flash movies. The set of classes enables you to load 3D models in the popular Collada file format (DAE file types). Swift 3D exports Collada files for PaperVision3D.

Using PaperVision3D you can bring Collada 3D models into Flash and have them behave in real 3D space. But, this comes at a cost. Currently, Flash is not enhanced to support real 3D models. The PaperVision3D framework achieves its goals because Flash can be extended using ActionScript. Using Collada models in your Android apps will generate jerky frame rate refresh.

The bottom line is: Don't use Collada until the core AIR framework is GPU accelerated to support 3D.

What You Have Learned

There are high expectations for Flash when it comes to animation, audio, and video. You might expect that the AIR for Android solution eliminates options for the sake of performance. The reality is that AIR for Android gives you access to the same visual eye candy as the desktop version.

Flash CS5 comes with support for three distinct animation tools: frame-based, Classic Tween, and Motion Tween.

Frame-based animation gives you the control to build, frame by frame, a sequence of images that, when played together, form an animation. The technique is very similar to the flip card technique used in classic cell animation or the Zoetrope of the late 1800s.

Classis Tween is a technique where Flash creates the animation sequence for you between two special frames called keyframes. The technique is an older format that goes back to the first release of Macromedia Flash.

The third and most flexible animation technique is the new Motion Tween technique. Unlike the Classic Tween technique you do not need to have keyframes to control your animation. A Motion Tween gives you the ability to apply much greater control over the animation sequence, including adding movement, changing elapsed time of the animation, and more. A new panel, the Motion Editor, enables you to apply exact control over your animation.

As you would expect, AIR for Android fully supports sound. This is particularly effective with phone-based applications where the user expects to have an audio response to any type of interactivity.

The web is dominated with video. As you would expect, Flash makes it very easy to add video to your Flash solutions using the video components. The AIR for Android player takes advantages of video accelerators in Flash. The end result is that you can broadcast video that scales from sub-DVD quality all the way up to HD. Also, with a click of the button, you can force your video to go full screen. This may not seem like a big deal for handheld phones, but full-screen video looks awesome on Android tablets and large form factor phones such as the Droid X and Evo.

The final motion technique you can leverage in Flash is 3D. The release of Flash Player 10 introduced simple 3D transformation. The transformation is applied to a 2D object, such as a graphic or movie, and allows the object to be skewed and pivoted in 3D space. For full 3D you need to leverage third-party frameworks such as PaperVision 3D.

The broad support for rich media is both a good and bad thing simultaneously. The good news is that you can duplicate the same animation completed for desktop computers. The bad news is that an Android simply does not have the same horsepower as a desktop system. So, test your Flash solutions on real hardware to ensure that you are getting the results you expect.

In this chapter you saw how you can add animation, audio, and video to your Flash AIR for Android projects without using code. In the next chapter you are going to be introduced to Flash components, tools that allow you add rich form-based functionality. By the end of the chapter we will introduce a little ActionScript to demonstrate how powerful the scripting engine in Flash really is.

PROJECT: OPTIMIZING ANIMATION, AUDIO, VIDEO, AND COMPONENT USE IN YOUR AIR FOR ANDROID APPS

The last couple of chapters have covered a whole batch of technologies, from animation, to sound, to video, and ending up with components. What you were learning is ways to add rich functionality to Flash with little or no ActionScript. Let's build out a solution that pulls all this together.

In this project you will learn how to:

- Structure images in Fireworks for use in Flash
- Import and convert art in Flash
- Mix Bitmap and Vector art to optimize animation on the screen
- Use Motion Tween to control the animation of objects on the stage
- Create, import, and apply sound files
- Create optimized video files for playback
- Use the Flash Video component

The goal of this project is to build a rich media solution in Flash that will run on your Android phone with a minimal amount of code. In fact, you are going to write just one line of code.

Your Building Blocks

Often you will find that the most complex part of your Flash projects is not the work you do in Flash, but the work you need to do to the files you import to Flash. The first stage of this project is to create all the files you need.

The first steps you need to complete are the following:

- Create the graphics
- Edit the audio
- Edit the video

You will not be using Flash CS5 to edit any of this work—we'll get to that soon enough.

 You can download all the files for this project at www.visualizetheweb. com/flashmobile.

Editing Your Graphics

The three editing tools you will use are:

- Fireworks
- Audacity
- iMovie (Mac) or Movie Maker (PC)

The first step is to create the graphic files you will be using in the project. The theme of the project is a baseball game. You are going to create four graphics:

- Baseball hat
- Baseball ball
- Baseball bat
- Stadium

You will find all the files in the project file. Open the graphic files in Adobe's Fireworks; you will see that all the files are Vector art (Figure 2.1Proj). Earlier I mentioned that you do not want to

Figure 2.1Proj Adobe's Fireworks CS5 is a great tool you can use to edit your images.

use Vector art too much in Flash; later you will see why we have Vector art here.

Collecting Your Audio

The next piece of preproduction you need to complete is capturing sound clips. It is getting easier to do Foley work. It used to be that you had to go out with a backpack of gear and try and get the right sound at the right time. The problem with sound is that it does not know it is being recorded. At any time there can be a great sound happening and you need a convenient tool to capture it. To this end, my new trusty tool is an iPhone. The microphone is actually a very good recorder. At a recent baseball tournament I captured the following sounds:

- Kids cheering
- Baseball hitting the bat
- Baseball being thrown

If you are like me, then you record more than you need. You can use the audio editing tool Audacity to edit down the three audio files. At the end, I exported the following WAV files:

- Pitch.wav
- Hit.wav
- kidsCheer.wav

These are the only audio files you will for this production.

Creating Your Video

The final step is to create a video. For this you can use any video editor that will export to MPEG-4 video. For this example I used Apple's iMovie (Figure 2.2Proj). The final export video that you will be using is called LiamBaseball.m4v.

Importing Files into Flash

Let's step through the process of getting your files set up in Flash.

1. Create a new AIR for Android application. Name the application baseball.xfl.
2. Select File → Import → Import to Library….
3. The Import window opens. Select Baseball hat, bat, and ball images (Figure 2.3Proj). Do *not* select the stadium image.
4. Select OK.

Figure 2.2Proj Editing video in Apple's iMovie.

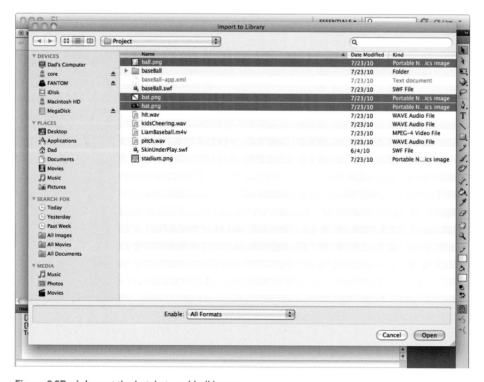

Figure 2.3Proj Import the hat, bat, and ball images.

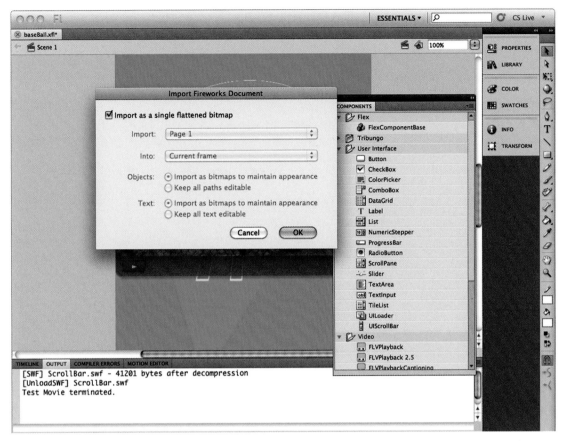

Figure 2.4Proj Selecting the Import as a single flattened bitmap option converts the Vector art into bitmap.

5. The Import Fireworks Document window will have an option labeled Import as a single flattened bitmap. Select the checkbox and then select OK. All three images will be imported as flattened images (Figure 2.4Proj).

6. Open the Library. You will see the three new bitmap images. Select each image. The bitmap images are now in your Library as flattened, bitmap images. They are no longer Vector images.

7. Select File → Import → Import to Library….

8. Choose the Stadium.png image. Uncheck the Import as a single flattened bitmap in the Import Fireworks Document window. You want to keep the Stadium as a Vector image.

9. Select File → Import → Import to Library….

10. Choose the three audio clips.

11. Save your Flash project.

You now have all the files you need for this project. Let's get cracking with the animation.

Adding Animation

For this project you are only going to use the Motion Tween method for animation. It is by far the easiest way to animate objects in Flash.

1. Select frame 1 of layer 1. Rename the layer "hat."
2. Open the library and drag the baseball hat image. Right-click and convert the image into a symbol. Name the Symbol "hat."
3. Place the hat in the lower left hand corner at –685 on the X axis and 761 on the Y axis.
4. Right-click on the timeline and select Motion Tween. A full second of animation will appear with a light blue background in the layer.
5. Select the final frame. Move the hat object to –586 X.
6. Play back the animation. You will see the baseball hat slide on.
   The previous animation is not too complicated. The animation is going to use the 3D transformation tools. 3D manipulation can be taxing on bitmap images. The bitmap object will often pixilate in unexpected ways. For this reason, we are going to use a Vector image: the stadium.
7. Above the "hat" layer on the timeline add a new layer and name it "stadium." Select the lock icon for the "hat" layer to prevent you from accidentally selecting the wrong item.
8. On frame 1 of the "stadium" layer drag an instance of the Stadium Vector art from the library onto the stage.
9. Right-click the Stadium art and convert it into Symbol. Name the new Movie Clip "Stadium."
10. Right-click on the stadium symbol on the stage and select Motion Tween.
11. Select the Free Transform tool (press V for the keyboard shortcut).
12. Select Stadium and, holding the SHIFT key, shrink up the stadium symbol. Holding the SHIFT key forces the width and height of the symbol to change uniformly.
13. Select frame 24. Resize the stadium symbol to the original size. You will see a diamond on the frame indicating that you have changed the size.
14. Test the movie. You will see the stadium symbol zoom in.
15. Press F5 to add a new frame after frame 24. You will notice that a new frame appears after frame 24 without a diamond. Keep adding frames until you reach frame 40.
16. Select frame 40.
17. Select the 3D Rotation tool (keyboard shortcut is W).
18. Select the Stadium on frame 40. You will see the cross hair Rotation Pitch and Skew tool appear. Push out the shape to bring the end of the home base close to the hat.
19. Test your movie. You will see the shape pivot. Using the Vector allows the animation to remain smooth.

20. Create a new layer and name it "ball."
21. On Frame 40 of the new ball layer add a keyframe. From the library, drag an instance of the baseball onto the center of the stage. Convert the image into a symbol.
22. The effect you want to create is the ball flying in. Select the Free Transform tool (press the Q button) and hold down the SHIFT key while you shrink ball down.
23. Right-click the keyframe on frame 40 and select Motion Tween.
24. Select frame 64. Resize the baseball back to full size and move the ball down to over home plate.
25. A baseball often curves as it is thrown. You can use the spline animation line to help with this effect.
26. Select a third of the way through the baseball animation and move the ball slightly to the left. Increase the curve even more at the two-thirds point. Motion Tween will fill in the gaps of the animation.
27. Play your animation. You will see the ball come curving in, finishing rapidly over the home plate.
28. You will also notice the other two animations on the screen vanishing. To bring them back, select the final frame for each animation. Press F5 to add new frames until all animation sequences are in sync.
29. The final step is to add a baseball bat hitting the ball out of the park. To do this, create a new layer and name it "bat."
30. Select frame 50 and add a new keyframe. You want your bat swinging at the ball just before it hits the ball.
31. From the library drag onto the stage a copy of the baseball bat. Convert the bat into a Movie Clip symbol.
32. All you need the bat to do is rotate on its central axis. Using the Free Transform tool, move the cursor over the top left-hand corner of the bat image and rotate the image until the bat does not show on the screen.
33. Move to frame 64. This is the same frame the ball stops over home plate.
34. Rotate the bat on frame 64 so that the bat is touching the ball.
35. Select frame 74, the final frame of the bat animation, and change the image property of the bat to a zero alpha level.
36. If you play the animation you will see the bat swing and the ball suddenly vanish. Add 10 frames to the end of the ball layer in the timeline.
37. On frame 74 of the ball layer, move the baseball to the top right-hand side of the screen and change the alpha level of the ball to zero.
38. Sync all the animation so the images stay in the screen and test.
39. To stop the animation from always repeating itself, you can add the ActionScript command "stop();" to frame 70. This is one piece of ActionScript.

What you now have is a sequence that uses the Motion Tween technique to quickly allow you to add complex animation with just a few keystrokes.

Adding Audio

The next step is to add some audio to give the presentation depth.

1. Create three new layers and call them pitch, hit, and crowd.
2. Select frame 40 of the pitch layer and create a new keyframe.
3. Now you can add a sound clip to the timeline. Add the pitch. wav sound clip in the Properties panel. The sound is in sync with the ball being thrown.
4. Select frame 58 of the "hit" layer and add a keyframe. Add the sound clip for hitting the ball. You add the ball hitting sound clip two frames before the ball hits the bat as an audio illusion.
5. Finally, add a keyframe to frame 62 of the crowd layer. Add the crowd cheering. You now have your crowd cheering.

Save and play back your movie. You should now see and hear your animation.

Adding Video

The final step in your app is to add video. In many ways, this is the easiest part of the whole application.

1. In the timeline add a new layer.
2. Name the layer "Components."
3. Open the Component panel and drag an instance of the FLVPlayBack 2.5 Component onto the center of the stage.
4. Select the FLVPlayBack Component and open the Properties panel. Select the property called "source" and locate the video file called LiamsBaseball.m4v, an MPEG-4 video.
5. Change the "skin" property to "SkinUnderPlay."

Test your movie. When you get to the final frame the video will open and begin playing the video (Figure 2.5Proj).

Testing on Your Android Phone

If you install this application as it is on your phone you will notice a couple of things not working, such as the video at the

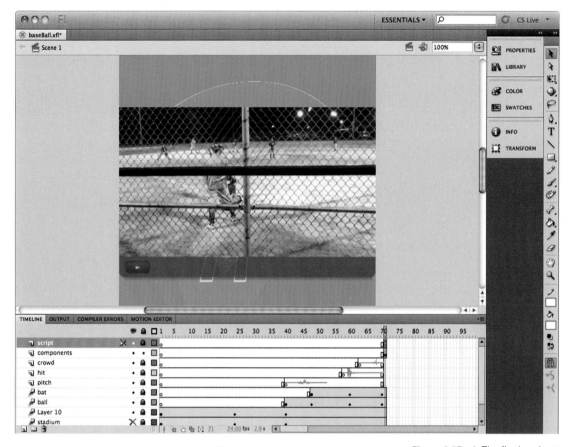

Figure 2.5Proj The final project includes 2D and 3D animation, sound, and video.

end. The reason for this is because the app needs to include additional files in the APK files.

1. Go to the Publish settings and select the AIR for Android settings.
2. On the General tab you will want to select the + symbol and add two additional files:
   - The linked video file
   - The SWF file called SkinUnderPlay.swf, which forms the skin to the video player
3. The rest of the settings should be OK for testing.

4. Connect your Android phone to the computer and press the Publish button.

5. The app should appear and work on your phone.

This project illustrates that you can add complex rich media, such as animation, video, and sound, with controls such as the FLVPlayBack video component. You do not necessarily need to know how to program Flash with ActionScript to have it do what you need it to do.

DEVELOPING MOBILE APPS USING ACTIONSCRIPT

Do you like Flash games and cool features on YouTube, like jumping from standard view to HD? There are two faces to Flash: the one you see and the complex scripting engine, called ActionScript, that you don't. Without ActionScript, Flash would not be interactive. ActionScript is the scripting language built within Flash that allows you to build interactive solutions. Any Flash movie where you need to click, drag, or pause requires ActionScript to instruct Flash what to do (Figure 3.1).

Flash CS5 allows you to build applications using two different versions of ActionScript. The older versions are ActionScript 1.0 and 2.0, or AS1 and AS2. AS2 is backward-compatible with AS1 applications. The release of Flash CS3 introduced ActionScript 3.0 (AS3), which was a significant overhaul of the scripting language. AS3 has adopted a true object-oriented approach to development, a technique that allows Flash applications to compete with solutions

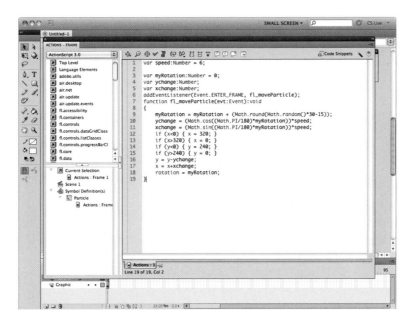

Figure 3.1 Here ActionScript is used to create a random animation effect.

developed with Microsoft's .NET or Oracle's Java. Complex solutions often require a lot of code, and older versions of ActionScript ran slowly with large and complex scripts. AS3 changed this. AS3 is as much as 10 times faster than AS2, and brings much more functionality to the party. In short, AS3 brings it on.

ActionScript 3.0 is the only way you can create solutions for the iPhone and Android OS. You will not be able to use AS1 or AS2 for this application.

In this chapter you will learn why you'll want to start using AS3, what has changed from and what is the same as earlier versions of ActionScript, and how you can make your applications rock by using AS3.

Enabling Flash to Execute Solutions Faster with AVM 2.0

Using ActionScript 3.0

 ActionScript has undergone significant changes. If you have worked with Flash AS1 or AS2 before, you won't be completely lost, but you will need to learn new ways to use your code.

The Flash Player, the plug-in you install in your web browser to playback Flash SWF files, is the key to success in building fast applications. To compile and then run any ActionScript in your Flash movies, the Flash Player uses a tool called the ActionScript Virtual Machine (AVM). For AS1 and AS2 the Flash Player uses AVM 1.0. The Flash Player 9 introduced a brand new AVM, called AVM 2.0, that is dedicated to running just AS3 application files. To put it simply, AVM 2.0 rocks: It makes your code zip along.

Developing AS3 solutions that are targeted at the AVM 2.0 rendering engine will ensure your have highly optimized Flash solutions.

What You Can Expect When You Use AS3

ActionScript 3.0 is a rewrite of ActionScript that brings it completely up to date with current development best practices. There are number of big changes that will take a while to get used to. The main changes are:

- ActionScript is located in Class files or in the Timeline.
- Code design is truly object-oriented.
- You cannot add ActionScript directly to movie clips or buttons instances.
- Triggering events has changed.
- Loading data has changed.
- XML is managed differently.

There are a score of smaller changes. As you dive directly into AS3 you will find a learning curve as you move from AS2. Is it all worthwhile to go through the pain? Absolutely. AS3 is simply so much faster and more powerful that it is worth the undertaking.

It is also the only way you can get your mobile apps to run on Android and iOS devices.

The Main Features of AS3

ActionScript is object-oriented in design concept. But what the heck does that mean? If you have developed for other programming languages, such as Java, C++, or C#, then you have heard of this term. Object-oriented essentially means that you break code into objects that can be easily reused. The idea is this: It is easier to manage an application that has a collection of smaller files than one large file.

There are two ways in which you can manage your ActionScript. The first, more traditional method is to add your ActionScript to the timeline (Figure 3.2). This will be familiar to earlier Flash developers. A good practice to establish is to have a layer in your timeline that is dedicated to working just with ActionScript. Adobe recommends that you label the ActionScript label "Actions." Locking the Actions layer will prevent you from accidentally adding movie clips into it.

The second method of inserting ActionScript into your Flash files is to use a Class file. Class files have a long history in the development world. With the Class file you can now specify both public and private classes. Using the Private keyword restricts the use of the attribute you defined to just that class and it will not be shared with other classes. This is useful as you develop instruction that needs to be executed privately in a closed environment.

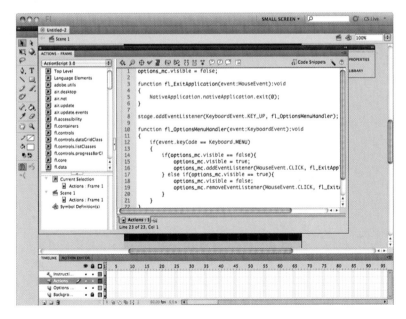

Figure 3.2 ActionScript running in the timeline.

Other major changes include:
- Developing solutions built with the DOM3 event model
- Using namespaces in your projects
- Controlling data
- Controlling text
- Drawing with the Shape Class
- The ability to easily work with external ActionScript libraries

All in all, these new changes to ActionScript ensure that you can develop even better solutions, ones that AS2 simply could not enable you to accomplish.

What Is the Same between AS2 and AS3?

With all the changes between AS3 and AS2 it important to remember that there is a lot of functionality that is the same between them. This will help as you transition from traditional AS1/2 Flash development to mobile app development using AS3.

For instance you still use the following in the same way:
- Variables
- Math objects
- If/Else statements
- Switch statements
- String
- Date to control the use of date and time
- Array to build a structured collection of data
- Boolean to specify a true or false

The following works in AS2 and AS3:

```
var str:String = new String("Hello, ");
var str2:String = new String("World");
trace (str + str2);
```

You can see that the overall syntax structure is the same between both versions of ActionScript. You still end your code with curly brackets, your variable names are still case sensitive, your variable names cannot start with a number, and you still use number class objects the same way.

Using Code Snippets to Get You Started

Transitioning to AS3 after your entire career has been spent working with AS2 does come with a learning curve. To help you through the transition, Adobe has included a great new tool in Flash CS5, the Code Snippets panel, which you can use to quickly add popular scripts to your movies. Here's what you do:

1. Create a new AS3 file.
2. Select Windows → Code Snippets. This will open the Code Snippets window (Figure 3.3).

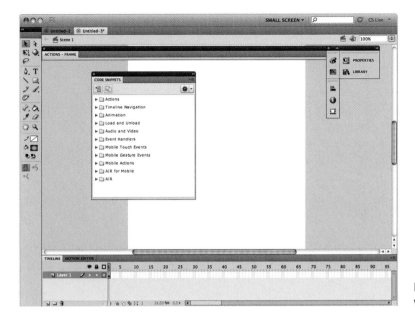

Figure 3.3 The Code Snippets window.

3. Code Snippets are organized in groups (Actions, Timeline Navigation, Animation, Load and Unload, Audio and Video, and Event Handlers).

4. Expand the Actions group and double-click Generate a Random Number.

Two things happen: a new layer, labeled Actions, is added to your timeline, and the new Actions layer has ActionScript added to it. The new script is automatically generated by Flash CS5.

The new ActionScript is true AS3. Check out the script by opening the Actions panel. Adobe has added some great inline comments to explain how you can use this script. Figure 3.4 contains a sample of the code that will be generated.

You will see that the code is split into two sections. The first section is a comment that explains how to modify and use the code that is generated. The second is the code itself. Test the movie and you will see a random number appear in the Output panel.

The Code Snippets panel really shows its power for allowing you to learn ActionScript quickly when you add code to movie clips on the stage. Let's go ahead and create a movie clip and then add a sound event.

1. Select the rectangle tool and draw a rectangle shape on the stage. Select the new shape and convert it to a movie clip.

2. Select the new movie on the stage and expand the Audio and Video submenu on the Code Snippets panel and double-click the Click to Play/Stop Sound Snippet (Figure 3.5).

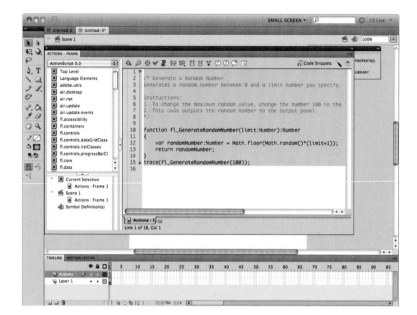

Figure 3.4 The AS3 code to generate a random number, which is created in the timeline.

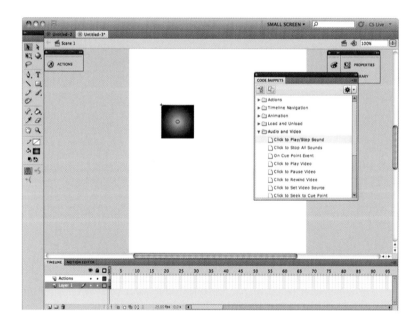

Figure 3.5 Many common actions are included in the Snippets panel, such as this Sound Snippet.

3. You will see a warning appear if you have not given your movie clip a name. Flash can do this automatically; select OK to automatically add the Code Snippet.

4. Open the Actions panel and you will see that the ActionScript to trigger the event has been added (Figure 3.6).

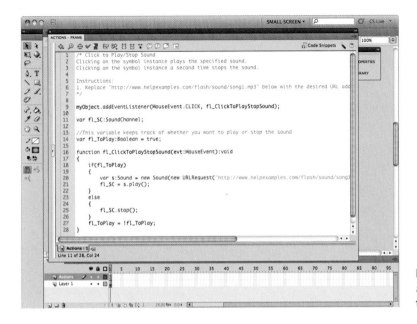

Figure 3.6 The Sound Snippet adds ActionScript directly into the timeline.

```
/* Click to Play/Stop Sound
Clicking on the symbol instance plays the specified sound.
Clicking on the symbol instance a second time stops the
sound.
Instructions:
1. Replace "http://www.helpexamples.com/flash/sound/
song1.mp3" below with the desired URL address of your
sound file. Keep the quotation marks ("").
*/
movieClip_1.addEventListener(MouseEvent.CLICK,
fl_ClickToPlayStopSound);
var fl_SC:SoundChannel;
//This variable keeps track of whether you want to play
or stop the sound
var fl_ToPlay:Boolean = true;
function fl_ClickToPlayStopSound(evt:MouseEvent):void
{
        if(fl_ToPlay)
        {
                var s:Sound = new Sound(new
URLRequest("http://www.helpexamples.com/flash/sound/
song1.mp3"));
                fl_SC = s.play();
        }
        else
        {
                fl_SC.stop();
        }
        fl_ToPlay = !fl_ToPlay;
}
```

Are Code Snippets and Behaviors the Same?

Hang on—these new Code Snippets look very similar to Behaviors. What is the difference? Behaviors were introduced with Flash MX 2004 as a way to easily allow designers to add ActionScript to their Flash. Behaviors are still there, but they work only for AS2. The Behaviors of the panel have not been updated for Flash CS5. You will find that the Code Snippets panel is much more versatile than the Behaviors panel.

5. Test your movie. Select your movie clip on the stage and the MP3 track will start to play.

You will see that the code is formatted to take advantage of the AS3 event model. For instance, the code is not added to the movie clip itself. The event is created as two parts: a function that explains what is going to happen, and a listener event that triggers the function. Without knowing it, you are using AS3. What you will find very helpful is that you can now go into your ActionScript code and modify it easily. For instance, you can change the path of the MP3 file to one on your own servers, or to point to a live, streamed MP3 file. For instance, you can change the URLRequest to point to *http://mp3-vr-128.as34763. net:80/*, a great radio station broadcasting out of London, U.K.

Developing Solutions Built with the DOM3 Event Model

ActionScript 3.0 now supports the ECMAScript, DOM3, event model syntax. In layman's terms, this means that you now use the Listener object to detect when you interact with your Flash movie using either a keyboard, mouse, or the new gesture interfaces used when touching the screen directly.

This is a big move from AS2. As an example, the following script is an AS2 instruction that instructs a movie clip to jump to frame 25 of a movie:

```
on (release) {
        this.gotoAndStop("25");
}
```

ActionScript 3.0 uses Listeners to trigger when an event occurs. Listeners are more complex to work with, but in the end, give you more flexibility. There are essentially two parts to a Listener: The first is a function that describes what is going to happen when you trigger an event, and the second is the Listener that waits for a specified event to happen, such as mouse clicking on a button.

The following steps will add an AS3 event that mimics the same event as the AS2 example earlier.

1. Create a new AS3 file. On the stage create a new movie clip.
2. Label the movie clip "myMovie."
3. Create a new layer in the timeline and name it Actions. Select the new layer.
4. Open the Actions panel. The first step is to create the function.

```
function gotoFunction(event:MouseEvent):void
{
        gotoAndStop(25);
}
```

5. The function is called "gotoFunction"; the parentheses dictate that it is looking for a mouse-driven event. There is only one instruction in the function, the gotoAndStop function that will move the Timeline to frame 25.

6. Add the listener that will look to trigger the function.

```
myMovie.addEventListener(MouseEvent.MOUSE_UP,
gotoFunction);
```

7. The first change is directly related to all AS3 needed placement in the timeline or in a Class file: On the stage is a movie clip labeled "myMovie." Use ActionScript to control the "myMovie" clip.

8. The second part of the Listener, addEventListener, instructs Flash that you are using the Listener object.

9. In parentheses are two parts, which explain that the event is a mouse event and to use the function gotoFunction.

At first blush, the new AS3 event model appears to be too complex. After all, AS2 is easier to use. The difference between the two is that the AS3 event model gives you flexibility to write more complex scripts and to extend the functionality of the event model beyond traditional mouse and keyboard interfaces. To do this you use the core object class controlling events on the screen, called the EventsDispatcher class. Through this you can not only leverage standard events such as mouse clicks and the keyboard, but you can extend the class with your event types.

Working with Classes

A common design pattern in object-oriented programs separates design, programming, and data elements. Flash CS5 adds this functionality with the inclusion of *classes*. A class is a packaged document that you can use to explain how UI components, business logic, and data elements will interact.

A class is a separate ActionScript file that is associated with the main Flash file and movie clips. You can use Flash CS5 as the class file editor or your favorite text editor such as Eclipse, Notepad, or TextEdit. A Class file is only a text file. It is very easy to create entire Flash movies using just Class files and not even add any content into a traditional timeline.

These steps will show you how to create a simple Class file for your Flash movies:

1. Create a new AS3 file. Save the file and name it "helloWorld.fla".

2. In the new, blank helloWorld.fla file open the Properties panel.

3. Expand the Publish setting. You will see a Class field. To the right-hand side of the Class field is a small pencil icon. Select the icon. A new window will open asking you if you want to create a new class. Create a new class and call it helloClass.

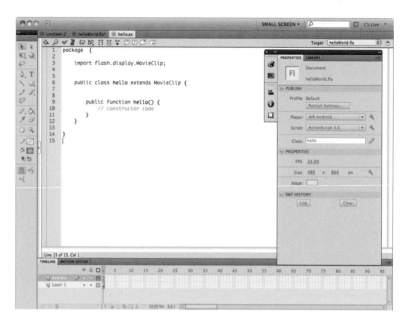

Figure 3.7 Class files can be edited directly in Flash Professional.

4. A new ActionScript file will open. Notice that the file is now labeled helloClass. The class is a default, blank class with the ActionScript shown in Figure 3.7.

```
package {
        import flash.display.MovieClip;
        public class helloClass extends MovieClip {
                public function helloClass() {
                        //constructor code
                }
        }
}
```

5. Remove the line that says //constructor code and replace it with: trace ("Hello, World");

6. Save your Class file.

7. Return to the helloWorld.fla file and test the movie. The result should be the words "Hello, World" posted to the Output panel.

Classes provide you a way in which you can create public and private class elements. The difference between the two is related to how you use the data. For instance, a public property can be shared throughout your whole Flash movie. A private property can only be used within the class in which it is defined.

Using Namespaces in Your Projects

Namespaces are ways in which you can define the visibility of properties you are creating. This is commonly used in XML when you are importing documents using a URI indicator.

Adding Class References to Movie Clips

Separate class references can be added directly to movie clips in your library. Open the Library panel and right-click on a movie clip and select the Properties option. The Symbol Properties window will open. In the Linkage group select the Export for ActionScript option. A class is automatically created for the symbol using the name of the movie clip. You can now modify the Class file for the movie clip in your favorite text editor.

The following example is built using a class called NamespaceExample. The role of this class is to pull in an XML document and step through the formatting of the code. Using namespaces you can instruct Flash where to find a definition of the document type you are using, in this case an RSS formatted document type.

1. Create a new ActionScript 3.0 movie. Create the class NamespaceExample.

2. Create a simple RSS formatted XML document. You can use the following formatted RSS document:

```
<rdf:RDF
xmlns:rdf="http://www.w3.org/1999/02/22-rdf-syntax-ns#"
xmlns="http://purl.org/rss/1.0/"
xmlns:dc="http://purl.org/dc/elements/1.1/">
<channel rdf:about="http://www.xml.com/cs/xml/
query/q/19">
    <title>This is an RSS feed</title>
    <link>http://www.bbc.co.uk/</link>
    <description>This is a test RSS document.
</description>
    <language>en-us</language>
    <items>
      <rdf:Seq>
    <rdf:li rdf:resource="http://www.bbc.co.uk/"/>
      </rdf:Seq>
    </items>
</channel>
<item rdf:about="http://news.bbc.co.uk/">
    <title>BBC News Center</title>
    <link>http://news.bbc.co.uk</link>
    <description>Welcome to the BBC News Center</description>
    <dc:creator>BBC</dc:creator>
    <dc:date>2010-02-12</dc:date>
</item>
<item rdf:about="http://www.bbc.co.uk/radio">
    <title>BBC Radio Center</title>
    <link>http://www.bbc.co.uk/radio</link>
    <description>Welcome to the BBC Radio Center
</description>
    <dc:creator>BBC</dc:creator>
    <dc:date>2010-02-12</dc:date>
</item> </rdf:RDF>
```

3. Open the NamespaceExample class. Start by defining the package with a public class called NamespaceExample that will extend the functionality of the Sprite object:

```
package
{
    import flash.display.Sprite;
    public class NamespaceExample extends Sprite
```

4. Insert the namespace reference that describes how to use RSS XML:

```
{
    private var rss:Namespace = new Namespace("http://purl.
org/rss/1.0/");
    private var rdf:Namespace = new Namespace("http://www.
w3.org/1999/02/22-rdf-syntax-ns#");
    private var dc:Namespace = new Namespace("http://purl.
org/dc/elements/1.1/");
    public function NamespaceExample()
```

5. RSS has several standard XML types. You are going to extract the following: title, creator, date, link, and description. Each of these items will be formatted in accordance to the namespace called RSS. You will see in the third line of the ActionScript that you reference the RSS namespace.

```
private function parseRSS(rssXML:XML):Array
    {
            default xml namespace = rss;
            var items:XMLList = rssXML.item;
            var arr:Array = new Array();
            var len:uint = items.length();
            for (var i:uint; i < len; i++)
            {
                    arr.push({title:items[i].title,
creator:items[i].dc::creator, date:items[i].dc::date,
link:items[i].link, description:items[i].description});
            }
            return arr;
    }
```

6. The final step is to add a Public function that will use the RSS namespace and send the content to the Output panel:

```
public function NamespaceExample()
    {
        var myXML:XML = getRSS();
        var rssItems:Array = parseRSS(myXML);
        var len:uint = rssItems.length;
        for (var i:uint; i < len; i++)
        {
            trace(rssItems[i].title);
            trace(rssItems[i].creator);
            trace(rssItems[i].date);
            trace(rssItems[i].link);
            trace(rssItems[i].description);
        }
    }
```

Run your Flash movie to see the RSS feed results sent to your Output panel.

Namespaces are an effective way to manage your control over XML data. As with all core classes in Flash, you can extend the namespace to use it in conjunction with other objects and data types.

Controlling Data

There are several key ways to control data in AS3. They include arrays, shared objects, and XML. An array is the first method you are likely to use in your ActionScript code. The role of an array is to create a list of data types in your code. For example, you may want to list the colors red, green, blue, and orange, as shown in Figure 3.8. To do this you need to define a new variable with the data type of Array:

```
var colorArray:Array = new Array("red", "green",
"blue", "orange");
```

You can see in this script that a set of four items have been inserted into the array. You can access the data in the array with the following trace statement:

```
trace (colorArray);
```

The "push" property will allow you to add a new item into your array:

```
colorArray.push("purple");
```

To remove the last item of an array you can use the Pop property.

```
colorArray.pop();
```

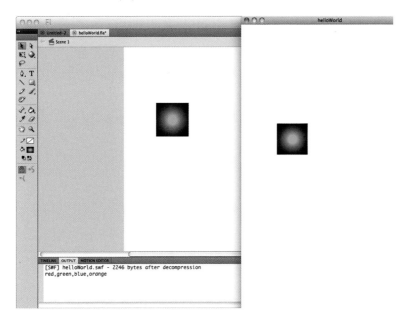

Figure 3.8 An array is a tool you can use to store data. Here you can see the data stored in an array posted to the Output panel.

Counting in Arrays

 When you are counting the number of values in an array you have to remember that arrays always start with 0. For instance, if you have five items in an array and tell the array to pull item 1, it will pull the second item. This is because the first item has the registered value of 0.

What you will find is that arrays are great for managing simple lists. Additional properties allow you to remove specific values, to count the number of values you have, and to sort your lists. For more complex data you will want to leverage the Local Data Storage or XML.

Using Flash Cookies

The Flash Player can store data locally in very much the same way that a cookie can be stored in a web browser. Flash does not call them cookies, but Shared Objects. An example of a Shared Object in AS3 is:

```
var mySO:SharedObject = SharedObject.
getLocal("myFlashCookie");
    mySO.data.now = new Date().time;
    trace(mySO.data.now);
```

The Shared Object is declared and given a name where it will be stored on the local computer. You can now effectively target data to this space that can be accessed if this computer comes back to this page at a later date.

Manipulating XML with E4X

Flash has supported XML in one fashion or another since Flash 5. Have you worked with XML in AS2? It's not pretty. To our relief, AS3 now supports the ECMA XML standard called E4X. You can now more easily step through your XML documents. The following will demonstrate how you can import an XML document into your Flash movie as a data type.

1. Before you can import an XML document, you need to have one you can use. You can copy the following code and save it as an XML document labeled "colors.xml":

```
<?xml version="1.0" encoding="UTF-8"?>
<pallette>
<color>Orange</color>
<color>Red</color>
<color>Yellow</color>
</pallette>
```

2. Create a new Flash AS3 movie and save it to the same folder as the XML document.
3. Create a new object to manage the XML:

```
var myXml:XML;
```

4. Now create a new URLLoader file that will load the XML file:

```
var xmlLoader = new URLLoader();
xmlLoader.addEventListener(Event.COMPLETE,onXMLLoaded);
xmlLoader.load(new URLRequest("colors.xml"));
```

5. At this point you have loaded the XML successfully into Flash. You can test this by adding the following function to trace the contents of the XML document into your Output window.

```
function onXMLLoaded(e:Event):void{
    myXml = new XML(e.target.data);
    trace(myXml);
}
```

6. The result should look just like your XML document.
7. You can now easily pull out a specific value. For instance, add the following to the onXMLLoaded function to extract the third value in the XML file:

```
trace(myXml..color[2]);
```

The double dots after the variable myXML allow you to step to the second value of your XML document. All of this is so much easier to accomplish with E4X than with the AS2 version.

Using Regular Expressions

Patterns are everywhere as you develop your code. This is clearly seen with the use of Regular Expressions, a method for describing the pattern of data you are looking to use. Using Regular Expressions you can now easily format form fields to correctly capture date, ZIP, or credit card numbers.

You can use a simple pattern with a string variable to validate the data:

```
var myColor = "Orange";
```

Now create a new Regular Expression that is looking for a simple pattern. In this instance, the pattern is that the myColor string value must start with an O.

```
var colorRegExp:RegExp = /O/;
```

You can write a trace script to test your movie:

```
trace( colorRegExp.test( myColor ) );
```

The value in the Output panel is True.

Let's extend what you can do with Regular Expressions by adding a pattern that looks for an e-mail address. Start by adding a new e-mail string with a valid e-mail address:

```
var email:String = "mdavid@matthewdavid.ws";
```

Next, create a new Regular Expression that is looking for a pattern structure in your e-mail:

```
var emailRegExp:RegExp = /^([a-zA-Z0-9_-]+)@
([a-zA-Z0-9.-]+)\.([a-zA-Z]{2,4})$/i;
```

Advanced Control of XML Data

A great feature in E4X is the ability to change the value of items into an XML document. What this means is that you can load an XML document and then modify the content. For instance, you can change Yellow to Blue.

The pattern is looking for a combination of alpha-numeric-special character formats separated by an @ sign and suffix ".". Add the following trace statement to see whether or not the pattern works:

```
trace( "Is this email valid? " + emailRegExp.test
( email ) )
```

Test the movie and you will get the following response in the Output panel:

```
Is this email valid? True
```

Change the e-mail address to just "Matthew David," a pattern that does not match the Regular Expression. When you test the movie you will see that the Regular Expression returns a false response.

Where to Get More Information on Regular Expressions

You can get great information on how to structure Regular Expressions at *www. regular-expressions.info*.

Controlling Text

In many ways you do not need to work on the stage at all when using AS3. All visual objects can be programmatically created. The easiest way to see this is in using the Text object to create dynamic text fields on the stage.

1. To create a dynamic text field, create a new AS3 file with an associated class called text.
2. The Actions panel will open showing you the text Class file. Add the libraries to be imported into your file:

```
import flash.display.Sprite;
import flash.text.TextField;
import flash.text.TextFieldAutoSize;
import flash.text.TextFormat;
```

3. Now you need to insert a private variable that will be used to define the dynamic text:

```
private var myTextField:TextField;
```

4. The following creates a basic string you can insert into your text field:

```
private var someText:String = "Hello world.";
```

5. A private function is used to define the physical position of the text field on the screen. You first need to declare the text field as a new object; then you can use the X and Y properties to place the text on the screen:

```
private function configuretext():void
  {
    myTextField = new TextField();
    myTextField.y = 200;
    myTextField.x = 100;
```

6. A TextFormat object is used to format the visual properties of the text. For instance, the following TextFormat object sets the font to "_sans", the color black, and font size 15:

```
var format:TextFormat = new TextFormat();
            format.font = "_sans";
            format.color = 0x000000;
            format.size = 15;
            myTextField.defaultTextFormat = format;
            addChild(myTextField);
```

7. The final two public functions tie the text string to the new formatted text field:

```
public function text()
    {
        configuretext();
        setValueOfTextField(someText);}
    public function setValueOfTextField(str:String):void
    {
        myTextField.text = str;
    }
```

8. Test your movie and you will see that you have a text string added to your screen.

So why would you go through the hard work of adding a scripted text field to the screen when you can do the same thing with the Flash text object with no scripting? The reason is that there may be times when you want to dynamically create text fields and the TextField object gives you this option.

Drawing with the Shape Class

As with the text object, you can create images dynamically in AS3. There are several different types of image you can create, including traditional movie clips and graphics. You can now also create a new type of image called a Sprite. Essentially, a Sprite is the same as a movie clip with the exception that it does not contain timeline functionality.

Sprites can be created by invoking the new Sprite Object Class and then adding properties to the object. The following steps will add a new square-shaped Sprite to the stage:

1. Add the following ActionScript to create a new Sprite labeled "myFirstSprite."

```
var myFirstSprite:Sprite = new Sprite();
addChild(myFirstSprite);
```

2. Format the size, fill/outline color, and position of the Sprite:

```
myFirstSprite.graphics.lineStyle(3,0xFF6600);
myFirstSprite.graphics.beginFill(0xFF0000);
myFirstSprite.graphics.drawRect(0,0,100,100);
myFirstSprite.graphics.endFill();
```

3. Now you can test the movie and see your rectangle on the screen.

4. Of course, this being ActionScript you can now add interactivity to your new Sprite. The following ActionScript will apply a fade-in transition effect to your new Sprite.

```
myFirstSprite.addEventListener(Event.ENTER_FRAME,
fadeInSprite);
myFirstSprite.alpha = 0;
function fadeInSprite(event:Event)
{
    myFirstSprite.alpha += 0.01;
    if(myFirstSprite.alpha >= 1)
    {
            myFirstSprite.removeEventListener(Event.
        ENTER_FRAME, fadeInSprite);
    }

}
```

You can do a lot with ActionScript constructed images. Working with all the different objects available to you in AS3, you have almost no limits to what you can create using Flash.

Using ActionScript to Control Animation, Audio, and Video in Your Android Apps

It can be argued that Adobe's Flash calling card is the easy implementation of rich animation, audio, and video. In many ways, it is these three technologies that are at the center of the argument between Apple and Adobe. The argument goes something like this: Animation and video can be played back through a web page using standards, so why use Flash?

Can you use alternative technologies to create animation in the Android/iPhone without using Flash? Of course, but the real power Adobe brings to the table is the ability to have exacting control over Animation Splines both visually and programmatically. Add to this mix, the world's leading video player to control your video and audio, then you see why Apple is so scared of Adobe's Flash.

The following sections are going to dig into the following rich media:

• Time management with ActionScript
• Animation control with ActionScript
• Audio and video control with ActionScript

You might be asking yourself, "I get it that you can control media with ActionScript, but Adobe has these great visual tools, so why do I need to learn code?" Good question, glad you asked. The designer tools Adobe provides are, indeed, very good. The challenge with the visual tools is that they are not very good when it comes to controlling dynamic data.

By dynamic data, I mean content that may come from a database, XML file, or array. For instance, you may want to create an MP3 player that loads content from an XML file. You have no way of knowing what the content is going to be before the XML file is loaded. For this reason, ActionScript gives you publicly accessible objects that allow you to make updates through ActionScript to dynamically loaded content—for instance, you can add a play button, mute, and volume control without ever having to use a visual editor.

Controlling Time with ActionScript

Time is important, especially when you need to sequence events in a game or an app on your phone. To support the control of time, Adobe includes a new class called Timer.

Essentially, a Timer is a custom listener that will trigger an event in time. The following is an example of a timer that waits for 2 seconds before displaying a message in the Output panel.

```
var aTimer:Timer = new Timer(2000,1);
aTimer.addEventListener(TimerEvent.TIMER,
timerListener);
function timerListener(e:TimerEvent):void
{
    trace("Hello, world");
}
aTimer.start();
```

The first line in this code block declares a new variable called "aTimer" to be a new Timer object. The values in the parenthesis dictates the thousandths of a second the timer needs to read before playing, with the second number specifying the number of times the event will repeat itself. In this case, the time elapsed is 2000 thousandths of a second (more commonly known as 2 seconds) and the repeat sequence is just 1 time.

The second line declares the listener for the aTimer variable. You will see in the parenthesis that the Listener is tied to a new function called timerListener. The function timerListener declares what will happen when the timer reaches 2 seconds. In this instance, a message is thrown to the Output panel.

The final line dictates when the timer will start. For this example, the timer starts when the app is loaded but there is no reason why you could not have a timer triggered with ActionScript when another event occurs on the screen such as when two objects collide.

Animating Your Content with ActionScript

Earlier you saw how you can use the Motion Editor to add exact control over your animation sequences. Let's go back to the Motion Editor and create a simple animation of 20 frames in a single diagonal. The timeline for the animation sequence is now shaded blue.

Here's a secret: The whole animation is being constructed in ActionScript using the AnimatorFactory object class. Don't believe me, check this out. Right-click on the blue shaded timeline and select Copy Motion as ActionScript 3.0. Open your favorite text editor and paste in the results. You will get something similar to the following code block:

```
import fl.motion.AnimatorFactory;
import fl.motion.MotionBase;
import fl.motion.Motion;
import flash.filters.*;
import flash.geom.Point;
var __motion_aniObject:MotionBase;
if(__motion_aniObject == null) {
    __motion_aniObject = new Motion();
    __motion_aniObject.duration = 24;
    // Call overrideTargetTransform to prevent the
scale, skew,
    // or rotation values from being made relative to
the target
    // object's original transform.
    // __motion_aniObject.overrideTargetTransform();
    // The following calls to addPropertyArray assign
data values
    // for each tweened property. There is one value in
the Array
    // for every frame in the tween, or fewer if the
last value
    // remains the same for the rest of the frames.
    __motion_aniObject.addPropertyArray("x", [0,12.5652,
25.1304,37.6957,50.2609,62.8261,75.3913,87.9565,100.522,
113.087,125.652,138.217,150.783,163.348,175.913,188.478,201
.043,213.609,226.174,238.739,251.304,263.87,276.435,289]);
    __motion_aniObject.addPropertyArray("y", [0,10.1717,2
0.3435,30.5152,40.687,50.8587,61.0304,71.2022,81.3739,
91.5457,101.717,111.889,122.061,132.233,142.404,152.576,162.7
48,172.92,183.091,193.263,203.435,213.607,223.778,233.95]);
    __motion_aniObject.addPropertyArray("scaleX",
[1.000000]);
    __motion_aniObject.addPropertyArray("scaleY",
[1.000000]);
    __motion_aniObject.addPropertyArray("skewX", [0]);
    __motion_aniObject.addPropertyArray("skewY", [0]);
    __motion_aniObject.addPropertyArray("rotationConcat",
[0]);
```

```
        __motion_aniObject.addPropertyArray("blendMode",
["normal"]);
        __motion_aniObject.addPropertyArray("cacheAsBitmap",
[false]);
        // Create an AnimatorFactory instance, which will
manage
        // targets for its corresponding Motion.
        var __animFactory_aniObject:AnimatorFactory = new
AnimatorFactory(__motion_aniObject);
        __animFactory_aniObject.transformationPoint = new
Point(0.500000, 0.500000);
        // Call the addTarget function on the
AnimatorFactory
        // instance to target a DisplayObject with this
Motion.
        // The second parameter is the number of times the
animation
        // will play - the default value of 0 means it will
loop.
        // __animFactory_aniObject.addTarget(<instance name
goes here>, 0);
    }
```

Adobe adds plenty of notes in this created animation ActionScript. Yes, this is a valid ActionScript. The object affected by this script is called aniObject. You can see it referenced throughout the script. With the animation sequence now exposed as ActionScript, you can now programmatically interact with the code. For instance, you may want to change the skew value.

Let's step through the code so you can see what is happening.

The first five lines point to additional frameworks that are supported in the animation sequence. The five frameworks are:

- motion.AnimatorFactory;
- motion.MotionBase;
- motion.Motion;
- flash.filters.*
- geom.Point;

These frameworks do much of the heavy lifting, allowing you to focus on the code.

The next major action you need to take on line 6 is declaring a new MotionBase object. Notice that the object is named var __ motion_aniObject. The object's name is pulled from the name of the object on the stage. In this instance, the object is called aniObject.

Line 7 is the start of an IF statement that details the animation movement and transformation of the aniObject.

Line 9 details the length of time of the animation. In this instance, the animation lasts for 24 frames.

The AnimatorFactory gives you access to interfacing ActionScript with your visual objects, but there are other ways for you to more easily control animation on the screen. Yes, we are going to go back to GreenSock's tools, which make controlling animation both fun and easy.

Lines 18 and 19 detail the vector points the animation moves to along the X and Y axes. The numbers are very precise, down to 0.001 of a pixel.

Line 20 adds information that explains if the object is scaled along the X axis, and line 21 adds information that explains if the object is scaled along the Y axis. Both have a value of 1.000000, indicating that there is no scaling.

Lines 22, 23, 24, 25, and 26 are additional parameters you can apply to the animated object to control skew along the X and Y axes, rotation, blend mode, and cacheAsBitmap.

Line 29 collects all the data you have supplied and creates an AnimatorFactory function. This will execute your command.

Again, all of this ActionScript can be automatically created for you in Flash. The following is a modified version of the earlier code, demonstrating how you can add skew, rotation, and other effects easily in ActionScript.

```
import fl.motion.AnimatorFactory;
import fl.motion.MotionBase;
import fl.motion.Motion;
import flash.filters.*;
import flash.geom.Point;
var __motion_mySquare:MotionBase;
if(__motion_mySquare == null) {
    __motion_mySquare = new Motion();
    __motion_mySquare.duration = 50;
    __motion_mySquare.addPropertyArray("x", [0,32.5051,
65.0102,97.5152,130.02,162.525,195.03,227.536,260.041,
292.546,272.297,252.048,231.799,211.55,191.301,171.052,
150.803,130.555,110.306,90.0568,69.8079,49.559,29.3101,
9.06122,23.7127,38.3642,53.0157,67.6672,82.3187,96.9702,
111.607,126.273,140.91,155.576,170.228,184.879,199.531,
214.167,228.819,243.485,258.137,272.773,287.425,302.091,
316.743,331.394,346.046,360.697,375.334,390]);
    __motion_mySquare.addPropertyArray("y", [0,
-2.51996,-5.03993,-7.55989,-10.0799,-12.5998,-15.1198,
-17.6398,-20.1597,-22.6797,-
        2.93893,16.8018,36.5426,56.2833,76.0241,95.7648,
115.506,135.246,154.987,174.728,194.469,214.209,233.95,
253.691,253.085,252.48,251.875,251.269,250.664,250.058,
249.454,248.847,248.243,247.637,247.031,246.426,245.82,
245.216,244.61,244.004,243.399,242.794,242.189,241.582,
240.977,240.372,239.766,239.161,238.556,237.95]);
    __motion_mySquare.addPropertyArray("scaleX",
[1.000000,0.958421,0.916843,0.875264,0.833686,0.792107,
```

```
0.750529,0.708950,0.667372,0.625793,0.631185,0.636577,0.641
969,0.647361,0.652753,0.658145,0.663537,0.668929,0.674321,
0.679713,0.685106,0.690498,0.695890,0.701282,0.706674,0.71
2066,0.717458,0.722850,0.728242,0.733634,0.739026,0.744418,
0.749810,0.755202,0.760594,0.765986,0.771378,0.760106,0.74
8834,0.737563,0.726291,0.715020,0.703748,0.692477,0.681205,
0.669934,0.658662,0.647391,0.636119,0.624847]);
        __motion_mySquare.addPropertyArray("scaleY",
[1.000000,0.958421,0.916843,0.875264,0.833686,0.792107,
0.750529,0.708950,0.667372,0.625793]);
        __motion_mySquare.addPropertyArray("skewX", [0,
4.87434e-005, 9.74867e-005, 0.00014623, 0.000194973,
0.000243717, 0.00029246,0.000341203, 0.000389947,
0.00043869, 0.000487434, 0.000536177,0.00058492,
0.000633664, 0.000682407, 0.00073115,
0.000779894,0.000828637, 0.00087738, 0.000926124,
0.000974867, 0.00102361, 0.00107235, 0.0011211,
0.00116984, 0.00121858, 0.00126733, 0.00131607,
0.00136481, 0.00141356, 0.0014623, 0.00151104, 0.00155979,
0.00160853, 0.00165727, 0.00170602, 0.00175476,
0.00182166, 0.00188857, 0.00195547, 0.00202238,
0.00208928, 0.00215618, 0.00222309, 0.00228999, 0.0023569,
0.0024238, 0.0024907, 0.00255761, 0.00262451]);
        __motion_mySquare.addPropertyArray("skewY",
[0,0.993964,1.98793,2.98189,3.97586,4.96982,5.96378,6.95775,
7.95171,8.94567,9.93964,10.9336,11.9276,12.9215,13.9155,14
.9095,15.9034,16.8974,17.8913,18.8853,19.8793,20.8732,21.86
72,22.8612,23.8551,24.8491,25.8431,26.837,27.831,28.825,
29.8189,30.8129,31.8068,32.8008,33.7948,34.7887,35.7827,
33.1802,30.5778,27.9753,25.3728,22.7704,20.1679,17.5654,14
.963,12.3605,9.75801,7.15554,4.55308,1.95061]);
        __motion_mySquare.addPropertyArray("rotationConcat",
[0,3.33325,6.66649,9.99974,13.333,16.6662,19.9995,23.3327,
26.666,29.9992,28.8829,27.7666,26.6502,25.5339,24.4176,23.3013,
22.1849,21.0686,19.9523,18.8359, 17.7196, 16.6033, 15.487,
14.3706, 13.2543, 12.138, 11.0216, 9.90532, 8.78899,
7.67266, 6.55634, 5.44001, 4.32368, 3.20735, 2.09102,
0.974696, -0.141632]);
        __motion_mySquare.addPropertyArray("blendMode",
["normal"]);
        __motion_mySquare.addPropertyArray("cacheAsBitmap",
[false]);
        var __animFactory_mySquare:AnimatorFactory = new
AnimatorFactory(__motion_mySquare);
        __animFactory_mySquare.transformationPoint = new
Point(0.499648, 0.500000);
        // __animFactory_mySquare.addTarget(<instance name
goes here>, 0);
    }
```

As you can see, adding complex animation using ActionScript can get, well, complex. Adding skews, different points of animation, and rotation to a single object can quickly add to the amount of ActionScript you need to write to add animation programmatically.

Ah, if only there was an easier way to animate objects across the state... Hang on, there is! GreenSock is a company that provides free animation frameworks you can use to reduce the amount of code you write. There are three different versions you can use:

- TweenNano
- TweenLite
- TweenMax

So, how do you apply these frameworks? Well, first you need to go to GreenSock.com and download the AS3 version of the library you will want to use. Be careful, GreenSock provides backward support for AS2, but you do not want that version as it will not work on the Android phone.

The good news is that the code is free. You can access special plug-ins that extend the code by becoming a GreenSock member (costing $25–$99). You can even get free membership if you offer to write an article for GreenSock—how cool is that?

Once you have the code downloaded, you will want to open the ZIP file and extract the folders and files within. You will see that there is a folder called COM. This is important. Copy the COM folder, and the files in it, to the directory where you have your Flash files.

Open your Flash Android movie. On the stage, create a rectangle with the drawing tools and convert it into a symbol. Name the symbol on the State myAnimation instance.

Open the Actions panel. First you need to call the frameworks that will do the heavy lifting for you. This is similar to the automatic ActionScript code created earlier by Adobe.

```
import com.greensock.*;
```

You can add a lot of properties to the animation path you want to create. But, for now, let's keep it simple. The first animation path you created earlier using Adobe's own ActionScript was a single path where the object moved from one position to another along a straight line. That created a lot of ActionScript. Here is the same animation created in one line:

```
TweenMax.to(myAnimation, 1.5, {x:82, y:107});
```

The first reference in this line is to the TweenMax library; the second reference is to the animated object on the stage (in this case, the object that you name myAnimation); the third property is the amount of time the animation will take to move from one location to another; and the final two X and Y coordinates dictate the final position of the object on the stage. Just one line! As you can see from this one, GreenSock provides a much leaner animation toolkit.

You can get even more complex by adding rotation, alpha blends, and different types of easing.

Each of the three different GreenSock Tween libraries inherits the features, methods, and properties of the previous library. The smallest library is TweenNano. TweenNano is a super lightweight library (only 1.6 Kb!). The functionality is very minimal but you get a *lot* for just 1.6Kb. TweenLite is a 4.7 Kb library, but gives you a much bigger selection of tools. The heavyweight is TweenMax (17.7 Kb). Both TweenLite and TweenMax can be extended with third-party plug-ins. Plug-ins are additional effects developed outside of the core framework. You can even mix different frameworks together.

The bottom line is that you need to have the ability to use ActionScript to programmatically add animation. This becomes even more important when it comes time to create games for your Android phone using ActionScript.

Extending Flash with Open Source Libraries

The core to AS3 is that it can be easily extended. To this end, you can use dozens of great open source libraries that can be used to extend the functionality of Flash. Great examples are:

- Box2D Physics Engine (*http://box2dflash.sourceforge.net/*)
- CoreLib (*http://code.google.com/p/as3corelib/*), a collection of basic utilities such as MD5 hashing, JSON serialization, and advanced data parsing
- Syndication Library (*http://code.google.com/p/as3syndication-lib/*), a library that allows you to parse all ATOM and RSS feeds easily
- AlivePDF (*www.fpdf.org/*), a library that allows you to convert your Flash screen content to PDF

These are some of the best libraries you can use. Each comes with its own level of documentation.

Summary

ActionScript is the core to all interactivity and logic built into Flash. AS3 is essential to our mobile app development. You will need to use it. Is there a learning curve to understanding AS3? You betcha! Is it worth it? Definitely.

Take advantage of self-help tools such as the Code Snippets. Check out YouTube for videos explaining how to add customized Code Snippets to meet your development needs. In addition, leverage the many open source ActionScript libraries that come populated with quick ways to add complex interaction to your apps easily.

At the end of the day, to be successful as a mobile app developer you will need to get comfortable with AS3. Might as well start now.

PROJECT: BUILDING SPRITE'S 123

In this section you have been introduced to ActionScript. You can do a lot with ActionScript, and the goal of this project is to illustrate how you can use ActionScript and Flash Professional to build a simple child's game called Sprite's 123. The game is an early learning game that teaches the numbers from 1 to 30, and is currently published in the iTunes App Store. Without getting into the specifics of using new gestures and mobile specific controls, you will see how I built the game using standard ActionScript 3.0 (AS3) techniques.

The code included in this game, as shown in Figure 3.1Proj, is available on the website for this book.

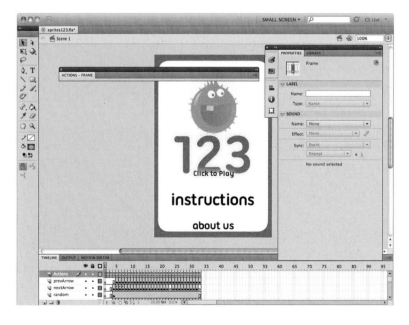

Figure 3.1Proj Classic Tween requires two keyframes.

Setting Up the Project to Run on an iPhone

The hardest part, for me, in building Sprite's 123 was not the code—it was the images and audio. There are a lot of images and audio cues used in the application; for this reason, it was important to set up my project correctly so I could easily access the files I needed, when I needed them.

1. Begin by creating a new iPhone Flash XFL project and name the solution sprites123. The code you are developing in this project will work on both the Android and iOS platform.

2. Open the Properties panel and select the Edit Application Settings icon for iPhone OS Player.

3. In the General Tap, you will see that the name of the output file IPA is sprites123.ipa. This file will be used as your final iOS app (Figure 3.2Proj).

4. Give your app a name; in this case we are using Sprite's 123.

5. Add a version number. It is important that the version number you write and the one you use in the final submit process are identical.

6. Select the app to be a full-screen solution.

7. Choose GPU for the rendering.

8. Choose the iPhone for the device.

9. In the Included files, you will need to select Default.png from the downloaded files (Figure 3.3Proj). The Default.png file is the document that loads immediately in iOS to inform the user that his or her app is loading in the background.

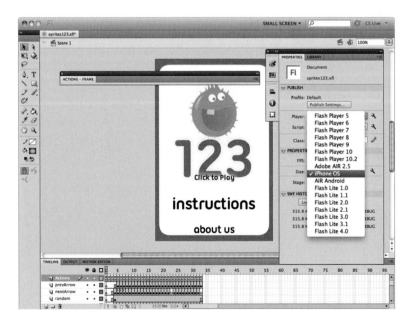

Figure 3.2Proj The Sprite's app will be converted into an iOS app.

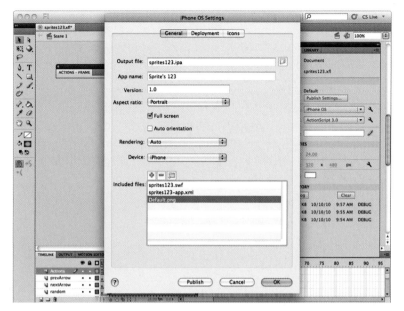

Figure 3.3Proj Use the Included files section to add a Default.png file to load when your application is launched on an iOS device.

10. You will need to add a developer certificate in the Deployment tab.
11. Select the Icons tab. In the downloaded folder you will find three icons: 29.png, 57.png, and 512.png. Choose these as the default icons for the project.
12. Save your project.

At this point you have applied the default settings for your application. The next step is to load the files you need to run the project.

Adding Files into the Library

To add the image and audio files to the library:
1. Select File → Import → Import to Library… and select all the images with the exception of the icon images.
2. All the images will populate the library. Create two folders in the library and name them numberImage and additionalImages. Move all the number images into the numberImages folder. Place the remaining images into the additionalImages folder.
3. Select File → Import → Import to Library and choose all the WAV audio files.
4. Create a new folder in the library and name it Sounds (Figure 3.4Proj). Move all the imported WAV files into the Sounds folder.
5. You will be referencing the sounds from within your ActionScript. A method for doing this is to give your sound file a class name (Figure 3.5Proj). The class name can be referenced from ActionScript.

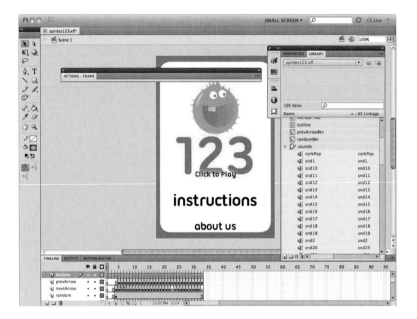

Figure 3.4Proj The Sounds folder will hold all your WAV files.

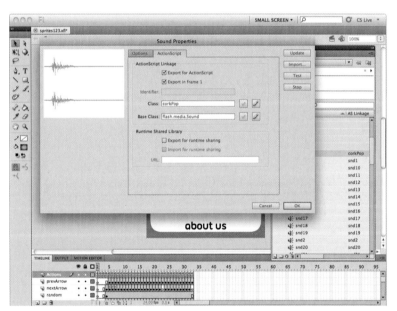

Figure 3.5Proj Adding a class name to your WAV file will allow you to reference the file from your ActionScript.

6. Right-click on the corkPop sound file and choose Properties. The Sound Properties window will open. Select the ActionsScript tab. Select the checkboxes alongside Export for ActionScript and Export in frame 1. Finally, enter corkPop into the Class ID field.

7. Repeat this for all the WAV files. Use the name of the file as the ID.

8. Save your file. At this time you are ready to start working in the timeline.

Setting Up the Timeline

You can use the traditional development process used in Flash applications to build your iPhone or Android app. To demonstrate this, we will use the timeline to manage your ActionScript and not Class files. This approach is how many Flash Professional designers have built solutions since ActionScript 1.0.

1. Go to the timeline and add a new layer named Actions (Figure 3.6Proj). You will add all of your ActionScript into this layer. Insert 33 keyframes into the Actions layer.

2. Add a new layer and call it Background. Drag the red border background image into this layer. Lock the layer so it is not moved accidentally.

3. Add three more layers and name them aboutUs, Instructions, and mainTitle. Add a single keyframe to frame 1 of these new layers.

4. Select the mainTitle layer. Find the 123Btn and drag it onto the stage. Convert the image into a movie clip (right-click and select Convert to symbol...). Open the Properties panel and insert the name btn123.

5. Open the Actions panel and insert the following ActionScript:

```
stop();
```

6. This script will stop the movie from playing the remaining frames. The next script will add a listener that will go to the frame that starts the learning tool on frame 4.

Tracking User Activity with Google Analytics

You can use the Google Analytics Flash Component to track how people use your application. Go to *http://code.google.com/ apis/analytics/docs/ tracking/flashTrackingIntro. html* to get the latest version of the components and instructions on how to add it to your Flash projects.

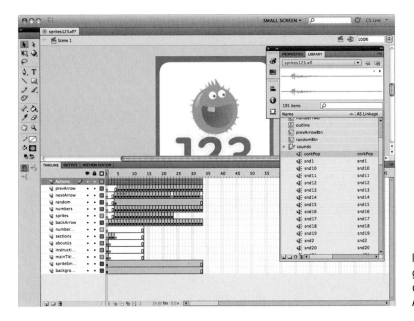

Figure 3.6Proj You are going to use the timeline to control where you place your ActionScript and graphics.

```
    btn123.addEventListener(MouseEvent.CLICK,
fl_ClickToGoToAndStopAtFrame_4);
    function fl_ClickToGoToAndStopAtFrame_4
(event:MouseEvent):void
    {

        gotoAndStop(4);
    }
```

7. Go ahead and repeat these steps to add the Instructions button and aboutUs button. Do not forget to label the buttons correctly. When you have done that, you can add the following ActionScript onto frame 1 of the Actions layer.

```
    instructionsBtn.addEventListener(MouseEvent.CLICK,
fl_ClickToGoToAndStopAtFrame_2);
    function fl_ClickToGoToAndStopAtFrame_2
(event:MouseEvent):void
    {

        gotoAndStop(2);
    }
```

The ActionScript above triggers an event that moves the movie from the current frame to frame two, as shown in Figure 3.7Proj.

```
    aboutUsBtn.addEventListener(MouseEvent.CLICK,
fl_ClickToGoToAndStopAtFrame_3);
    function fl_ClickToGoToAndStopAtFrame_3
(event:MouseEvent):void
    {

        gotoAndStop(3);
    }
```

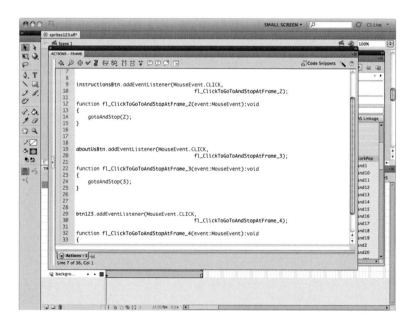

Figure 3.7Proj You can use the Code Snippets to quickly generate the code used in these steps.

This ActionScript is very similar to the previous example in that it moves the user to a new frame; in this instance it is frame 3.

Frame 2 is a screen that contains the instructions for how to play Sprite's 123. For this screen, create a new layer and label it backArrow. From the library drag an instance of the backArrow image onto the stage into the top left-hand corner. Convert the image into a movie clip. Name the clip backArrowBtn. You now want to add a function that will send the user back to the home screen when the arrow is selected.

The following ActionScript will do this for you:

```
backArrow.addEventListener(MouseEvent.CLICK,
fl_ClickToGoToAndStopAtFrame);
    function fl_ClickToGoToAndStopAtFrame
(event:MouseEvent):void
    {
        gotoAndStop(1);
    }
```

Save your work and then test the movie. You should be able to jump back and forth between frame 1 and the instructions frame using the buttons on the screen.

The next screen to work on is the About screen. Like the Instructions page, the About screen has a button in the top left-hand corner that sends the user back to the first screen in the app. In addition, however, you also have two buttons that link you to a website and to an e-mail address.

To add the web and e-mail links you will use the same navi-gateToURL property in a Click event listener. The following will open a web page and take you to a website (Figure 3.8Proj):

```
webSiteBtn.addEventListener(MouseEvent.CLICK,
ClickToGoToWebPage);
    function ClickToGoToWebPage(event:MouseEvent):void
    {
        navigateToURL(new URLRequest("http://www.
madlearning.net"), "_blank");
    }
```

The following ActionScript uses the navigateToURL to open a blank e-mail. The trick is to use the mailto command in the URLRequest.

```
emailBtn.addEventListener(MouseEvent.CLICK,
fl_ClickToGoToWebPage);
    function fl_ClickToGoToWebPage(event:MouseEvent):void
    {
        navigateToURL(new URLRequest("mailto:info@
madlearning.net"), "_blank");
    }
```

Save your work and test the links to make sure they work.

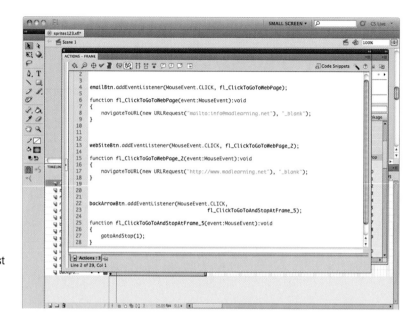

Figure 3.8Proj The URLRequest property is used to create e-mail and to send the customer to a web address.

Adding Interaction to Your Number Screens

The screens that the numbers are on get complicated very quickly. You have a lot going on, so we will step through one screen in detail so you can see what is happening.

Here is what you can expect:

- Forward and backward buttons
- Random screen button
- Animation
- Audio

Let's break down the ActionScript so you can see what is happening on the first number screen. The first screen has a forward button, but no backward button. The button that takes you to the next screen has the label nextArrowBtn1. The following ActionScript will take you to next screen (frame 5):

```
nextArrowBtn1.addEventListener(MouseEvent.CLICK,
next_ClickToGoToAndStopAtFrame_1);
    function next_ClickToGoToAndStopAtFrame_1
(event:MouseEvent):void
    {
        gotoAndStop(5);
    }
```

In the bottom center of the screen is a button that, when you select it, will send you to a random page. You are able to accomplish the random number by creating a random number function.

Let's create the function first and add the listener second. Here is the ActionScript:

```
function fl_GenerateRandomNumber(limit:Number):Number
{
        var randomNumber:Number = Math.floor
(Math.random()*(limit+1)+4);
        return randomNumber;
}
```

The first line in the function declares the new function as a number. The third line uses the Math.random property to generate a random number. By default, the random property will use a value of 0. The +1 prevents the final value from coming out as 0; otherwise you run into the problem of navigating a user to frame 0, which does not exist. The final +4 forces the final random number to add an additional 4. The numbers game starts on frame 4. Next add the listener that will use this function to generate a random number:

```
randomBtn.addEventListener(MouseEvent.CLICK,
fl_ClickToGoToAndStopAtFrame_27);
    function fl_ClickToGoToAndStopAtFrame_27
(event:MouseEvent):void
    {
            gotoAndStop(fl_GenerateRandomNumber(20));
    }
```

Now, when you select the random button, you will be randomly linked from frame 4 to 27.

A visual cue that you have landed on a screen is a spinning, animated Sprite. In reality, the Sprite is a single image using the Flash transition class to animate on the screen.

The animation will be controlled using the Transition class. To activate this into the project, add the following imports into your ActionScript:

```
import fl.transitions.*;
import fl.transitions.easing.*;
```

The next step is to drag a spriteBlue75 from the library and drop it onto the stage where you want the animation to take place. Convert spriteBlue75 to a movie clip and name the clip sprite1.

By default, you want sprite1 to be invisible when the screen loads. This will add to the animation effect. To do this, add the following ActionScript into the Actions panel for frame 4.

```
sprite1.visible = false;
```

You will also want to play a "cork pop" sound when the Sprite animates onto the screen. You will need a new function associated with the SoundChannel class. The following will do that:

```
var fl_SC:SoundChannel;
```

The next step is to add a second variable that triggers the animation to load 200 milliseconds after the screen loads. The delay allows a user to see a brief blank screen, the number on the screen, and then the animation (one animated object for the number 1, two animated objects for the number 2, etc.). You will control the time using a Timer.

```
var myTimerNumberOne1:Timer = new Timer(200,1);// 1 second
```

The following listener will now run when you load the frame:

```
myTimerNumberOne1.addEventListener(TimerEvent.TIMER,
firstAnimationNumberOne);
   myTimerNumberOne1.start();
   function firstAnimationNumberOne(event:TimerEvent):void
   {
   sprite1.visible = true;
   TransitionManager.start(sprite1, {type:Zoom,
direction:Transition.IN, duration:3, easing:Elastic.
easeOut});
   TransitionManager.start(sprite1, {type:Rotate,
direction:Transition.IN, duration:1, easing:None.easeIn});
   var s:Sound = new corkPop();
   fl_SC = s.play();
   }
```

The first line is a listener event. The Timer labeled myTimerNumberOne1 is used to control when the listener should start.

The third line starts the function that is run when the listener is active. The first action in the function is to make sprite1 visible. The two lines starting with TransitionManager trigger two different animation sequences (zoom and rotate).

A new Sound variable is declared with s:Sound. In this instance, the variable is pointing to corkPop, a class name given to the corkPop sound in the library.

The final command is to use the Sound Channel to play the sound variable.

You can also shake things up by allowing the user to press the screen to hear the number read out to them. To do this you will need to create a second CLICK event listener, as shown:

```
numberOne.addEventListener(MouseEvent.CLICK,
numberOneAni);
   function numberOneAni(event:MouseEvent):void
   {
   TransitionManager.start(sprite1, {type:Rotate,
direction:Transition.IN, duration:2, easing:Elastic.
easeOut});
   var s:Sound = new snd1();
   fl_SC = s.play();
   }
```

The function in this event triggers a rotation animation and plays the WAV file in the library called snd1.

Save your work and preview the application.

Completing the Application

You will want to step through the rest of the code for Sprite's 123. You will see that the code pattern for the rest of the application is very similar to frame 4. The main difference is the number of sounds, animations, and events happening on the screen. It can get complicated because, well, there's a lot happening.

The end result, however, is that you can test and run this application as is on your iPhone or Android device using ActionScript skills you already have. The only difference is that you are running the app on a phone instead of a desktop. Nothing else changed. How cool is that?

LEVERAGING CUSTOM IPHONE AND ANDROID INTERFACE CALLS WITH ACTIONSCRIPT

The Android Phone gives you a lot of additional controls such as Multitouch, gestures, Accelerometer, and Geolocation. In this section you will learn how you can tap into the Android specific extensions with ActionScript to add a rich level of control to your apps. Most of the content in this chapter will also work on iOS devices, with a few exceptions: WebView, microphone, and camera. At the time of writing this book, these additional features had not been added to the iOS apps. Check out the website *www.visualizetheweb.com/flashmobile* for updated information on this. The mobile world is changing fast.

Specifically, we are going to review the following:
- Gestures
- Orientation
- Geolocation
- Loading data into Flash
- Loading web pages into the WebView
- Microphone
- Camera/video

The Adobe Integrated Runtime (AIR) platform is maturing at a rapid clip. Newer features, such as Vibration, will likely be included in the final release of AIR 2.5 for Android, but are currently not available for the version I am using for this book. Crazy, isn't?

With that said, the mobile features covered in this chapter will get you up and running very quickly.

The first set of changes you will make will allow you to load data from remote sites onto your Android device. Following this, you will start to interact directly with the hardware on the phone itself.

141

Using Gestures in Your Apps

Adobe includes many programmable interfaces you can use through ActionScript. Multitouch is a feature you may use in many of your applications. This section explains how Multitouch is programmed into your apps.

- Using your finger instead of a mouse to interact with applications
- Using two or more fingers in your app

In many ways, it is the use of your fingers that makes touch so compelling on iOS and Android devices. But there are some caveats you need to keep in mind as your little digits tap on your OLED screen.

- Not all touch screens are the same. The king of sensitivity is the iPhone 4; no matter where you touch the screen, you will get the desired response. In contrast, the original Motorola Droid was a big disappointment for sensitivity. You often find yourself repeatedly tapping the same area before you get the desired responses. (Note: The new Droid Incredible is much better.)
- Your fingers are not as delicate as a mouse. The reality is that a mouse or stylus is a much more accurate pointing device than your fingers. Keep this in mind as you design you apps.
- Fingers tend to be big. Apple states in its human design guidelines that you should allow for 44 × 44 px (height and width) to accommodate the average finger.
- Simultaneous tap. You can have up to 11 fingers tapping the screen simultaneously. Not sure why it is 11 and not 12 or just 10, but I did not develop the code.

Keep these four rules in mind as you use control content on the screen.

Using a Single Finger to Interact with Content

There is a lot of hoopla about gestures and multitouch development. But we have been getting away with just a single tap of the mouse button for many years. You will also find that most of the time a single tap from one finger is really all you need. The great thing with using a single tap is that the event is exactly the same as a single mouse click. You use the MouseEvent.CLICK to trigger a single tap interaction. Let's see this in action.

1. Open a new Flash Android or iPhone application.
2. On the stage draw a rectangle. Press the F8 button to convert the drawing into an object.
3. Name the instance of the rectangle on the "myObject".
4. Select frame 1 on the timeline.

5. Open the Actions panel. Paste the following ActionScript into the screen:

```
    myObject.addEventListener(MouseEvent.CLICK,
fl_MouseClickHandler);
    function fl_MouseClickHandler(event:MouseEvent):void
    {
        myObject.alpha *= 0.5;
    }
```

This code is essentially a simple listener that is looking for a mouse click. The good news is that a single click is the same action your finger is applying to the screen. Test your movie in either your Android or iOS device. You will see that as you tap on the screen the Alpha level of the rectangle of the screen will change.

Using the MouseClick event is a great trick when you want to quickly migrate code from a standard desktop app to a web app. There is, however, a better way to do this using the TouchEvent listener.

Flash 10 introduced a slew of Multitouch events you can use, the simplest of which is a single tap. The following code will duplicate the exact same action as seen using the MouseClick but using the TouchEvent class:

```
    Multitouch.inputMode = MultitouchInputMode.TOUCH_POINT;
    myObject.addEventListener(TouchEvent.TOUCH_TAP,
fl_TapHandler_2);
    function fl_TapHandler_2(event:TouchEvent):void
    {
        myObject.alpha *= 0.5;
    }
```

The main difference you'll see is that the TouchEvent is specifically looking for a single tap on the screen (the TOUCH_TAP event).

Dragging Objects across the Stage

A common practice when you are building interactive applications is to drag objects across the stage. This has been successfully done with the mouse for more than a decade in Flash. So, can you do the same with your finger?

The action you are looking to create is called a gesture. You tap, hold, and drag an object across the stage. That's it. The Multitouch class used in the previous TouchEvent is once again leveraged to add this gesture.

A drag event is defined by two events: the place you start to drag your object and the place where you finish dragging the object. You do this in Flash by using two event listeners (one for the Begin Event and the second for the End Event) that trigger two separate functions.

For instance, you can use the same instance created earlier and add the following code:

```
Multitouch.inputMode = MultitouchInputMode.TOUCH_POINT;
myObject.addEventListener(TouchEvent.TOUCH_BEGIN,
fl_TouchBeginHandler);
myObject.addEventListener(TouchEvent.TOUCH_END,
fl_TouchEndHandler);
var fl_DragBounds:Rectangle = new Rectangle(0, 0,
stage.stageWidth, stage.stageHeight);
function fl_TouchBeginHandler(event:TouchEvent):void
{
    event.target.startTouchDrag(event.touchPointID,
false, fl_DragBounds);
}
function fl_TouchEndHandler(event:TouchEvent):void
{
    event.target.stopTouchDrag(event.touchPointID);
}
```

The first line declares that you are using a new Multitouch event. In this case, the event is called TOUCH_POINT. By declaring TOUCH_POINT you can now allow the object on the stage to be dragged around.

The second line is the first event listener. In this case, the first event listener controls the start of the drag. You will see that the TOUCH_BEGIN event is paired with the function fl_TouchBeginHandler. The fl_TouchBeginHandler function is triggered on the fifth line. You will want to define where you can drag your movie clip in the TOUCH_BEGIN event. The fl_TouchBeginHandler function calls a variable on line 5 that controls the area where you can move your object to an invisible rectangle the size of the screen.

The final line on the screen is the TOUCH_END event, or what happens when you have dragged your object around the screen and now are letting go. As with the first listener, the TOUCH_END listener is linked to a function. Here the function is stopping the drag action.

You can test this code in your movies to drag labeled objects around the stage.

Adding a Long Press Event to Your Code

What if you want to add a function such as holding a button down? There are many apps that are designed to measure how long you can hold a button on the screen. Fortunately, this is very easy to duplicate in Flash by mixing up your knowledge of ActionScript: using Multitouch and Timers.

A Timer, as covered earlier, is an event that is controlled by time. In the following example you will add the code needed to increase the size of the main object on the stage after one second of the object being tapped.

1. Let's just use the movie setup earlier. You should have a shape on the screen with the ID of myObject.

2. Open the Actions panel. Begin by adding the ActionScript that will trigger a function when the movie clip is selected:

```
Multitouch.inputMode = MultitouchInputMode.TOUCH_POINT;
myObject.addEventListener(TouchEvent.TOUCH_BEGIN,
fl_PressBeginHandler);
```

3. The following is the function being called by the TOUCH_ BEGIN event:

```
function fl_PressBeginHandler(event:TouchEvent):void
{
        fl_PressTimer.start();
}
```

4. The function is calling a variable called fl_PressTimer. This variable is associated to a Timer listener. The following Timer listener is set to a delay of 1000 milliseconds. You will see that the listener calls a function named fl_PressTimerHandler, which changes the size of the movie clip.

```
var fl_PressTimer:Timer = new Timer(1000);
fl_PressTimer.addEventListener(TimerEvent.TIMER,
fl_PressTimerHandler);
function fl_PressTimerHandler(event:TimerEvent):void
{
        myObject.scaleX = 2;
        myObject.scaleY = 2;
}
```

5. The final step in your code is to add a second touch event that listens for when you lift your finger off the screen. The following does exactly that, and runs a function that returns your movie clip to its original size.

```
myObject.addEventListener(TouchEvent.TOUCH_END,
fl_PressEndHandler);
function fl_PressEndHandler(event:TouchEvent):void
{
        fl_PressTimer.stop();
        myObject.scaleX = 1;
        myObject.scaleY = 1;
}
```

6. At this point, save your file and publish to either your iPhone or Android device.

As you can see, Adobe gives you many different ways to control a single finger's interaction on the screen.

Working with Gestures

The iPhone brought a new way of controlling your screen: gestures. A gesture is a term where you use two or more fingers simultaneously on the screen. Common gestures include:

- Two-finger tap
- Pinch and zoom
- Rotate
- Swipe

Each of these actions can be duplicated in Flash for use on your Android or iOS device.

Adding Two-Finger Tap Control

The two-finger tap is very similar to a single-finger tap. Of course, the main difference is that you use two fingers. I know, give me a prize for pointing out the obvious. Let's jump into the code.

As you expect by now, the Multitouch class controls the event. The first line of code declares a new GESTURE event:

```
Multitouch.inputMode = MultitouchInputMode.GESTURE;
```

The second line of code states where the gesture is to be applied and what type of gesture it will be. In this case, the whole stage is listening for the GESTURE_TWO_FINGER_TAP event.

```
stage.addEventListener(GestureEvent.GESTURE_TWO_FINGER_
TAP, fl_TwoFingerTapHandler);
```

An event is triggered when two fingers tap the screen:

```
function fl_TwoFingerTapHandler(event:GestureEvent):void
{
    myObject.scaleX *= 2;
    myObject.scaleY *= 2;
}
```

You can swap out your code in the function for your own action.

That's it. As you can see, Flash has made it very easy for you to add a two-finger gesture.

Adding Pinch and Zoom

Apple's inclusion of pinch and zoom has become almost a must-have for any photo album. Good thing you can do this in Flash.

As you would expect, you use a gesture to zoom an object on the stage. Two fingers are required to pincer in and out. ActionScript refers to this as a TransformGestureEvent. The actual event is called GESTURE_ZOOM. You will see from the following example that the code is very similar to a single-tap Multitouch event with the exception of the event type in line two:

```
Multitouch.inputMode = MultitouchInputMode.GESTURE;
stage.addEventListener(TransformGestureEvent.
GESTURE_ZOOM, fl_ZoomHandler);
    function fl_ZoomHandler(event:TransformGestureEvent):
void
    {
        myObject.scaleX *= event.scaleX;
        myObject.scaleY *= event.scaleY;
    }
```

You can test this on an object on the stage. Just change the function to call the object you are manipulating.

Rotating a Movie Clip on the Stage

This will come as no shock, but a rotate gesture is almost identical to a zoom gesture. As with the zoom gesture, you are using two fingers. The difference is that your two fingers are anchor points around which you can rotate an object.

In the following code, the event you are looking for is TransformGestureEvent.GESTURE_ROTATE. That's it. The function uses the rotation property in ActionScript to rotate the selected object.

```
Multitouch.inputMode = MultitouchInputMode.GESTURE;
    myObject.addEventListener(TransformGestureEvent.
GESTURE_ROTATE, fl_RotateHandler);
    function fl_RotateHandler(event:TransformGestureEvent):
void
    {
        event.target.rotation += event.rotation;
    }
```

It is certainly a lot easier to add rotation in Flash than in Java for Android or Objective-C for iOS.

Swiping Objects on the Screen

In many ways, the most complex gesture you will accomplish on a mobile device involves swiping objects on the screen. The swipe gesture has the basic rule of dragging your finger across the screen. This is a common activity in data driven applications on the iPhone.

What is really happening with a swipe event? When you swipe your finger on the screen, what you are sending to the device is an instruction to move select content on the screen either to the left or right a specific number of pixels. In the following example you are going to move a movie clip to the left or right (depending how you swipe) by 40 pixels. You will also be able to swipe up and down moving the object 40 pixels.

The difficulty using the swipe gesture comes in controlling whether you swipe horizontally or vertically. You will define this in the gesture's event function, where you will look for either an X (horizontal) or Y (vertical) interaction.

1. The first line of code you need to add triggers the gesture.

   ```
   Multitouch.inputMode = MultitouchInputMode.GESTURE;
   ```

2. The second line triggers the TransformGestureEvent for a GESTURE_SWIPE. The GESTURE_SWIPE is the event defined for a swipe. At this point, the ActionScript does not know the direction of the swipe.

   ```
   stage.addEventListener (TransformGestureEvent.
   GESTURE_SWIPE, fl_SwipeHandler);
   ```

3. The gesture's function is broken into two Switch statements. The first statement examines if the swipe action is left or right and then moves the object on the stage accordingly.

   ```
   function fl_SwipeHandler(event:TransformGestureEvent):
   void
      {
           switch(event.offsetX)
           {
                case 1:
                {
                     myObject.x += 40;
                     break;
                }
                case -1:
                {
                     myObject.x -= 40;
                     break;
                }
           }
           switch(event.offsetY)
           {
                case 1:
                {
                     myObject.y += 40;
                     break;
                }
                case -1:
                {
                     myObject.y -= 40;
                     break;
                }
           }
      }
   ```

4. The second Switch statement examines if the swipe is up or down.

5. Save your file and test.

As you can see, swiping does require additional code. With that said, it is not too complex.

Adding Two or More Gestures Together

Are you restricted to adding just one gesture to an object? No, you are not. The following script demonstrates how you can add a left/right swipe, rotate, and pinch/zoom gesture to the same object on the stage:

```
Multitouch.inputMode = MultitouchInputMode.GESTURE;
stage.addEventListener (TransformGestureEvent.
GESTURE_SWIPE, fl_SwipeHandler);
    function fl_SwipeHandler(event:TransformGestureEvent):
void
    {
        switch(event.offsetX)
        {
            case 1:
            {
                myObject.x += 40;
                break;
            }
            case -1:
            {
                myObject.x -= 40;
                break;
            }
        }
    }
    myObject.addEventListener(TransformGestureEvent.
GESTURE_ROTATE, fl_RotateHandler);
    function fl_RotateHandler(event:TransformGestureEvent):
void
    {
        event.target.rotation += event.rotation;
    }
    stage.addEventListener(TransformGestureEvent.
GESTURE_ZOOM, fl_ZoomHandler);
    function fl_ZoomHandler(event:TransformGestureEvent):
void
    {
        myObject.scaleX *= event.scaleX;
        myObject.scaleY *= event.scaleY;
    }
```

Test this code to see it run on your device.

Gestures are huge part of your interactive development whether on the iPhone, Android, or BlackBerry.

Which Way Is Up? Controlling Orientation with the Android Accelerometer

The Android Accelerometer controls the orientation of the device. The same is true for iOS. In this section you will learn how you can interpret orientation through ActionScript to change the display for the correct screen position.

There are two ways in which you can control orientation in your Android apps:

- Publish settings
- ActionScript

The easiest way to detect orientation is through the AIR Android publish settings. Select the Properties panel and choose AIR Android Settings. The Application & Installer Settings window will open. On the General tab, select the check mark for Auto orientation (Figure 4.1). Now, when you rotate the Android device, you will see your AIR app also rotate.

This is the easiest orientation tool, but it does not give you a lot of control. For this, you need to use ActionScript.

Adding the Accelerometer to Your Apps with ActionScript

With the release of the Flash Player 10.1 and AIR 2.5, the Flash team added several new core features. Access to the

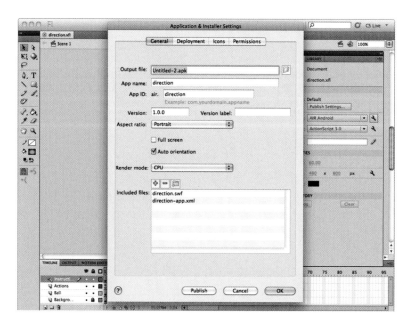

Figure 4.1 Select Auto orientation to have your app rotate as you rotate your device.

Accelerometer is one of those. The role of the Accelerometer is to detect when you move your phone. The Accelerometer is a listener that is triggered when it is used. The following example adds an Accelerometer listener to your iPhone app.

1. Start by creating a new iPhone app and adding the necessary development properties in the iPhone settings.
2. Add a dynamic text field to the stage. Name the new text field "myTextField" in the properties panel.
3. Create a new layer on the timeline and name it "Actions". Select the "Actions" layer and open the Actions panel. You need to import the libraries for the Accelerometer to work correctly:

```
import flash.events.AccelerometerEvent
import flash.sensors.Accelerometer;
```

4. Now you need to create a new Accelerometer object:

```
var acc1:Accelerometer = new Accelerometer();
```

5. A new Boolean object will be used to test whether the Accelerometer works or not:

```
var isSupported:Boolean = Accelerometer.isSupported;
checksupport();
```

6. The following function contains the event listener that waits for the Accelerometer to be triggered:

```
function checksupport():void {
    if (isSupported) {
        myTextField.text = "Accelerometer feature
supported";
        acc1.addEventListener(AccelerometerEvent.
UPDATE, updateHandler);
    } else {
        myTextField.text = "howdy "; }
    }
```

7. The final function posts a message to the text field to tell what direction the device has moved to:

```
function updateHandler(evt:AccelerometerEvent):void {
    myTextField.text = String("at: " + evt.timestamp
+ "\n" + "acceleration X: " + evt.accelerationX + "\n"
+ "acceleration Y: " + evt.accelerationY + "\n" +
"acceleration Z: " + evt.accelerationZ);
    }
```

8. The final step is to package your code into an Android app and test it on your phone.

The Accelerometer gives you new ways for your customers to interface with your applications.

Using Accelerometer in Flash Player Apps

The Accelerometer works great on Android devices but the same code can be used for Adobe AIR apps running Palm's WebOS and RIM's BlackBerry phones. Yes, that's right. Develop one app and have it deployed to multiple mobile devices. How cool is that?

Knowing Where You Are, Using Geolocation

Location awareness is key to mobile devices. In this chapter you will use ActionScript to communicate with the Android's Geolocation services to determine where you are located.

Geolocation works by using Satellite GPS coordinates to pinpoint your location within 4 feet of your current position. This can be useful for solutions where you need to know where you are in relation to other coordinates.

Adobe's AIR 2.5 gives you access to GPS data through the Geolocation class. Common properties you can read include:

- Latitude
- Longitude
- Altitude
- HorizontalAccuracy

In addition to these commonly accessed properties you can also test the speed at which the phone is moving by measuring distance moved over a specific period of time.

The following example will simply post your location to your phone. What you can do with this, however, is take the data and apply it to location data. For instance, you might be writing an app where you want to see how far you are from the nearest campground.

1. Create a new Flash movie and name it Geo.fla.
2. In the Properties panel choose the AIR Android Settings button. Select the Permissions tab.
3. From the Permissions screen choose the hardware permission ACCESS_FINE_LOCATION to access the phone's GPS hardware.
4. On the stage create a new text field and label it "myTxt".
5. Select frame 1 on the timeline and open the Actions panel.
6. The first step in your code is to import the frameworks you need for this example to work. In this case, the two frameworks are Geolocation and GeolocationEvent.

```
import flash.events.GeolocationEvent;
import flash.sensors.Geolocation;
```

7. Declare a new Geolocation variable. In this instance, you are going to name the new variable "myGeo".

```
var myGeo:Geolocation;
```

8. The following IF/ELSE statement is looking to see if Geolocation is supported. If Geolocation is supported then Flash triggers the myGeolocationUpdateHandler to access GPS information on your current location.

```
if (Geolocation.isSupported)
{
        myGeo = new Geolocation();
        myGeo.setRequestedUpdateInterval(100);
        myGeo.addEventListener(GeolocationEvent.UPDATE,
myGeolocationUpdateHandler);
}
else
{
        myTxt.text = "No geolocation support.";
}
```

9. The following function extracts data from the GPS hardware and posts the results to the text field on the stage.

```
function myGeolocationUpdateHandler
(event:GeolocationEvent):void
{
        myTxt.text = "Geolocation is supported!" + "\n";
        myTxt.appendText("latitude:" + event.latitude.
toString() + "°\n");
        myTxt.appendText("longitude:" + event.longitude.
toString() + "°\n");
        myTxt.appendText("Altitude:" + event.altitude.
toString() + " m\n");
        myTxt.appendText("horizontal accuracy:" + event.
horizontalAccuracy.toString() + " m");
}
```

10. Save your file and then publish to your Android phone. You will notice a slight pause after your app loads as it collects the GPS coordinates.

As you can see, this is a very simple example of using GPS. You can now build solutions from these basics.

Loading RSS Data into Flash

The challenge with connecting to RSS readers is the number of different RSS technologies you have out in the wild (ATOM, RSS 1, and RSS2). This is where your knowledge of Flash can really come into play.

ActionScript 3.0 (AS3) is not a new technology. It has been around for many years. To this end, you have a large collection of open source libraries you can use to make it much easier to create your ActionScript. We are going to do just this for the following RSS reader.

The open source code is called as3syndicationlib and is hosted at Google's Code Repository (*http://code.google.com/p/ as3syndicationlib/*). This may sound alarming, but the latest update was in 2006. Yes, that seems like eons ago, but AS3 is at a point where it is mature. All you have to do is look in the right places.

Go to the Downloads page and download the code, and place the code in the folder where you will be creating the RSS feed. Now, open Flash CS5 and create a new AIR for Android application.

1. Save your new file. Open the AIR Android Settings and select the Permissions tab. Select the INTERNET permission. This will allow the app to load the external RSS feed.

2. On the stage draw a text field and add the ID "rssContent."

3. Draw a new image on the stage. Convert the image to a symbol. Give the new symbol the ID "rssButton."

4. Open the Actions panel. The first step is to identify which frameworks you are going to need in this project:

```
import com.adobe.utils.XMLUtil;
import com.adobe.xml.syndication.rss.Item20;
import com.adobe.xml.syndication.rss.RSS20;
import flash.events.Event;
import flash.events.IOErrorEvent;
import flash.events.SecurityErrorEvent;
import flash.net.URLLoader;
import flash.net.URLRequest;
import flash.net.URLRequestMethod;
```

5. The first ActionScript function will define the RSS feed you want to load.

```
var loader:URLLoader;
static const RSS_URL:String = " http://i3dot0.blogspot.
com/feeds/posts/default";
function onLoadPress():void
{
        rssLoader = new URLLoader();
        var rssRequest:URLRequest = new URLRequest
(RSS_URL);
        rssRequest.method = URLRequestMethod.GET;
        rssLoader.addEventListener(Event.COMPLETE,
onDataLoad);
        rssLoader.addEventListener(IOErrorEvent.
IO_ERROR, onIOError);
        rssLoader.addEventListener(SecurityErrorEvent.
SECURITY_ERROR, onSecurityError);
        rssLoader.load(request);
}
```

6. The following action is called when the RSS data is fully loaded:

```
function onDataLoad(e:Event):void
{
        var rawRSS:String = URLLoader(e.target).data;
        parseRSS(rawRSS);
}
```

7. Now you can parse out data from the loaded RSS feed. The following will post the title from the RSS feeds into the text field.

```
function parseRSS(data:String):void
{
        if(!XMLUtil.isValidXML(data))
        {
                writeOutput("Feed does not contain valid
XML.");
                return;
        }
        var rss:RSS20 = new RSS20();
                rss.parse(data);
                var items:Array = rss.items;
                for each(var item:Item20 in items)
                {
                        writeOutput(item.title);
                }
}
```

8. The following function will post the data to the text field on the stage.

```
function writeOutput(data:String):void
{
        rssContent.text += data + "\n";
}
```

9. The following functions will output any errors you receive to the text field:

```
function onIOError(e:IOErrorEvent):void
{
        writeOutput("IOError : " + e.text);
}
function onSecurityError(e:SecurityErrorEvent):void
{
        writeOutput("SecurityError : " + e.text);
}
```

10. The final step is to add a listener that will trigger the RSS feed to load.

```
rssButton.addEventListener(MouseEvent.CLICK,
buttonClick);
function buttonClick (e:MouseEvent):void{
onLoadPress();
}
```

11. Save your file and test on your Android device.

You can now load external data, in the form of RSS, from a different website. This is a really big deal for your development as it demonstrates that you can integrate data from different sources.

Adding Permissions to Your Apps

Developing iOS and Android apps can be slightly different. The main difference is that you can currently do more with Android apps hardware than with iOS. Will this change over time? I am certain it will, but this is where we are for now.

Many of the Android-specific features listed in the following examples require you activate specific permissions in your code. Fortunately, this is easy to do (Figure 4.2). Select AIR ANDROID settings on the Properties panel. The Application & Installer window opens. Choose the fourth tab along the top labeled Permissions. You will see a whole list of permissions you must select if you are going to use the hardware on the device.

The following is a list of permissions you can select:
- INTERNET
- WRITE_EXTERNAL_STORAGE
- READ_PHONE_STATE
- ACCESS_FINE_LOCATION
- ACCESS COARSE LOCATION
- CAMERA
- RECORD_AUDIO
- DISABLE_KEYBOARD
- WAKE_LOCK
- ACCESS_NETWORK_STATE
- ACCESS_WIFI_STATE

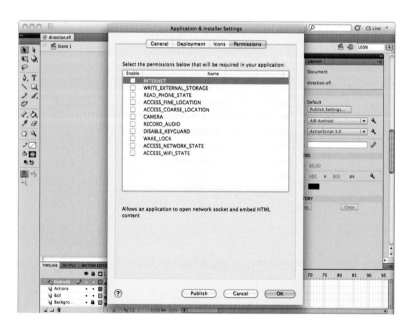

Figure 4.2 Adding permissions for Android apps.

Each of these hardware-specific permissions control different elements of your Android phone. Some are obvious, such as RECORD_AUDIO to control the microphone. Some are less obvious, such as ACCESS_FINE_LOCATION to activate the GPS settings.

You can select which permission you need for your application. You do, however, have another way to modify which permissions you can use.

Each application you develop will create an XML configuration file. The role of the file is to define launch settings, code location, and other features. One element is called the MANIFEST. The Android manifest lists in XML the hardware permissions you can use. The following demonstrates adding permission to use the CAMERA:

```
<android>
  <manifestAdditions>
    <manifest>
      <data><![CDATA[<uses-permission
android:name="android.permission.CAMERA"/>]]></data>
    </manifest>
  </manifestAdditions>
</android>
```

It is certainly easier to use the UI in Flash to state which permissions you want to use, but knowing that you can manually access and modify the permissions with your favorite notepad does have its benefits. For instance, you can add reference to a new hardware permission that may not have made its way to Flash CS5 UI. An example of this is support for VIBRATE.

Loading Web Pages into the StageWebView

It is important to remember that AIR for Android is not just a crippled version of the Adobe Integrated Runtime, but almost the complete version of AIR 2.5. A key part of AIR on the desktop is the ability to launch web ports and pull complete web pages into your Flash world. Well, AIR on Android will do the same, and it is crazy-easy to implement.

There are two key elements you need to keep in mind when using StageWebView:
- Ensure you have set your app permissions correctly
- Use the StageWebView object

The first step is to create a new AIR for Android application and open the AIR for Android settings in the Properties panel.

Choose the fourth tab, labeled Permissions. The WebView object will load an external web page. For this to occur you must select the INTERNET permission option on the Permissions tab. If you do not do this then you will *not* be able to load a web page.

Alternatively, you can manually update the XML manifest document. The following will allow the INTERNET permission to work:

```
<android>
  <manifestAdditions>
    <manifest>
      <data><![CDATA[<uses-permission
android:name="android.permission.INTERNET"/>]]></data>
    </manifest>
  </manifestAdditions>
</android>
```

The next step is to add the ActionScript that will load a StageWebView. Let's do that right now.

1. Select frame 1 in the timeline. Open the Actions panel.
2. Create a new StageWebView object and name it "webView".

   ```
   var webView:StageWebView = new StageWebView();
   ```

3. The following code states that the new StageWebView object will reside on the current stage:

   ```
   webView.stage = this.stage;
   ```

4. You can define the position and size of the WebView you load. This is called the viewport. The following ActionScript creates a new rectangular viewport and places it in the top left-hand corner with a width of 470 px and height of 300 px.

   ```
   webView.viewPort = new Rectangle(0,0,470,300);
   ```

5. Finally, you need to state the web page you want to load using the loadURL property.

   ```
   webView.loadURL("http://www.google.com");
   ```

6. Save your file and then load it onto your Android phone. You will see that the AIR app opens and reveals Google's home page.

   There are some caveats when working with StageWebView. The first is that you cannot communicate between Flash and the web page. Second, the web browser used to load the page is *not* the default Android browser but a branched version of WebKit. This means you do not have the JavaScript acceleration the V8-powered Android browser has. Finally, the StageWebView does take over the area of the stage it is loaded onto. This means you lose space you could otherwise use for application development.

There are, however, lots of benefits to running StageWebView. It is, after all, an easy way to integrate Flash and HTML together. In addition, you can load two or more viewports to a screen. For instance, you can add the following code to include a second viewport:

```
var webViewTwo:StageWebView = new StageWebView();
webViewTwo.stage = this.stage;
webViewTwo.viewPort = new Rectangle(0,305,470,300);
webViewTwo.loadURL("http://www.focalpress.com");
```

You are also not restricted to loading web pages on external sites. You can load pages local to the application. For this, however, you must remember to include the local HTML as part of your application when you build the app. This is done through the AIR Android settings tab. Choose the folder with the included HTML you want to include in the final package.

Controlling the Use of the Microphone

The microphone is arguably the most used part of a phone. You need it for every call you make. You can also use it to record audio. The following section demonstrates how you can leverage the microphone in your solutions.

1. Start by creating a new Flash AIR for Android solution.
2. Open the AIR Android settings and select Permissions. Check the AUDIO permission.
3. On the stage, select frame 1 from the timeline and open the Actions panel. Add the following to create a 4-second delay in your project:

```
const DELAY_LENGTH:int = 4000;
```

4. The next step is to create the new microphone object. Here you will see that it has been abbreviated to mic.

```
var mic:Microphone = Microphone.getMicrophone();
```

5. Two properties for the microphone include gain (loudness) and rate (sound quality). The following sets the gain and rate for the new mic object.

```
mic.gain = 100;
mic.rate = 44;
```

6. The following sets the microphone to stop working (silence level of 0) after the DELAY_LENGTH period has passed. In this instance, DELAY_LENGTH is 4000 milliseconds, or 4 seconds.

```
mic.setSilenceLevel(0, DELAY_LENGTH);
```

7. The following line triggers the microphone object listener.

```
mic.addEventListener(SampleDataEvent.SAMPLE_DATA,
micSampleDataHandler);
```

8. The following timer object uses the same time-based technology in ActionScript covered in the previous section, demonstrating that you do not need to relearn Flash to build Android apps.

```
var timer:Timer = new Timer(DELAY_LENGTH);
timer.addEventListener(TimerEvent.TIMER, timerHandler);
timer.start();
var soundBytes:ByteArray = new ByteArray();
```

9. The following function captures the sound to the phone's memory.

```
function micSampleDataHandler(event:SampleDataEvent):
void
      {
            while (event.data.bytesAvailable)
            {
                  var sample:Number = event.data.readFloat();
                  soundBytes.writeFloat(sample);
            }
      }
```

10. The following uses the mic object to record a new sound file.

```
function timerHandler(event:TimerEvent):void
      {
            mic.removeEventListener(SampleDataEvent.
SAMPLE_DATA, micSampleDataHandler);
            timer.stop();
            soundBytes.position = 0;
            var sound:Sound = new Sound();
            sound.addEventListener(SampleDataEvent.
SAMPLE_DATA, playbackSampleHandler);
            sound.play();
      }
```

11. The following function will play back the 4 seconds of record audio.

```
function playbackSampleHandler(event:SampleDataEvent):void
      {
            for (var i:int = 0; i < 8192 && soundBytes.
bytesAvailable > 0; i++)
            {
                  var sample:Number = soundBytes.readFloat();
                  event.data.writeFloat(sample);
                  event.data.writeFloat(sample);
            }
      }
```

12. Save your work. Compile and load the APK file onto your Android phone. Select the app and talk into your microphone. After 4 seconds, the audio will stop and will play back to you.

You can easily extend this example. For instance, you can add a button that allows you to click and record the audio; audio files can be saved to the physical hard drive on the Android phone. You can even use the many ActionScript libraries that modify sound files to create a sound modulator. In other words, you can do a lot.

Controlling the Camera

For me, one of the coolest features you can access on your phone is the camera. The goal of this section is to demonstrate how you can access the camera on your Android phone. As with the microphone example earlier, you can add additional ActionScript that will allow you to save your video for playback later or even add color correction controls.

But enough of that; let's jump right into the project.

1. The first thing is to create a new Android Flash project and then associate the correct hardware permissions. You should be comfortable doing this by now. The hardware that needs permission is the CAMERA.
2. Instead of adding the code into the Timeline, let's go ahead and create a simple class for the AIR solution. Name a new class in the Properties panel takeVideoTest and select Flash as the code environment.
3. After the opening package add the following references to different frameworks.

```
package
{
        import flash.display.Sprite;
        import flash.media.Camera;
        import flash.media.Video;
        import flash.text.TextField;
        import flash.text.TextFieldAutoSize;
        import flash.text.TextFormat;
        import flash.utils.Timer;
        import flash.events.TimerEvent;
        import flash.events.StatusEvent;
        import flash.events.MouseEvent;
        import flash.system.SecurityPanel;
        import flash.system.Security;
```

4. Next, let's declare the variables you will be using:

```
public class takeVideoTest extends Sprite
{
        private var myTxt:TextField;
        private var headerTxt:TextField;
        private var cam:Camera;
        private var t:Timer = new Timer(1000);
        public function takeVideoTest()
```

5. The variables just listed will control two different text fields, the camera and a timer control.

6. The next block defines the size, position, and other properties of the myTxt field.

```
{
myTxt = new TextField();
myTxt.x = 10;
myTxt.y = 10;
myTxt.background = true;
myTxt.selectable = false;
myTxt.autoSize = TextFieldAutoSize.LEFT;
```

7. The following ActionScript defines the properties of the headerTxt field.

```
headerTxt = new TextField();
headerTxt.x = 120;
headerTxt.y = 220;
headerTxt.autoSize = TextFieldAutoSize.LEFT;
```

8. The following is a style document that formats the visual presentation of the text fields:

```
var format:TextFormat = new TextFormat();
format.font = "_Sans";
format.color = 0xFF0000;
format.size = 24;
format.bold = true;
headerTxt.defaultTextFormat = format;
addChild(headerTxt);
```

9. The following IF/ELSE statement is looking to see if the camera is installed. Remember, although it is common for Android phones to have a camera, it is not mandatory. The first part of the IF statement will throw a message if there is no camera installed.

```
cam = Camera.getCamera();
if (! cam)
{
myTxt.text = "No camera is installed.";
}
```

10. If the camera is installed and is working, the following message will be sent to the myTxt field informing the user that the camera is connecting.

```
else
{
myTxt.text = "Connecting";
connectCamera();
}
addChild(myTxt);
```

```
t.addEventListener(TimerEvent.TIMER, timerHandler);
}
private function clickHandler(e:MouseEvent):void
private function statusHandler(event:StatusEvent):void
{
if (event.code == "Camera.Unmuted")
{
connectCamera();
cam.removeEventListener(StatusEvent.STATUS,
statusHandler);
}
}
```

11. The following function controls the size and position of the video playback.

```
private function connectCamera():void
{
var vid:Video = new Video(cam.width,cam.height);
vid.x = 10;
vid.y = 10;
vid.width = 120;
vid.height = 120;
vid.attachCamera(cam);
addChild(vid);
t.start();
}
```

12. Finally, the following function will send data about the video camera's performance to the myTxt screen. Video frames per second playback will vary depending on your hardware.

```
private function timerHandler(event:TimerEvent):void
{
myTxt.y = cam.height + 20;
myTxt.text = "";
myTxt.appendText("bandwidth: " + cam.bandwidth + "\n");
myTxt.appendText("currentFPS: " + Math.round(cam.
currentFPS) + "\n");
myTxt.appendText("fps: " + cam.fps + "\n");
myTxt.appendText("keyFrameInterval: " + cam.
keyFrameInterval + "\n");
headerTxt.text = "Video Camera Test";
}
}
}
```

13. The final step is to save your work and then test it on your Android phone.

Video support in AIR is going to be a big deal. Through access to the camera you can add augmented reality to your AIR apps, video editing, and video conference similar to Apple's FaceTime.

Additional Features on AIR 2.5 for Android

There are additional software features that are specific to Android. The following allow you cache images so they play back more efficiently on the screen and demonstrate how you can load external data directly into your AIR project.

Working with cacheAsBitmapMatrix

Another optimization trick you can do is to restrict your use of vector-based images inside of Flash. Where possible use PNG formatted images. The good news is that that Android has great support for PNG files, allowing you to include transparency.

If you do need to use vector images you can fool the iPhone into thinking that the image is a bitmap by using the cacheAsBitmapMatrix.

1. The first step is to create a new image. You will need to import the Flash Geom Matrix:

```
import flash.geom.Matrix;
```

2. Create a new shape:

```
var my_shape :MyShape = new MyShape();
addChild(my_shape);
```

3. Now use the cacheAsBitmap property to ensure that all objects that are created are cached:

```
my_shape.cacheAsBitmap = true;
my_shape.cacheAsBitmapMatrix = new Matrix();
```

4. You can now create images on the screen that the iPhone thinks are bitmaps.

Audio files can have a short delay between an event happening and the sound playing. This is because the audio file is not in the iPhone's cache for playback. You can avoid this by exporting your audio file to be triggered in the first frame of your movie.

Summary

A mobile platform gives you many different ways you can interact with your applications: you have fingers pointing, gestures, and hardware interactivity. Throwing these all together provides you with new opportunities to interact with your app. Pulling together your knowledge of ActionScript, you now have the foundation knowledge you need to build applications for iOS and Android devices.

PROJECT: BUILDING A GESTURE-DRIVEN APPLICATION

The focus of this chapter is to get you comfortable working with gestures on your Android and iPhone device. By the time you are done with the chapter you will have created a slide show application that includes on-screen tap, swipe, drag and drop, and Geolocation.

Getting Started

You will need to download the files for the project at *www .visualizetheweb.com/flashmobile* (click the Book tab). It is important to download the files for this project; I will be jumping over some of the basic setup features (such as importing images into the library) so we can focus on the interactive elements in ActionScript. Make sense? Great.

Let's begin by looking into the basic construction of the project.

Begin by opening Project.fla (Figure 4.1Proj). You will see that the project is a short presentation discussing the beauty of hiking. There are two parts that make up the app: the first screen and the movie clip labeled slides_mc, which is a four-frame movie. Each frame will be a different section of the presentation.

The main timeline has two other main features: navigation buttons (forward and backward) and a text box to let you know which frame you are on. The forward and backward buttons are labeled prev_btn and next_btn, with the text field named slide-Number_txt (Figure 4.2Proj).

The goals of this next section are to:

- Allow a user to tap on the buttons to go forward and backward
- Dynamically change the page transition from one screen to the next
- Post back to the text field which screen you are on

  Later in the chapter you will add more complex interaction.

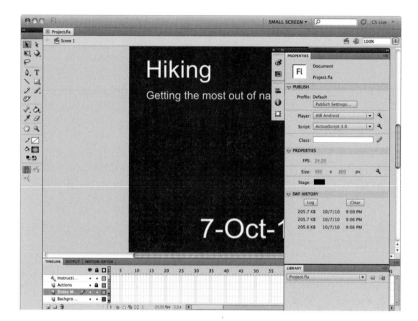

Figure 4.1Proj The hiking project you will create.

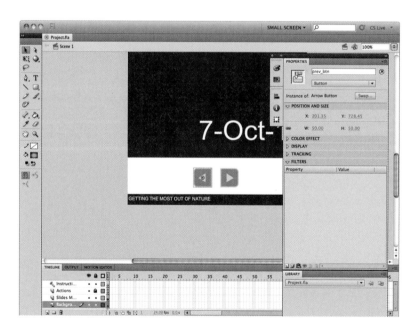

Figure 4.2Proj Label the forward, backward, and text fields.

Navigating Using the Tap Gesture

You will need the Actions panel open for most of this, and you will be adding the ActionScript to frame 1 of the main timeline.

1. Create a new frame and name it Actions.
2. Add the first Action to the Actions panel: Stop();
3. Instruct Flash that you will be using gestures with the following code:

```
Multitouch.inputMode = MultitouchInputMode.TOUCH_POINT;
```

4. Add an event listener for the next button. Notice that listener is calling nextSlideButton as the function that will activate when the event is triggered by a single tap on the screen.

```
next_btn.addEventListener(TouchEvent.TOUCH_TAP,
fl_nextSlideButton);
```

5. The fl_nextSlideButton function in turns calls a second function that is used to determine where in the movie clip you are currently located (Figure 4.3Proj).

```
function fl_nextSlideButton(evt:TouchEvent):void
{
        fl_nextSlide();
}
```

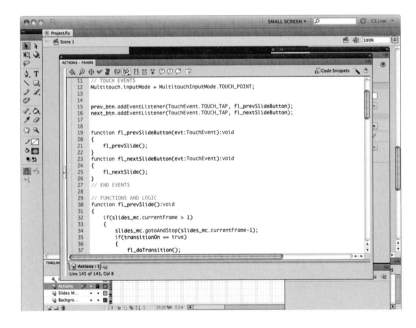

Figure 4.3Proj Add a nextSlide action.

The following function, fl_nextSlide, examines where you are in the slides_mc movie clip.

```
function fl_nextSlide():void
{
    if(slides_mc.currentFrame < slides_mc.totalFrames)
    {
        slides_mc.gotoAndStop(slides_mc.currentFrame+1);
        if(transitionOn == true)
        {
            fl_doTransition();
        }
        if(pageNumberOn == false)
        {
            slideNumber_txt.text = "";
        } else {
            slideNumber_txt.text = String(slides_
mc.currentFrame + "/" + slides_mc.totalFrames);
        }
    }
}
```

The whole function is an IF statement. Line 3 of the function examines if you are on the final frame of the slides_mc, as shown in Figure 4.4Proj. If you are, then nothing will happen. If you are not, three things will be triggered:

- You will move to the next slide.
- A transition from screen to screen will happen if the setting is set to True.
- Text informing the presenter which screen you are on will be updated.

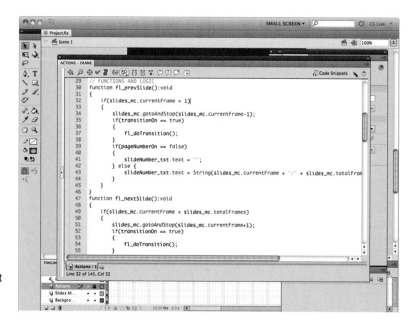

Figure 4.4Proj The ActionScript will update the text along the bottom of the screen.

Moving from one screen to the next is controlled through the first line:

```
slides_mc.gotoAndStop(slides_mc.currentFrame+1);
```

Here you are looking at the current frame you are on and simply adding 1 to that number to move you forward. We'll come back to the transition code in a moment.

The third IF statement in the block of code is looking to see if you want to add text. You will notice that the block of code is looking for a True/False value. You can control whether you want this statement turned on or off by setting a True/False variable, as shown:

```
var pageNumberOn:Boolean = true; // true, false
```

Transitions are a little more complicated, simply because you can change the different transitions you want in the presentation (Figure 4.5Proj).

Start by adding an import action to include the transition functions onto the screen:

```
import fl.transitions.*;
```

You can choose to include or exclude transitions by adding the following ActionScript:

```
var transitionOn:Boolean = true; // true, false
```

Let's assume you want to add transitions (keeping your value at True); you can also choose a specific type of transition:

```
var transitionType:String = "Fade"; // Blinds, Fade,
Fly, Iris, Photo, PixelDissolve, Rotate, Squeeze, Wipe,
Zoom, Random
```

As you can see, there are 10 transitions and each has to have its own definition, depending on which you choose (Figure 4.6Proj).

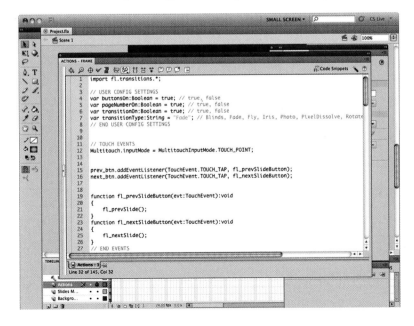

Figure 4.5Proj You can set default scripts to turn on and off different features in the presentation.

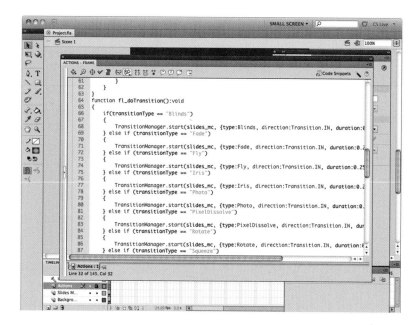

Figure 4.6Proj There are 10 different transitions you can add to the presentation.

This is handled through a fl_doTransition function. The following is an IF statement:

```
function fl_doTransition():void
{
    if(transitionType == "Blinds")
    {
        TransitionManager.start(slides_mc, {type:Blinds,
direction:Transition.IN, duration:0.25});
    } else if (transitionType == "Fade")
    {
        TransitionManager.start(slides_mc, {type:Fade,
direction:Transition.IN, duration:0.25});
    } else if (transitionType == "Fly")
    {
        TransitionManager.start(slides_mc, {type:Fly,
direction:Transition.IN, duration:0.25});
    } else if (transitionType == "Iris")
    {
        TransitionManager.start(slides_mc, {type:Iris,
direction:Transition.IN, duration:0.25});
    } else if (transitionType == "Photo")
    {
        TransitionManager.start(slides_mc, {type:Photo,
direction:Transition.IN, duration:0.25});
    } else if (transitionType == "PixelDissolve")
    {
        TransitionManager.start(slides_mc,
{type:PixelDissolve, direction:Transition.IN,
duration:0.25});
```

```
    } else if (transitionType == "Rotate")
    {
        TransitionManager.start(slides_mc, {type:Rotate,
direction:Transition.IN, duration:0.25});
    } else if (transitionType == "Squeeze")
    {
        TransitionManager.start(slides_mc,
{type:Squeeze, direction:Transition.IN, duration:0.25});
    } else if (transitionType == "Wipe")
    {
        TransitionManager.start(slides_mc, {type:Wipe,
direction:Transition.IN, duration:0.25});
    } else if (transitionType == "Zoom")
```

A final option you have with your transitions is to add a random feature to change the transitions for each screen. This is handled by adding a little random math magic to a switch statement:

```
    {
        TransitionManager.start(slides_mc, {type:Zoom,
direction:Transition.IN, duration:0.25});
    } else if (transitionType == "Random")
    {
        var randomNumber:Number = Math.round(Math.
random()*9) + 1;
        switch (randomNumber) {
            case 1:
                TransitionManager.start(slides_mc,
{type:Blinds, direction:Transition.IN, duration:0.25});
                break;
            case 2:
                TransitionManager.start(slides_mc,
{type:Fade, direction:Transition.IN, duration:0.25});
                break;
            case 3:
                TransitionManager.start(slides_mc,
{type:Fly, direction:Transition.IN, duration:0.25});
                break;
            case 4:
                TransitionManager.start(slides_mc,
{type:Iris, direction:Transition.IN, duration:0.25});
                break;
            case 5:
                TransitionManager.start(slides_mc,
{type:Photo, direction:Transition.IN, duration:0.25});
                break;
            case 6:
                TransitionManager.start(slides_
mc, {type:PixelDissolve, direction:Transition.IN,
duration:0.25});
                break;
```

```
                case 7:
                        TransitionManager.start(slides_mc,
{type:Rotate, direction:Transition.IN, duration:0.25});
                        break;
                case 8:
                        TransitionManager.start(slides_mc,
{type:Squeeze, direction:Transition.IN, duration:0.25});
                        break;
                case 9:
                        TransitionManager.start(slides_mc,
{type:Wipe, direction:Transition.IN, duration:0.25});
                        break;
                case 10:
                        TransitionManager.start(slides_mc,
{type:Zoom, direction:Transition.IN, duration:0.25});
                        break;
                }
        }
```

At this point you can test your movie. You will be able to click forward on each screen, but will not be able to move backward. Following is the code that will allow you to go back to the previous screen:

```
function fl_prevSlide():void
{
    if(slides_mc.currentFrame > 1)
    {
        slides_mc.gotoAndStop(slides_mc.currentFrame-1);
        if(transitionOn == true)
        {
            fl_doTransition();
        }
        if(pageNumberOn == false)
        {
            slideNumber_txt.text = "";
        } else {
            slideNumber_txt.text = String(slides_
mc.currentFrame + "/" + slides_mc.totalFrames);
        }
    }
}
```

At this point you will want to test your movie. Using the tap gesture on the buttons, you can now move from one screen to the next in your movie clip.

Adding a Swipe Gesture to Move from One Screen to the Next

The next gesture to add to the app is a swipe gesture to move from one screen to the next. You can add this to the home page, but let's take a deeper look at the swipe gesture and add it to each frame of the Slides movie clip.

Go to frame 1 of the Slides movie clip. The following ActionScript sets the gesture mode:

```
Multitouch.inputMode = MultitouchInputMode.GESTURE;
```

Following this you need to declare the type of gesture you want to use in the event listener. You will see in the following that you are using a GESTURE_SWIPE, or swipe gesture, that references the whole stage. When the swipe gesture is done, the fl_SwipeToGoToNextPreviousFrame_2 function is called:

```
stage.addEventListener (TransformGestureEvent.GESTURE_
SWIPE, fl_SwipeToGoToNextPreviousFrame_2);
```

The following function looks to see if you are swiping to the left (offsetX value is set to –1). If the event is true, then you will go to frame 2 (Figure 4.7Proj).

```
function fl_SwipeToGoToNextPreviousFrame_2
(event:TransformGestureEvent):void
    {
    if(event.offsetX == -1)
        {
            gotoAndStop(2);
        }
    }
```

The swipe gesture for frame 2 is very similar. The exception, as you will see next, is that you can swipe left (offsetX value is

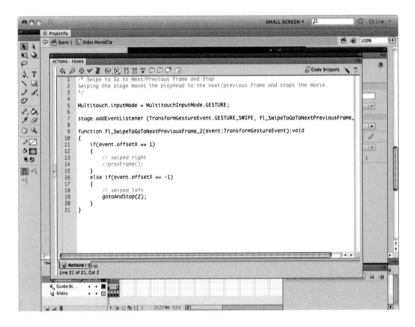

Figure 4.7Proj The ActionScript shows you a swipe gesture that will take you to the next screen.

set to −1) or right (offsetX value is set to 1), sending you forward or backward one frame.

```
stage.addEventListener (TransformGestureEvent.GESTURE_
SWIPE, fl_SwipeToGoToNextPreviousFrame);
    function fl_SwipeToGoToNextPreviousFrame
(event:TransformGestureEvent):void
    {
        if(event.offsetX == 1)
        {
           gotoAndStop(1);
        }
        else if(event.offsetX == -1)
        {
           gotoAndStop(3);
        }
    }
```

Frame 3 is very similar. Frame 4 will only allow you to swipe from the left:

```
stage.addEventListener (TransformGestureEvent.GESTURE_
SWIPE, fl_SwipeToGoToNextPreviousFrame_4);
    function fl_SwipeToGoToNextPreviousFrame_4
(event:TransformGestureEvent):void
    {
        if(event.offsetX == 1)
        {
          gotoAndStop(3);
        }
    }
```

Save your files and test the movie. You can now swipe from one frame to the next.

Adding Drag and Drop Gestures

The drag and drop gesture is very similar to the tap gesture. You will use drag and drop on the third frame of the presentation to move the different photos around (Figure 4.8Proj).

Frame 3 has three photos. Each photo is a movie clip, with the names pictureOne, pictureTwo, and pictureThree.

The drag and drop event is created by a starting and ending event (called TOUCH_BEGIN and TOUCH_END). The following declares the input type of TOUCH_POINT.

```
Multitouch.inputMode = MultitouchInputMode.TOUCH_POINT;
```

A TOUCH_BEGIN listener is created to declare the starting point of the touch event:

```
pictureOne.addEventListener(TouchEvent.TOUCH_BEGIN,
fl_TouchBeginHandler_5);
```

As you might expect, a function in the listener is called to determine what will happen if you use this listener. In this instance you want to be able to move the photo around the screen. To do this you first need to define the area of the screen and then call that area in your new function. The following variable will hold the values of the screen size:

```
var fl_DragBounds_5:Rectangle = new Rectangle(0, 0,
stage.stageWidth, stage.stageHeight);
```

Now that you know the screen size you can now use it in your function:

```
function fl_TouchBeginHandler_5(event:TouchEvent):void
{
        event.target.startTouchDrag(event.touchPointID,
false, fl_DragBounds_5);
}
```

The following listener and function will control what happens when you stop moving the photo around the screen. In this instance, the stopTouchDrag property is triggered.

```
pictureOne.addEventListener(TouchEvent.TOUCH_END,
fl_TouchEndHandler_5);
function fl_TouchEndHandler_5(event:TouchEvent):void
{
        event.target.stopTouchDrag(event.touchPointID);
}
```

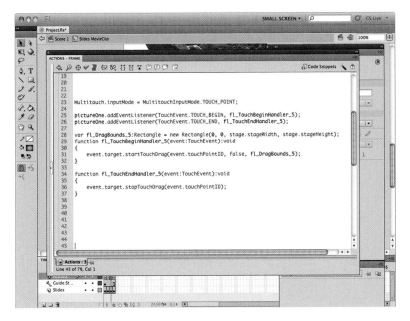

Figure 4.8Proj The drag and drop gesture allows you to move objects, such as this picture, around the screen.

The pictureTwo movie clip has similar events:

```
pictureTwo.addEventListener(TouchEvent.TOUCH_BEGIN,
fl_TouchBeginHandler_7);
    pictureTwo.addEventListener(TouchEvent.TOUCH_END,
fl_TouchEndHandler_7);
    var fl_DragBounds_7:Rectangle = new Rectangle(0, 0,
stage.stageWidth, stage.stageHeight);
    function fl_TouchBeginHandler_7(event:TouchEvent):void
    {
        event.target.startTouchDrag(event.touchPointID,
false, fl_DragBounds_7);
    }
    function fl_TouchEndHandler_7(event:TouchEvent):void
    {
        event.target.stopTouchDrag(event.touchPointID);
    }
```

The differences in the code are the names of the functions and the movie clip that is being referenced.

Finally, here is the code for pictureThree:

```
pictureThree.addEventListener(TouchEvent.TOUCH_BEGIN,
fl_TouchBeginHandler_6);
    pictureThree.addEventListener(TouchEvent.TOUCH_END,
fl_TouchEndHandler_6);
    var fl_DragBounds_6:Rectangle = new Rectangle(0, 0,
stage.stageWidth, stage.stageHeight);
    function fl_TouchBeginHandler_6(event:TouchEvent):
void
    {
        event.target.startTouchDrag(event.touchPointID,
false, fl_DragBounds_6);
    }
    function fl_TouchEndHandler_6(event:TouchEvent):void
    {
        event.target.stopTouchDrag(event.touchPointID);
    }
```

Save your project. Publish your files to your Android or iPhone device. Swipe until you get to the third screen of the presentation. You can now drag the pictures around the screen.

Using Geolocation to Find Where You Are

The final frame of the movie used the Geolocation hardware on your phone to determine where you are. When using Geolocation, first you need to change your Android publishing permissions to allow for Fine and Coarse location detection. If you do not set these, then you cannot use the GPS or WiFi location tools on your phone.

Go to frame 4 of the presentation. On the screen is a text field with the name of myTxt. The Geolocation information will be posted to this screen.

In the Actions panel import the namespaces you need to leverage the Geolocation tools:

```
import flash.events.GeolocationEvent;
import flash.sensors.Geolocation;
Next, add the following variable and declare the object
to be a Geolocation object.
var myGeo:Geolocation;
```

You can now use this variable in the following if/else statement. In the following statement, you are looking to see if Geolocation is supported. If Geolocation is *not* supported then a message is sent to the myTxt field on the screen.

If Geolocation *is* supported then you will update the screen 10 times a second. Remember that the GPS tool will drain a battery quickly.

```
if (Geolocation.isSupported)
{
        myGeo = new Geolocation();
        myGeo.setRequestedUpdateInterval(100);
        myGeo.addEventListener(GeolocationEvent.UPDATE,
myGeolocationUpdateHandler);
}
else
{
        myTxt.text = "No geolocation support.";
}
```

The following function is called if Geolocation is supported to print information to the screen, letting you know what the latitude, longitude, altitude, and horizontal accuracy are, as shown in Figure 4.9Proj.

```
function myGeolocationUpdateHandler
(event:GeolocationEvent):void
    {
        myTxt.text = ("latitude: " + event.latitude.
toString() + "°\n");
        myTxt.appendText("longitude: " + event.
longitude.toString() + " m\n");
        myTxt.appendText("Altitude: " + event.altitude.
toString() + " m\n");
        myTxt.appendText("horizontal accuracy:
" + event.horizontalAccuracy.toString() + " m");
    }
```

At this point you can save and test your movie in your iPhone or Android device.

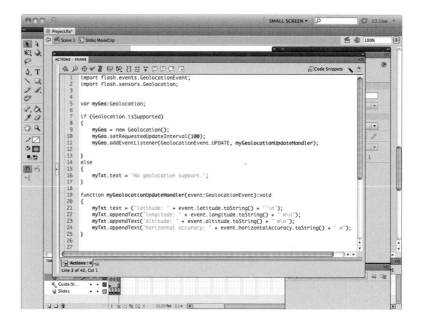

Figure 4.9Proj Geolocation uses both GPS and WiFi to determine where you are located on the planet.

Summary

In this project you have seen how you can use your phone's hardware to manage touch-screen gestures and GPS coordinates. This just scratches the surface of what you can do. But it is fun to have a fully functioning app running on your phone, isn't it?

BUILDING GAMES WITH FLASH FOR THE MOBILE MARKET

Almost a third of all apps developed for the Android and iOS are games. In this section we introduce you to game development on the Android and iOS.

Getting Started with Game Development

There are more than 50,000 games in the iTunes App Store and 20,000 in the Android Market Place (Figure 5.1). They range from simple word puzzles to complex 3D strategy games. In this section you will learn the basics needed for game development:

Figure 5.1 A small selection of the thousands of games available for iOS.

- Understanding what you want your game to be
- Planning, planning, planning
- Using Flash to do the heavy work
- Developing your game to work on all devices

Often the biggest decision you need to make when developing a game is, what do I want the game to do? Think about this long and hard. The reality is that no game is created quickly; you will spend a lot of time on your game and you want to ensure that the game is worth your time.

In many ways, Flash is maturing into an ideal platform for game development. Advances in the Flash Player and the work the Flash Team at Adobe have put into AIR allow you to perform almost limitless tasks in Flash. For instance, you can create simple card games, logic games, or even complex multiplayer games. In fact, the most popular game on the planet, FarmVille, is written in Flash. Want to take it up a notch with 3D, no problem. Flash will handle your 3D worlds just fine.

When you have decided what type of game you want to develop, the next stage is planning. OK, I know this may not be the most thrilling part of game design, but it is in many ways the most important. You simply don't want to just jump in and begin coding. With the OOP program structure in AS3, you do need to think ahead.

With that said, you can break down the structure of your game into the following sections:

- For whom is the game intended?
- What type of game is it?
- What will the screens of the game look like?
- What sounds and visuals do you need for the game?
- What is the target device for your game?

Understanding your audience is a big part of game design. Are you building a game that is for anyone, such as your mother or aunt, or are you targeting a specific group, such as teen boys (yeah, we want lots of blood and violence!). Get it down on paper, in an e-mail, or a tweet, just so you know who you want buying your game. This will keep your focus through the game development life cycle. The following screen shot shows a selection of games available on Apple's iTunes App Store.

When you know your intended audience, you next need to know what type of game you want to develop. There are simply loads of game options for Flash, as mentioned earlier. Some common types include parlor games (games that can be played and learned in 30 seconds or less); role-playing games, such as FarmVille, where you can play the game for the rest of your life; and even complex physics games where you are colliding with objects all over the place.

The reason why you have so many choices when it comes to game development is simple: ActionScript 3.0 (AS3). The AS3

Figure 5.2 A subselection of iOS games that target puzzle fans.

AVM is simply very powerful and gives you the opportunity to flex your programming muscles.

Screen design and development is a lot of fun. You will enjoy this part of your game development. There are lots of ways to develop your screen; the way I like to approach screen design is simply to get a notepad, permanent marker, and an open mind. Draw screens out on the notepad. Scratch out and restart as many times as needed until you have the designs that make you feel most comfortable. The objective is to get ideas down on paper.

When you have your ideas on paper you have a choice: either leave them as draft ideas or flesh them out with greater detail. My personal preference is to leave them as rough drawings. Tweaks and modifications can be made later.

Games are multisensory. You will want to ensure that you address this by adding audio and visual feedback to your audience as they play your games. It is worth buying some good graphics. Don't use clip art—it always looks like you used clip art and looks shoddy. There are lots of ways of getting sounds. Some of the best resources are the collections of sounds you can buy from the BBC, Sony, or Warner Bros. Each company has sound effect files you can download and use in your project (Figure 5.3).

The final choice you need to make is to decide for which device you will design your game. Is this an iPad game, an

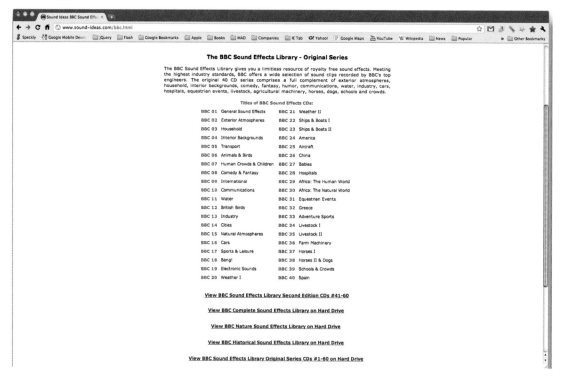

Figure 5.3 A selection of sound effects organized by category that the BBC offers.

Android game, or one for the BlackBerry PlayBook? Each device is different in shape, the speed of the CPU/GPU, and technology. Flash can handle a lot, but a game for the iPod Touch is going to look different when run on a tablet.

After you have gone through this process you are now ready to start developing your game.

Making It Easier to Write Code with Libraries

Code development is a lot of work. Creating simple scripts takes time. As you can imagine, game development gets even more complicated. To help you get through this problem you will want to leverage code libraries. A library is a collection of AS3 classes that perform specific functions: they may be animation, collision detection, physics, 3D, or more. There are a lot of libraries you can use.

Before jumping into specific Game Engine libraries, let's look at some general code libraries that will help you in your game development.

There are essentially three groups of libraries you should be concerned about as a game developer:

- Utilities
- Animation
- 3D

This game does not contain more specific game engine tools, such as physics engines, but we will get to that soon enough. In many ways, this collection of libraries can be used for any application you develop for your mobile device—they all run on AS3. The news keeps getting better. All of these libraries are free and open source. You can start using them in your projects right now without spending a single penny.

Adding a Library to Your Project

Libraries can be added quite easily to your project. Generally, you will download a library in a single ZIP file. The file will contain a folder or collection of folders with the code. Find your application folder and include the new library folders in the same directory.

The next step is to link to the library from your ActionScript code. The following example demonstrates how you can do this with GreenSock's TweenMax animation library. The first step is to download the AS3 library (Figure 5.4). Depending on which library you use will depend on where you can find it. For TweenMax you can go straight to *www.greensock.com*

Figure 5.4 GreenSock's animation library is arguably the most popular tween tool for Flash projects.

and find the link right off the home page. Make sure you select the AS3 version of TweenMax. As with many libraries, TweenMax comes in AS2 and AS3 flavors. As we said earlier in this book, AS2 is not supported in mobile devices.

The file you download will be a ZIP folder (Figure 5.5). The folder contains *a lot* of content, but most of it is documentation and you do not need it in your project. What you *do* need is the folder called COM. Locate the COM folder and copy it to the same folder as your Flash project.

What is inside the COM folder? It is all the classes and goodness that you need for adding dozens of different types of animation to your projects. You do not need to add complexity when you have these classes. For example, the TweenMax class structure manages all the events, getters/setters, animation types (there are a lot), layout, loading, data, motion paths, and much, much more. The following is just one small example of the work GreenSock has done for you. This is the class library that allows you to add Elastic animation type to your project:

```
package com.greensock.easing {
    public class Elastic {
        private static const _2PI:Number = Math.PI * 2;
```

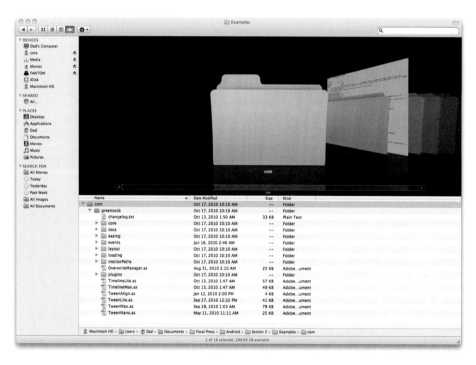

Figure 5.5 The folder structure for GreenSock's library.

```
        public static function easeIn (t:Number,
b:Number, c:Number, d:Number, a:Number = 0, p:Number =
0):Number {
            var s:Number;
            if (t==0) return b; if ((t/=d)==1) return
b+c; if (!p) p=d*.3;
            if (!a || (c > 0 && a < c) || (c < 0 && a <
-c)) { a=c; s = p/4; }
            else s = p/_2PI * Math.asin (c/a);
            return -(a*Math.pow(2,10*(t-=1)) * Math.sin(
(t*d-s)*_2PI/p )) + b;
            }
        public static function easeOut (t:Number,
b:Number, c:Number, d:Number, a:Number = 0, p:Number =
0):Number {
            var s:Number;
            if (t==0) return b; if ((t/=d)==1) return
b+c; if (!p) p=d*.3;
            if (!a || (c > 0 && a < c) || (c < 0 && a <
-c)) { a=c; s = p/4; }
            else s = p/_2PI * Math.asin (c/a);
            return (a*Math.pow(2,-10*t) * Math.sin(
(t*d-s)*_2PI/p ) + c + b);
            }
        public static function easeInOut (t:Number,
b:Number, c:Number, d:Number, a:Number = 0, p:Number =
0):Number {
            var s:Number;
            if (t==0) return b; if ((t/=d*0.5)==2)
return b+c; if (!p) p=d*(.3*1.5);
            if (!a || (c > 0 && a < c) || (c < 0 && a <
-c)) { a=c; s = p/4; }
            else s = p/_2PI * Math.asin (c/a);
            if (t < 1) return -.5*(a*Math.pow(2,10*(t-=1))
* Math.sin( (t*d-s)*_2PI/p )) + b;
            return a*Math.pow(2,-10*(t-=1)) * Math.sin(
(t*d-s)*_2PI/p )*.5 + c + b;
            }
        }
    }
```

That is *a lot* of complex code. And you do not need to write it. To get this type of animation into your project you simply need to reference the library, its exposed classes, and add it to your own project.

To do this, you will need to save a Flash Professional file into the same directory as your library, the folder with the COM folder.

Open the Actions panel and add the following:

```
import com.greensock.TweenMax;
```

This command will import that TweenMax class. In turn, the TweenMax class will then import all the other Class files and allow you to add them to your project.

Now, let's see how easy it is to add the Elastic animation to your project.

Create a simple drawing in Flash and convert it into a movie clip instance. Name the instance myAnimation. Place the movie clip in the center of the stage. The objective will be to use the Elastic animation sequence to add animation to move the movie clip named myAnimation into the top left-hand corner.

In the Actions panel add the following:

```
TweenMax.to(myAnimation, 1, {x:0, y:0, ease:Elastic.
easeIn});
```

Test your animation. Your animation should now work using just two lines of code.

As you can see, libraries can dramatically reduce the amount of work needed to add core functionality.

Working with Utility Libraries

A utility is a tool that performs a function that is under the hood. This group includes data control, security, and other functions that the user does not see.

Using AS3CoreLib

The first library you will want to use is AS3CoreLib (Figure 5.6). The library is written by some of the leading Flash evangelists— Mike Chambers, Christian Cantrell, Tinic Uro, et al.—and covers

Figure 5.6 AS3CoreLib contains many core assets for your projects.

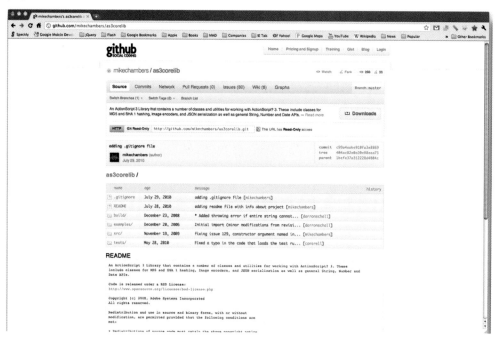

some very important behind-the-scenes features around security. AS3CoreLib allows you to easily leverage the following in your code:

- MD5 hash
- SHA1 hash
- JSON library (serialization and deserialization)
- JPEG and PNG encoding
- HTTP Utility and Helper Classes
- Array, String, Date, Number, and XML Utility APIs

The AS3CoreLib can be downloaded at *http://github.com/ mikechambers/as3corelib*.

Using AS3Crypto

As the name suggests, AS3Crypto is a library designed to add ways in which you can encrypt your data coming in and out of Flash (Figure 5.7). This library includes the ability to connect with SSL. The list of supported cryptography is very impressive. You can use the following:

- Protocols: TLS 1.0 support (partial)
- Certificates: X.509 Certificate parsing and validation, built-in Root CAs

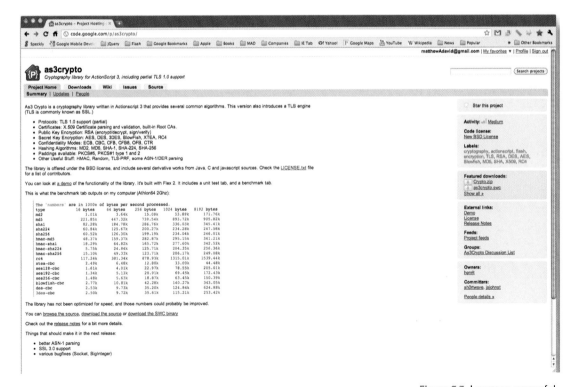

Figure 5.7 Leverage powerful encryption tools in your apps.

- Public key encryption: RSA (encrypt/decrypt, sign/verify)
- Secret key encryption: AES, DES, 3DES, BlowFish, XTEA, RC4
- Confidentiality modes: ECB, CBC, CFB, CFB8, OFB, CTR
- Hashing algorithms: MD2, MD5, SHA-1, SHA-224, SHA-256
- Paddings available: PKCS#5, PKCS#1 type 1 and 2
- Other useful stuff: HMAC, Random, TLS-PRF, some ASN-1/ DER parsing

The library can be downloaded at *http://code.google.com/p/ as3crypto/*.

One note of caution when building iOS apps with cryptography: You must ensure that you declare what type of cryptography you are using when you submit your app to the App Store. If you do not, Apple will reject your app.

Using AS3eBayLib

The AS3eBayLib allows you to easily connect to eBay's public XML API files. This allows you to create novel and unique experiences with eBay's massive amount of content and ecommerce.

You can download the library (Figure 5.8) at *http://code.google .com/p/as3ebaylib/*.

Figure 5.8 Add the eBay Store to your site.

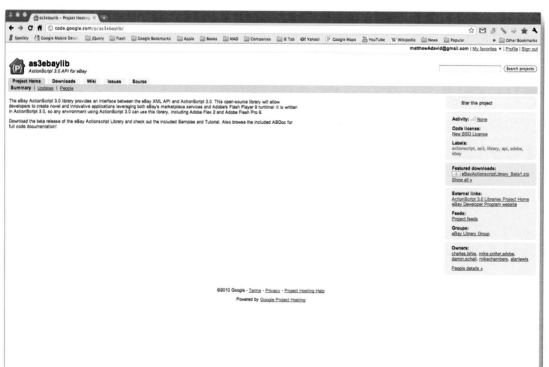

Using PureMVC

Model View Controller (MVC) is a classic architecture (Figure 5.9) where you separate all elements of your code, UI, and data. Typically, if you are writing Class files and using XML, then you are indirectly doing this in Flash already. *But,* you can always do better. This set of classes forces a set of best practices when using MVC in your development.

You can download the code at *http://puremvc.org/*.

Figure 5.9 MVC is a model for developing applications. PureMVC helps guide your development to support the MVC model.

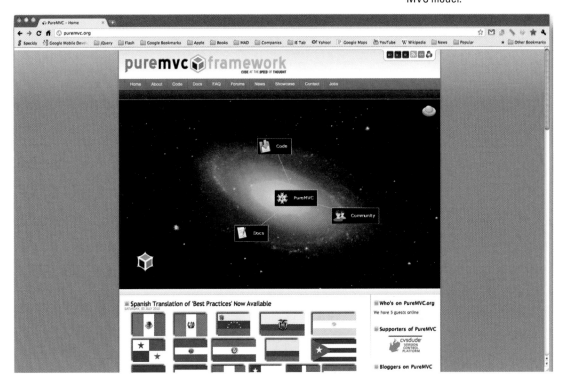

Using Yahoo! ASTRA

ASTRA (Figure 5.10) is a collection of tools, web APIs, and more. With ASTRA you can easily build solutions that tap into Yahoo's Web Services such as Answers and Weather.

You can download the code at *http://developer.yahoo.com/flash/*.

Using Animation Libraries

The following represent some of the most popular animation libraries. The goal of each library is to simply make animation much easier. Earlier you have seen how TweenMax reduced hundreds of lines of code down to just two. The following are all built on this principle.

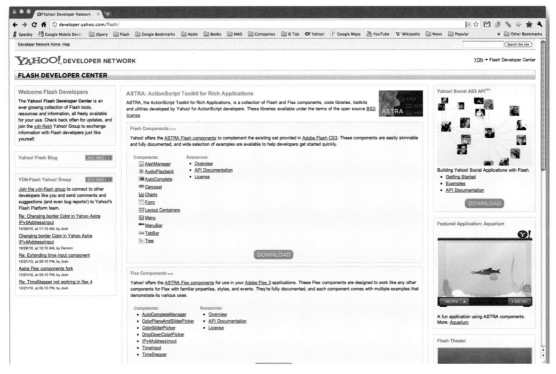

Figure 5.10 Yahoo! ASTRA allows you to add components, data sources, and social integration into your apps.

Using GreenSock's TweenMax, TweenLite, and TweenNano

GreenSock could almost have its own subcategory when it comes to animation. In addition to TweenMax, GreenSock also has TweenLite and TweenNano. The big difference between the different animation libraries is functionality versus file size.

For instance, you can do crazy animations in TweenMax that you cannot do in TweenNano—but, the TweenNano file will be much smaller. Size is a big factor when you are building apps.

In addition to the core animation solutions you get with TweenMax and TweenLite, you can also extend both of these libraries with custom plug-ins (Figure 5.11). The list is crazy long. Here are some of the animation techniques you can perform:

- Filters
- Hex colors
- Volume
- Tint
- Frames
- Saturation
- Contrast
- Hue
- Colorization
- Brightness

Figure 5.11 GreenSock gives you access to dozens of different animation and tween tools.

- Bezier tweening
- OrientToBezier
- Round values
- Jump to any point in the tween with the currentTime or currentProgress property, and automatically rotate in the shortest direction

The list goes on and on! The list of plug-ins is equally long. I know, crazy isn't it?

You can download all this animation goodness at the following web address: *www.greensock.com/*.

Using KitchenSync

KitchenSync is a versatile animation library (Figure 5.12). The thing I like about KitchenSync is that it hosts its documentation on Wonderfl.net. Wonderfl.net is great for showing and sharing AS3 code because you can play around with the code and see what it does right in your web page.

KitchenSync is downloaded and installed exactly the same as any other library. The following example builds a Sprite that you then animate in a simple tween:

```
KitchenSync.initialize(this);
ar sprite:Sprite = new Sprite();
```

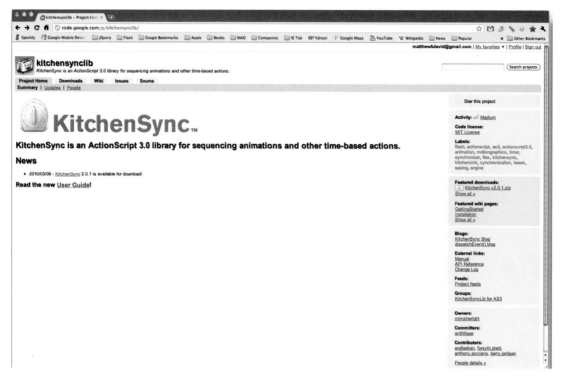

Figure 5.12 KitchenSync is a
more advanced tween library.

```
sprite.graphics.beginFill(0);
sprite.graphics.drawRect(10, 10, 25, 25);
addChild(sprite);
new KSSimpleTween (sprite, "x", 0, 400, 3000, 500,
Cubic.easeInOut).start();
```

There is more code here than with TweenMax, but KitchenSync
does get the job done the same way.

You can download KitchenSync at *http://code.google.com/p/
kitchensynclib/*.

Using AS3 Animation System 2.0

When you get a little more comfortable with animation, you
will reach a point where you want to do more complex work.
This is where you will want to turn to AS3 Animation System 2.0
(Figure 5.13). Animation System is designed for developers to gain
tighter control over virtual timelines and animation sequences.
As a game developer you will need this.

The following example demonstrates how you create Sprites,
animation paths, and timelines controls all through script.
Nothing is added to the main FLA file.

Start by downloading the files and copying the COM folder
into the same folder as your project.

Figure 5.13 AS3 Animation System 2.0 is an advanced animation library tool for advanced developers.

Open Flash Professional and save an FLA to the same folder as the COM object.

In Flash set the FLA class to point to SequenceValueMapExample. A blank Class file will open. The first step is to import all the classes you will use:

```
package
{
    import flash.display.Sprite;
    import flash.display.StageAlign;
    import flash.display.StageScaleMode;
    import flash.events.Event;
    import flash.events.MouseEvent;
    import com.boostworthy.animation.easing.
Transitions;
    import com.boostworthy.animation.rendering.
RenderMethod;
    import com.boostworthy.animation.sequence.
Timeline;
    import com.boostworthy.animation.sequence.tweens.
AdvancedTween;
    import com.boostworthy.animation.sequence.tweens.
PathTween;
    import com.boostworthy.core.Global;
    import com.boostworthy.geom.Path;
```

The following setting controls the size of the stage, frame rate and color.

```
[SWF(backgroundColor="#111111", frameRate="15",
width="480", height="800")]
```

Next, you configure the color, width, and height of the box Sprite:

```
protected const BOX_COLOR:uint = 0x006666;
protected const BOX_WIDTH:Number = 60;
protected const BOX_HEIGHT:Number = 60;
```

Now configure the color and radius of a circle Sprite:

```
protected const CIRCLE_COLOR:uint = 0x006666;
protected const CIRCLE_RADIUS:Number = 5;
```

Now you need to set up the timeline and the method to reference the Sprites. We are not going to go too far into the details as you can get a lot more information from the website, which tells you how much control you have:

```
protected var m_objTimeline:Timeline;
protected var m_spGraph:Sprite;
protected var m_spBox:Sprite;
protected var m_spCircle:Sprite;
protected var m_objPath:Path;
```

Now you can set up the Event Handlers. Here the events are mouse-driven, but as mentioned earlier, this works just fine in simple touch-driven solutions.

```
public function SequenceValueMapExample()
{
init();
}
protected function onMouseDown(objEvent:MouseEvent):void
{
m_objTimeline.play();
}
protected function onMouseUp(objEvent:MouseEvent):void
{
m_objTimeline.playReverse();
}
protected function init():void
{
setDefaultValues();
Global.stage = stage;
m_objTimeline = new Timeline(RenderMethod.TIMER, 60);
createAnimationGraph();
createBox();
createCircle();
createAnimation();
stage.addEventListener(MouseEvent.MOUSE_DOWN,
onMouseDown);
```

```
stage.addEventListener(MouseEvent.MOUSE_UP, onMouseUp);
}
protected function setDefaultValues():void
{
stage.scaleMode = StageScaleMode.NO_SCALE;
stage.align = StageAlign.TOP_LEFT;
}
```

The following code creates all the visuals for your animation:

```
protected function createBox():void
{
m_spBox = new Sprite();
m_spBox.name = "m_spBox";
m_spBox.graphics.beginFill(BOX_COLOR);
m_spBox.graphics.drawRect(-BOX_WIDTH / 2, -BOX_HEIGHT / 2,
BOX_WIDTH, BOX_HEIGHT);
addChild(m_spBox);
m_spBox.x = Math.floor(stage.stageWidth / 2);
m_spBox.y = Math.floor(stage.stageHeight / 2) + 50;
}
protected function createCircle():void
{
m_spCircle = new Sprite();
m_spCircle.name = "m_spCircle";
m_spCircle.graphics.beginFill(CIRCLE_COLOR);
m_spCircle.graphics.drawCircle(0, 0, CIRCLE_RADIUS);
m_spGraph.addChild(m_spCircle);
m_spCircle.x = m_objPath.start.x;
m_spCircle.y = m_objPath.start.y;
}
```

Up to this point you have been setting up core functionality. Now you can add animation.

```
protected function createAnimationGraph():void
{
m_spGraph = new Sprite();
var nY:Number = Math.floor(stage.stageHeight / 4);
m_objPath = new Path();
m_objPath.moveTo(0, nY);
m_objPath.curveTo(30, nY - 50, 60, nY);
m_objPath.curveTo(90, nY + 50, 120, nY);
m_objPath.curveTo(180, nY - 100, 240, nY);
m_objPath.curveTo(270, nY + 50, 300, nY);
m_objPath.curveTo(330, nY - 50, 360, nY);
var objGraphics:Sprite = new Sprite();
objGraphics.graphics.lineStyle(1, 0x555555);
m_objPath.draw(objGraphics.graphics);
m_spGraph.addChild(objGraphics);
m_spGraph.x = Math.floor(stage.stageWidth / 2 - m_
spGraph.width / 2);
addChild(m_spGraph);
```

```
    }
    protected function createAnimation():void
    {
    m_objTimeline.addTween(new PathTween(m_spCircle,
m_objPath, false, m_objPath.start.x, m_objPath.end.x,
Transitions.SINE_IN_AND_OUT));
    m_objTimeline.addTween(new AdvancedTween(m_spBox,
"width", m_objPath, Transitions.SINE_IN_AND_OUT));
    m_objTimeline.addTween(new AdvancedTween(m_spBox,
"height", m_objPath, Transitions.SINE_IN_AND_OUT));
    }
    }
    }
```

As you can see, AS3 Animation Studio gives you a lot of control that other animation programs do not offer.

You can download the code at *www.boostworthy.com/blog/ ?p=170.*

Adding 3D to Apps

Figure 5.14 3D can be added to Flash. The website for PaperVision3D's daily sample will provide you with some inspiration.

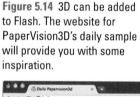

There are several very popular 3D libraries for Flash (Figure 5.14). Can you use them in your projects? Yes, but with caution. Technically, each of these engines will render 3D Flash on your phone but the results will not be good.

3D requires a lot of GPU assistance and phones are struggling to get that kind of power when running Flash. That is likely to change as AIR 2.5 is more tightly integrated into the GPU, but for now, use 3D with caution.

Using PaperVision3D

Arguably, the granddaddy of 3D libraries for Flash is PaperVision3D. You will see that many of the game engines covered later in the chapter use PaperVision3D as their core 3D engine (Figure 5.15).

There is a simple reason for PaperVision3D's popularity: it is very complete in its execution. With PaperVision3D you create real 3D worlds that can import 3D Collada objects. The following example demonstrates a spinning 3D cube with a loaded external Collada object. Collada is a standard 3D file type. Out of the box, Flash does not support Collada, but with a little PaperVision3D love you now can load these files.

The first step is to create the Flash project and link it to the following class:

```
package com.dehash.pv3d.examples.dae {
```

Figure 5.15 *www. optuswhalesong.com.au/* uses 3D from PaperVision to create an interactive Whale Song game.

Next, import all the PaperVision3D class libraries. Remember you need to keep the libraries in the same folder as the Flash project. In this instance, the library does *not* start with COM, but with ORG.

```
import org.papervision3d.objects.parsers.Collada;
import org.papervision3d.view.BasicView;
import org.papervision3d.events.FileLoadEvent;
import flash.events.Event;
```

The following code defines the size of the Flash viewport. In this instance, the settings are set for Android:

```
[SWF(width="480", height="800",
backgroundColor="0x000000")]
    public class CubeDemo extends BasicView {
    The following will import the Collada object you need:
    private var cube:Collada;
    public function DaeCubeDemo(viewportWidth:Number = 480,
viewportHeight:Number = 800,
    scaleToStage:Boolean=true, interactive:Boolean=false,
cameraType:String="CAMERA3D")
    {
    super(viewportWidth, viewportHeight, scaleToStage,
interactive, cameraType);
```

Here, the Collada object is a simple square:

```
cube = new Collada("cube.dae", null, 2, true);
```

The following are events to control loading the Collada cube:

```
    cube.addEventListener(FileLoadEvent.COLLADA_MATERIALS_
DONE, colladaMaterialsDoneHandler, false, 0, true);
    cube.addEventListener(FileLoadEvent.LOAD_COMPLETE,
loadCompleteHandler, false, 0, true);
    cube.addEventListener(FileLoadEvent.LOAD_ERROR,
loadErrorHandler, false, 0, true);
    cube.addEventListener(FileLoadEvent.LOAD_PROGRESS,
loadProgressHandler, false, 0, true);
    cube.addEventListener(FileLoadEvent.SECURITY_LOAD_
ERROR, securityLoadErrorHandler, false, 0, true);
    renderer.renderScene(scene, camera, viewport);
    }
```

The following will control how the cube moves in the screen and the position of the camera to view the cube:

```
    protected override function onRenderTick(event:Event =
null):void {
    cube.yaw((mouseY-(stage.stageHeight/2))/(stage.
height/2)*5);
    cube.roll((mouseX - (stage.stageWidth/2))/(stage.width
/ 2) * -5);
```

```
    renderer.renderScene(scene, camera, viewport)
    }
    private function securityLoadErrorHandler(event:FileLoad
Event):void {
    }
    private function loadProgressHandler(event:FileLoadEvent)
:void {
    }
    private function loadErrorHandler(event:FileLoadEvent)
:void {
    }
    private function loadCompleteHandler(event:FileLoadEvent)
:void {
    }
    private function colladaMaterialsDoneHandler(event:File
LoadEvent):void {
    The following adds the loaded cube onto the screen:
    scene.addChild(cube);
    this.startRendering();
    }
    }
    }
```

You can download PaperVision3D (Figure 5.16) at *http:// papervision3d.googlecode.com/. svn/trunk/as3/trunk*

Figure 5.16 PaperVision is an open source project.

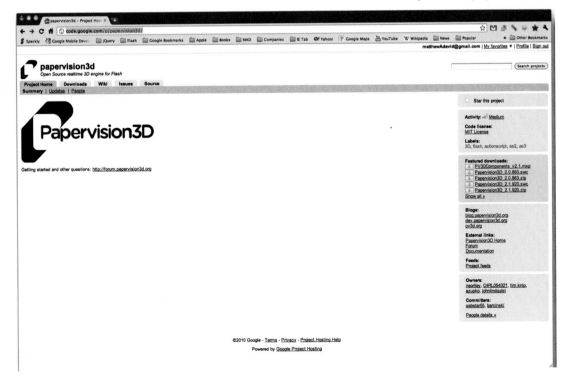

Additional 3D Libraries You Can Use

PaperVision3D is not the only game in town. You can also use Sandy 3D Engine and Away3D (Figure 5.17). Both frameworks are very good and build on the success of PaperVision3D. You can download these frameworks here:

- Sandy 3D Engine: *www.flashsandy.org/*
- Away 3D: *http://away3d.com/*

My personal preference right now is Away3D, but these engines keep leap-frogging each other. Make sure you keep you eyes open to what these engines can provide you.

Figure 5.17 Away3D is a rapidly maturing framework for 3D on the web and your mobile devices.

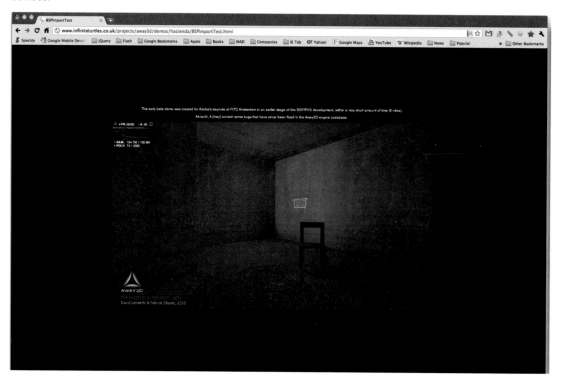

Creating 3D Objects

There is no good using 3D if you can't import your own 3D models. Fortunately there is a company that has your back: Electric Rain (*www.erain.com*) (Figure 5.18).

Electric Rain specializes in creating tools that make developing 3D very easy. The latest release of Swift 3D, its Flash 3D modeling tool, allows you to export your 3D models as true Collada files. Just open PaperVision 3D and bring that puppy into your project and you are good to go.

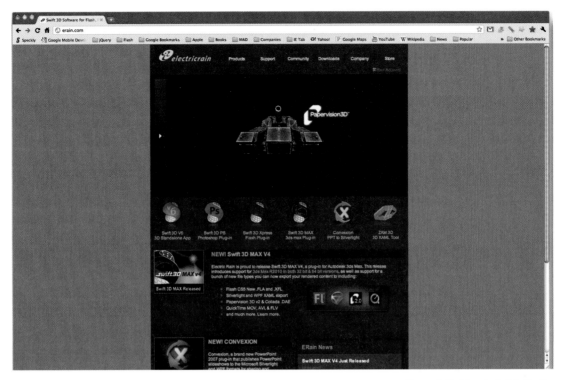

Figure 5.18 Electric Rain's Swift 3D comes packed with Paper-Vision and Collada support.

Using Game Engines

A fast way to get started in game development is to work with established game engines. This allows you to focus on the game instead of learning how to write a physics engine for each game. There are several classes of game libraries you can use. They are broken down into the following:

- 2D game environments
- Social network integration
- Full game environments

I have intentionally kept 3D game engines out of this group due to performance issues. At the time of writing this book, there is a lot of rumor and speculation that Adobe will address the issue of 3D performance in mobile apps, but it is not there yet.

Working in 2D

Many successful games on the web built with Flash start in 2D, as shown in the FarmVille screen shot below. This is an area that you will also want to focus on with mobile game development for a simple reason: 2D processes faster than 3D. To this end, games where you realistically bump into stuff, like ragdoll or canon games, dominate this category. There are some great 2D game engines you can leverage.

Figure 5.19 FarmVille's technology can be ported to Android and iOS devices very easily.

Using Box2DAS3 for Physics

There is a great physics engine for your games that you can use for free. It is called Box2DAS3 (Figure 5.20). The framework is based on the Java project called Box2D, and it is awesome. Realistic Physics is difficult to accomplish in games: you have objects colliding with each other; gravity affects the objects, and each object can have a different density and elasticity. In other words, there is a lot of number crunching.

Box2DAS3 is comprised of a number of key classes, including Common, Collision, and Dynamics.

- The Common library is a collection of utility files such as color and settings you need for your Box2DAS3 projects.
- The Collision collection controls the different ways in which objects can hit each other, such as distance, time of impact, and bounding area.
- Dynamics allows you to add joints to a collection of objects to create ragdoll-like objects.

Throw all these together and you have a powerful platform for game development.

You are not going to get a detailed analysis of game development with Box2DAS3 here, but I will step through a simple project to illustrate how you can add physics into your game.

Figure 5.20 Physics is an important element of any game. Box2DAS3 is a mature platform for ragdoll physics.

As with previous libraries, the code is contained in a Class file associated with the FLA. Start by opening a new Flash movie and associating a Class file called HelloWorld. In addition, you will want to have the Box2D folder in the same folder as your project.

The objective of the HelloWorld Box2DAS3 project is to demonstrate a simple environment that contains physics.

Let's jump into the Class file.

The first step is to import all the Class files you will use in this project. Here you will see all the Box2D Class files being imported into your project:

```
package{
    import flash.display.Sprite;
    import flash.events.Event;
    // Classes used in this example
    import Box2D.Dynamics.*;
    import Box2D.Collision.*;
    import Box2D.Collision.Shapes.*;
    import Box2D.Common.Math.*;
    public class HelloWorld extends Sprite{
    public function HelloWorld(){
```

Below is the event loop that adds new content into the project:

```
addEventListener(Event.ENTER_FRAME, Update, false, 0, true);
```

BOX2D creates a world in which you place your objects. The following sets the lower and upper boundaries of the game:

```
var worldAABB:b2AABB = new b2AABB();
worldAABB.lowerBound.Set(-100.0, -100.0);
worldAABB.upperBound.Set(100.0, 100.0);
```

The following value defined the gravity you use in your game. A value of 0.0 is equal to Earth gravity. Changing this value will add some interesting game physics.

```
var gravity:b2Vec2 = new b2Vec2(0.0, 10.0);
// Allow bodies to sleep
var doSleep:Boolean = true;
```

The following code allows you to construct a world object:

```
m_world = new b2World(worldAABB, gravity, doSleep);
```

The following variables are used for the objects that are on the stage:

```
var body:b2Body;
var bodyDef:b2BodyDef;
var boxDef:b2PolygonDef;
var circleDef:b2CircleDef;
```

The following code adds the values for the ground:

```
bodyDef = new b2BodyDef();
bodyDef.position.Set(10, 12);
boxDef = new b2PolygonDef();
boxDef.SetAsBox(30, 3);
boxDef.friction = 0.3;
boxDef.density = 0;
```

Now you get to add the Sprite to the physical environment:

```
bodyDef.userData = new PhysGround();
bodyDef.userData.width = 30 * 2 * 30;
bodyDef.userData.height = 30 * 2 * 3;
addChild(bodyDef.userData);
body = m_world.CreateBody(bodyDef);
body.CreateShape(boxDef);
body.SetMassFromShapes();
// Add some objects
for (var i:int = 1; i < 10; i++){
bodyDef = new b2BodyDef();
bodyDef.position.x = Math.random() * 15 + 5;
bodyDef.position.y = Math.random() * 10;
var rX:Number = Math.random() + 0.5;
var rY:Number = Math.random() + 0.5;
```

The following code defines the physical characteristics of the box shapes that fall onto the stage:

```
if (Math.random() < 0.5){
    boxDef = new b2PolygonDef();
    boxDef.SetAsBox(rX, rY);
```

```
        boxDef.density = 1.0;
        boxDef.friction = 0.5;
        boxDef.restitution = 0.2;
        bodyDef.userData = new PhysBox();
        bodyDef.userData.width = rX * 2 * 30;
        bodyDef.userData.height = rY * 2 * 30;
        body = m_world.CreateBody(bodyDef);
        body.CreateShape(boxDef);
    }
```

Now you need to define the circle objects that will fall on the stage. Notice in the following description you can set the density, radius, and friction level of the circles. Here the values are constant, however you could easily set up the values to be dynamic using a little math logic.

```
    else {
        circleDef = new b2CircleDef();
        circleDef.radius = rX;
        circleDef.density = 1.0;
        circleDef.friction = 0.5;
        circleDef.restitution = 0.2
        bodyDef.userData = new PhysCircle();
        bodyDef.userData.width = rX * 2 * 30;
        bodyDef.userData.height = rX * 2 * 30;
        body = m_world.CreateBody(bodyDef);
        body.CreateShape(circleDef);
    }
    body.SetMassFromShapes();
    addChild(bodyDef.userData);
    }
}
public function Update(e:Event):void{
        m_world.Step(m_timeStep, m_iterations);
```

The following will run through the code and update the position of the objects on the screen. It is this section of code that forces you to have fewer objects being animated for a mobile device. This will chew up your CPU cycles.

```
    for (var bb:b2Body = m_world.m_bodyList; bb; bb = bb.m_
next){
    if (bb.m_userData is Sprite){
    bb.m_userData.x = bb.GetPosition().x * 30;
    bb.m_userData.y = bb.GetPosition().y * 30;
    bb.m_userData.rotation = bb.GetAngle() * (180/Math.PI);
    }
    }
    }
    public var m_world:b2World;
    public var m_iterations:int = 10;
    public var m_timeStep:Number = 1.0/30.0;
    }
}
```

Now you can test your movie on your device. Voilà! Physics in action!

As with any animation library you use for a mobile device, be careful how much action is happening on the screen at once. The previous example has a small collection of objects colliding with each other. If you have more than 15 objects on the screen at once then you will see the frame rate of your game drop from 20 down to one or two per second. This will obviously change as more powerful phones and tablets reach the market, but for now, beware.

You can download Box2DAS3 at *http://box2dflash.sourceforge .net/*.

Verlet Physics Engine

From the same developer who brought you Box2DAS3 comes a Verlet physics engine, a tool you can use to create ragdoll-like physics.

The engine is fully documented with the source code available at *http://code.google.com/p/ape/*.

Adding Physics to Your 3D Worlds

Physics is not simply the realm of 2D—you can bring it to 3D, too. JigLib for Flash is arguably the best physics engine that integrates with 3D tools such as PaperVision and Away3D. but be warned, the solutions are very CPU intensive. Test and refine your code frequently to enable the games to run smoothly on an iPhone or Android device.

You can download JigLib from *www.jiglibflash.com/blog/ source/*.

Making Your Games Social

Have you heard of FarmVille? More likely, who hasn't? At last check, FarmVille has more players than registered users of Twitter—77+ million players. How nuts is that?

It is clear that social network is a big deal for game development. You need your game to connect to social networks to allow game players to promote your game for you.

Good thing this can be done in ActionScript.

Adding Facebook to Your Games

Adobe partnered with Facebook to develop Open Source Flash classes that enable you to connect your Flash games to the Facebook platform. Adobe has done a great job integrating Flash into Facebook. You can do a lot with it.

The following example is one of the most basic: connecting Flash with Facebook to show your friends. Sounds simple but it is important.

Note

 You will need to be registered as a Facebook developer for the example to work.

The structure of the Class file should be very familiar to you by now. You will need to create a Flash project and, in the Properties panel, associate a class with the following code. In this case, the class is called FriendList.

The first step is to import all the libraries you will need. As with Box2DAS3 and GreenSock's animation libraries, you will need to place all the library files for the project into the same folder.

Let's step through Adobe's basic example of integrating Flash with Facebook. The first step is importing all the Class files:

```
package {
import com.facebook.graph.net.FacebookRequest;
import com.facebook.graph.utils.FacebookDataUtils;
import fl.controls.ScrollBar;
import fl.controls.TextArea;
import fl.data.DataProvider;
import fl.text.TLFTextField;
import flash.display.MovieClip;
import flash.display.NativeWindow;
import flash.display.NativeWindowInitOptions;
import flash.display.Sprite;
import flash.display.StageAlign;
import flash.display.StageScaleMode;
import flash.events.Event;
import flash.events.MouseEvent;
import flash.text.TextField;
import flash.text.TextFieldAutoSize;       .
import flash.text.TextFormat;
import flashx.textLayout.factory.TextLineFactoryBase;
import flash.display.Loader;
import flash.net.URLRequest;
import com.facebook.graph.controls.Distractor;
import fl.events.ListEvent;
import com.facebook.graph.FacebookDesktop;
```

When you have imported the Class files you will want to create a DataProvider object to hold the Friend List data you receive from Facebook. The following creates a new dp variable that will be your DataProvider object.

```
public class FriendList extends MovieClip {
protected var dp:DataProvider;
```

Next, define the window where the data will be displayed:

```
protected var win:NativeWindow;
```

The following is a public function named FriendList. You will use this in conjunction with the DataProvider to create the display on the screen, and assign the content correctly:

```
public function FriendList() {
dp = new DataProvider();
```

There are two buttons on the screen, loginBtn and logOutBtn, that allow you to connect to Facebook. The following two listeners are associated with the two buttons:

```
    loginBtn.addEventListener(MouseEvent.CLICK,
handleLoginClick, false, 0, true);
    logOutBtn.addEventListener(MouseEvent.CLICK,
handleLogOutClick, false, 0, true);
```

In addition to the two buttons, you have a List component on the stage named friendList. The objective of this list is to display the data you receive from Facebook:

```
    friendList.labelField = "name";
    friendList.addEventListener(ListEvent.ITEM_CLICK,
handleListChange, false, 0, true);
    detailsBtn.addEventListener(MouseEvent.CLICK,
handleDetailsClick, false, 0, true);
```

The following code block is essential in connecting to Facebook. This is where you add your developer application ID. You will need to review Facebook's API instructions to acquire an Application ID. When you do, replace APPLICATION_ID in the following ActionScript with your ID. Without it, your code will not work.

```
    FacebookDesktop.init('APPLICATION_ID', handleLogin);
    }
```

The following two functions are associated with the two buttons to log you in or out of Facebook:

```
    protected function handleLoginClick(event:MouseEvent):
void {
    FacebookDesktop.login(handleLogin);
    }
    protected function handleLogOutClick(event:MouseEvent)
:void {
    FacebookDesktop.logout();
    resetUI();
    }
```

The following function creates a new button that will be used in a modeless window when you log in.

```
    protected function resetUI():void {
    loginBtn.label = 'Login';
    loginBtn.enabled = true;
    detailsBtn.label = 'Show details';
    detailsBtn.setSize(100, 22);
    dp.removeAll();
    friendList.dataProvider = dp;
    }
```

The following ActionScript informs you that you are "logged in" to Facebook:

```
    protected function handleLogin(response:Object,
fail:Object):void {
    if (response) {
    loginBtn.label = 'You are logged in.';
    loginBtn.enabled = false;
    detailsBtn.enabled = false;
    loadFriends();
    }
    }
```

The next block of code loads the data you receive from Facebook into Flash. Notice that you are stepping through an XML tree structure. You are targeting the repeating values in the XML group called friends:

```
    protected function loadFriends():void {
    FacebookDesktop.api('/me/friends', handleFriendsLoad);
    }
```

The following code is used to manage a failure in the code:

```
    protected function handleFriendsLoad(response:Object,
fail:Object):void {
    if (fail) { return; }
    dp.removeAll();
```

Now that you have all the data from your "friends," you can post that data into an Array. In turn, that Array can post the data into the dp DataProvider.

```
    var friends:Array = response as Array;
    var l:int = friends.length;
    for (var i:int=0; i < l; i++) {
    dp.addItem(friends[i]);
    }
    friendList.dataProvider = dp;
    }
```

Values can be selected from the List Component. The following ActionScript will enable the detailsBtn to display additional details from a friend:

```
    protected function handleListChange(event:ListEvent):void {
    detailsBtn.enabled = true;
    detailsBtn.label = 'Show details ' + event.item.name;
    var w:Number = 150 + (detailsBtn.label).length;
    detailsBtn.setSize(w, 22);
    }
    protected function handleDetailsClick(event:MouseEvent)
:void {
```

```
    if (!friendList.selectedItem) { return; }
    FacebookDesktop.api('/'+friendList.selectedItem.id,
handleDetailsLoad);
    }
```

The following script creates a new text box to display the friend details. Notice that the TextFormat option has been used to define the presentation of the text:

```
    protected function handleDetailsLoad(response:Object,
fail:Object):void {
    var df:TextFormat = new TextFormat('_sans', 12);
    var tf:TextField = new TextField();
    tf.autoSize = TextFieldAutoSize.LEFT;
    tf.defaultTextFormat = df;
    var textToDisplay:Array = [];
    var d:Object = response;
    for (var n:String in d) {
    var displayValue:Object = d[n];
```

The following switch statement allows you to change your update status:

```
    switch (n) {
    case 'updated_time':
    displayValue = FacebookDataUtils.
stringToDate(displayValue as String); break;
    case 'work':
    case 'hometown':
    case 'location':
    displayValue = objectToString(displayValue); break;
    case 'education':
    displayValue = arrayToString(displayValue as Array);
break;
    }
    textToDisplay.push(n + ': ' + displayValue);
    }
    tf.text = textToDisplay.join('\n');
    tf.x = 200;
    var init:NativeWindowInitOptions = new
NativeWindowInitOptions();
    The following loads the Facebook logo into your app:
    var img:Loader = new Loader();
    var imgURL:String = FacebookDesktop.getImageUrl(d.id,
'large');
    var distractor:Distractor = new Distractor();
    distractor.text = 'loading';
    img.load(new URLRequest(imgURL));
    img.contentLoaderInfo.addEventListener(Event.COMPLETE,
onImageReady, false, 0, true);
```

A modeless pop-up window is used to allow you to enter your Facebook credentials. The following creates this window. Again, you are using the same standard ActionScript you have been applying throughout this book:

```
win = new NativeWindow(init);
win.width = 600;
win.height = tf.textHeight + 120;
win.stage.scaleMode = StageScaleMode.NO_SCALE;
win.stage.align = StageAlign.TOP_LEFT;
win.stage.addChild(tf);
win.stage.addChild(img);
win.stage.addChild(distractor);
win.activate();
}
```

The following adds the Facebook logo into the new window:

```
protected function onImageReady(event:Event):void {
win.stage.removeChildAt(win.stage.numChildren-1);
}
```

The final two functions push the value you captured in your Arrays (the data holding the details information on a friend) to the new modeless window.

```
    protected function objectToString(value:Object):
String {
   var arr:Array = [];
   for (var n:String in value) {
   arr.push(n + ': ' + value[n]);
   }
   return '\n\t' + arr.join('\n\t');
   }
    protected function arrayToString(value:Array):
String {
   var arr:Array = [];
   var l:uint = value.length;
   for (var i:uint=0;i<l;i++) {
   arr.push(objectToString(value[i]));
   }
   return arr.join('\n');
   }
   }
   }
```

There is a lot more you can do with Facebook integration with ActionScript. This is just a taste to get you excited.

To get all the code, jump over to *http://code.google.com/p/ facebook-actionscript-api/* as shown in the screen shot below.

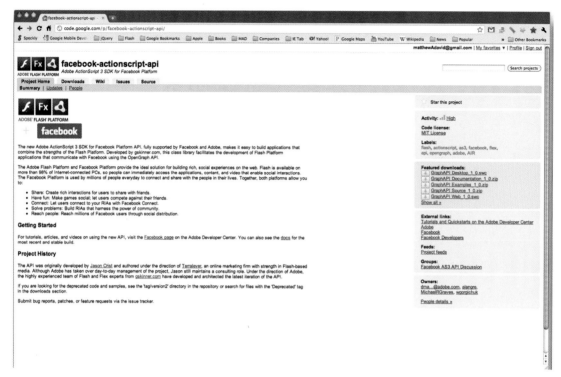

Figure 5.21 Make your games social with Facebook.

Adding Leader Board Services with MochiAds

It is not good getting the highest score in a game if you cannot tell the whole world. MochiAds is the very tool you need to easily add a leader board service to your games. The concept of MochiAds is similar to Xbox Live or Apple's Game Center in that you have a tool that shows who is doing the best in a game.

You can get all the code and samples on how to integrate MochiAds at *http://mochiland.com/articles/introducing-mochiads-leaderboards.*

Tweeting from Flash

Although FarmVille today has more registered users than Twitter, it is clear from the growth curve of adoption that Twitter will be the largest social network on the planet within the next five years. Its goal is one billion registered users. Ambitious? Yes, but I think they will do it.

So, with that said, having Twitter in your games it almost as important as Facebook. It will come as no surprise, then, that there is a great Open Source AS3 project you can use to build games that use Twitter. Fancy that? You can get the code at *http://wiki.swfjunkie.com/tweetr.*

As with Facebook, you must register yourself as a developer with Twitter to use its service and integrate the AS3 code.

Using Full Game Environments

Up to this point, you have seen how you can use third-party products to help build out what you need to develop a game. You have not used a single environment, such as Unity, to build your games. Well, it seems that game development with Flash is a big deal. There are several companies that are looking to fill the need of providing a complete game environment.

Using PushButtonLabs.com

In my opinion, the current leader of full game development environments is PushButtonLabs with its PushButton Engine (PBE) open source game engine (Figure 5.22). It simply has a very comprehensive set of libraries that allow you to develop complex games. The games library includes physics engines, animation engines, game libraries, and more. There is a lot to learn. If you plan on using PBL then put aside a good chunk of time to learn how the environment works. It will be worth it.

Figure 5.22 PushButtonEngine has one of the most complete game engines you can use for your projects.

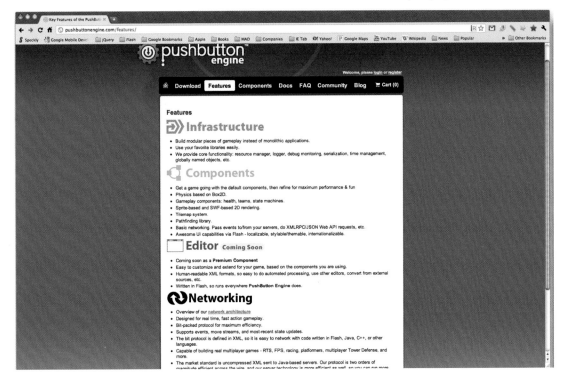

Download the files from PushButtonLabs and open the PBFlashCS4Demo (it will work in CS5) to get a flavor of how these games work. There are a lot of libraries used in PushButton Engine games. You are importing the following classes:

- Box2D (yes, the same Box2DAS3 used earlier in the chapter)
- A specialized animation class
- Core engine
- Sprite management
- 2D rendering
- Class objects for the game

Getting Started with PushButtonEngine

PushButtonLabs' PushButtonEngine is a game engine. What that infers is that the code does *a lot*! Physics, interaction, animation styles, level logic and more are built into PBE. Leveraging additional Open Source projects, such as Box2D, you have the tools needed for your game environment. PBE does a huge amount of the work for you; all that is left is for you to write the custom code, graphics, and logic specific to your game.

Setup for PBE is not hard for you to do. Let's go through the steps for creating a simple "Hello World" solution.

For this demo you are not going to build the final solution for Android. The reason is simple: When you are running AIR for Android you cannot see the Output window. It's a known bug and Adobe is working on a solution. With that said, we will set up the whole program as if we were going to build an AIR for Android solution.

1. Start by creating a new Adobe Flash Professional AIR project.
2. Save the Flash project as PBEHelloWorld.fla.
3. Set the size of the movie to 800 × 480 and with a frame rate of 20 fps.
4. Download the latest version of PushButtonEngine from *http:// pushbuttonengine.com/*.
5. Extract the folders and files from the PBE ZIP file and save them to the same folder as the FLA file. Your folder structure should look like the following:
   - PBEHelloWorld.fla
   - SRC folder
   - Box2D folder
     ○ Collision folder containing all the Class files for collision
     ○ Common folder containing Box2D common Class files and Math subfolder
     ○ Dynamics folders containing Class files and Contacts and Joints subfolder
   - Br folder
     ○ Containing subfolders for loading files

- Com folder
  - Animation classes
  - Box2d classes
  - Components classes
  - Engine classes
  - Rendering2D classes
  - Screens classes
  - Sound classes
  - Tweaker classes

6. Open the Flash FLA file. Go to the Properties panel and add a new class. Name the class PBEHelloWorld. Open the Class file in Flash Professional. The file will look something like this:

```
package {
        import flash.display.MovieClip;
        public class PBEHelloWorld extends MovieClip {
                public function PBEHelloWorld() {
                        // constructor code
                }
        }
}
```

7. Save the Flash Class file as PBEHelloWorld.as.
8. You will need to edit the Class file to use PBE. The first action is to ensure you are importing the correct files into the Class file. Delete line two in the preceding ActionScript (import flash.display.MovieClip) and replace it with the following, the import commands that will import the Class files for PushButtonEngine into your sample application:

```
import com.pblabs.engine.PBE;
import com.pblabs.engine.debug.Logger;
import flash.display.Sprite;
```

9. Modify the public class extension from the original code (public class PBEHelloWorld extends MovieClip). You will not actually see anything on the Stage for this example. We are going to change the extension to the smallest image type, a Sprite.

```
public class PBEHelloWorld extends Sprite
```

10. Define the class. Let's start by declaring a public class:

```
public class PBEHelloWorld extends Sprite
{
```

11. Declare the static setters for the ViewPort (what you see on the screen) for width and height:

```
public static var WIDTH : Number = 800;
public static var HEIGHT: Number = 480;
```

12. Create the Flash SWF file width, height, and frameRate:

```
[SWF(width="800", height="480", frameRate="20")]
public function PBEHelloWorld ()
{
//SUPER
super ();
```

13. At the end of this script you will want to run a test that posts a message to the Output panel. You will need to initialize the PBE Logger for this action:

```
PBE.startup(this);
```

14. The final line of script will run a simple message when the app is run in test/debug mode:

```
Logger.print(this, "PushButtonEngine wants to say:
Hello World!");
}}}
```

15. The final step is to save your work in the Class file and test your movie. The PBE code will load and post a message to the Output window.

This script might seem like a lot of work to generate a message to the Output window (after all, you can do the same thing using a simple "trace" statement), but you have now completed this task with a full game engine. The next section will step you through creating the level for a game using XML and PBE. The final section on PBE will demonstrate how you can create a Frogger-style game using PBE.

Creating a Level Configurator in PBE using XML

A key feature you can take advantage of in PushButtonEngine is the ability to load levels created in readable XML. Following is an example of how you can do this.

```
import com.pblabs.animation.AnimatorComponent;
import com.pblabs.box2D.Box2DDebugComponent;
import com.pblabs.box2D.Box2DManagerComponent;
import com.pblabs.box2D.Box2DSpatialComponent;
import com.pblabs.box2D.CircleCollisionShape;
import com.pblabs.box2D.PolygonCollisionShape;
import com.pblabs.engine.PBE;
import com.pblabs.engine.core.LevelManager;
import com.pblabs.engine.resource.Resource;
import com.pblabs.rendering2D.BasicSpatialManager2D;
import com.pblabs.rendering2D.DisplayObjectScene;
import com.pblabs.rendering2D.SimpleSpatialComponent;
import com.pblabs.rendering2D.SpriteSheetRenderer;
import com.pblabs.rendering2D.spritesheet.
CellCountDivider;
```

```
    import com.pblabs.rendering2D.spritesheet.
SpriteSheetComponent;
    import com.pblabs.rendering2D.ui.SceneView;
    import com.pblabs.stupidSampleGame.DudeController;
    import flash.display.Sprite;
    import flash.utils.*;
```

PushButton Engine makes extensive use of XML to describe custom elements. Next the ActionScript validates that all the XML files have loaded correctly:

```
    PBE.registerType(com.pblabs.rendering2D.
DisplayObjectScene);
    PBE.registerType(com.pblabs.rendering2D.
SpriteSheetRenderer);
    PBE.registerType(com.pblabs.rendering2D.spritesheet.
SpriteSheetComponent);
    PBE.registerType(com.pblabs.rendering2D.
SimpleSpatialComponent);
    PBE.registerType(com.pblabs.rendering2D.
BasicSpatialManager2D);
    PBE.registerType(com.pblabs.rendering2D.spritesheet.
CellCountDivider);
    PBE.registerType(com.pblabs.rendering2D.ui.SceneView);
    PBE.registerType(com.pblabs.box2D.Box2DDebugComponent);
    PBE.registerType(com.pblabs.box2D.
Box2DManagerComponent);
    PBE.registerType(com.pblabs.box2D.
Box2DSpatialComponent);
    PBE.registerType(com.pblabs.box2D.
PolygonCollisionShape);
    PBE.registerType(com.pblabs.box2D.
CircleCollisionShape);
    PBE.registerType(com.pblabs.stupidSampleGame.
DudeController);
    PBE.registerType(com.pblabs.animation.
AnimatorComponent);
```

You have all the files loaded into Flash; now you need to initialize the engine. Time to rock and roll.

```
    PBE.startup(this);
```

The following scene is set up for an Android phone. You can play around with the view settings to match the device you are targeting.

```
    var sv:SceneView = new SceneView();
    sv.name = "MainView";
    sv.x = 0;
    sv.y = 0;
    sv.width = 800;
    sv.height = 480;
    addChild(sv);
```

The most important part of the code is the XML document that describes your world. This is an instance of the LevelManager. We'll get into more details about why this is important in a bit:

```
LevelManager.instance.load("levelDescriptions.xml", 1);
```

The following stops the playback in the timeline:

```
stop();
```

You will use XML to develop your games. This gives you an edge over other game worlds. XML is easy to edit (you just need Notepad), but XML is also a data source. This means you can load external XML from a database. Want to create a new world on the fly? Create a tool that allows the XML to be edited in a web page and reloaded from the database. Here is an example of a game level description in XML for PushButtonLabs:

```
<things version="1">
  <entity name="Platform1" template="Platform">
    <component name="Spatial">
      <position type="">
        <x>94</x>
        <y>450</y>
      </position>
    </component>
  </entity>
<entity name="Platform2" template="Platform">
  <component name="Spatial">
    <position type="">
      <x>400</x>
      <y>500</y>
    </position>
  </component>
</entity>
<entity name="Platform3" template="Platform">
  <component name="Spatial">
    <position type="">
      <x>706</x>
      <y>450</y>
    </position>
  </component>
</entity>
<group name="LevelData">
    <objectReference name="Platform1"/>
    <objectReference name="Platform2"/>
    <objectReference name="Platform3"/>
  </group>
</things>
```

What we have here are descriptions for three platforms on the screen and their position. You can add many, many more to create a dynamic platform game. Cool, huh?

You can now run the test game. What you will see is a basic world with a jumping Sprite. Nothing special, but it does show you that you do not need to do a lot to get a game started.

The Game Mechanics of a Frogger-Style Game

One of my favorite games in the mid-1980s was Frogger, the game where you try to rescue a frog by moving him forward and backward across a road and stream. The mechanics of Frogger (movement, collision, random enemy generation) are fundamentals for all games. As you would imagine, PBE allows you to tap into these mechanics.

The following section takes you further into game development. What you will be doing is reproducing the core game play features of Frogger. What you will cover includes:

- Leveraging PBE for core game mechanics
- Using Flash SWF files to manage visual/audio assets
- Extending PBE with your own custom classes
- Adding a custom to manage objects on the screen (screen wrapping, horizontal movement and collision detection)

At this point you will not be adding a scoring mechanism or life counter. The project covered in the next chapter explores those features in greater detail.

Getting Started with Your Game Structure

A good starting point for any game is to first sit down and identify what you are going to accomplish in the game. For the Frogger-style game, the mechanics come down to the following story line:

- There is a frog.
- The frog has to move forward/backward and left/right.
- You move the frog from the bottom of the screen to the top.
- Blocking your path as you move are enemies moving from left to right along horizontal paths.
- If the frog hits an enemy a sound is played.
- You win when the frog is able to get to the top of the screen.

Although this is not much of a story compared to modern games such as Call of Duty, this story does reveal three core asset groups:

- Visual assets (the drawings)
- Audio assets (the sound effects of the game starting and the frog hitting an enemy)
- Game Code (this is where you extend PBE with your own custom ActionScript)

The visual and audio assets can be shared with a linked library in Flash. There is nothing new about linked libraries in Flash—they have been around since Flash 6. But, this does not diminish how useful they are. For instance, you can now create a single Flash

Note

 At the time of this writing, only Android and BlackBerry PlayBook fully support AIR 2.5. The iPhone/iPad running iOS will not allow you to use linked libraries. Hopefully, by the time you are reading this, Adobe will have resolved this issue. Check out the companion website for updates.

movie that contains all the assets for your project, save the file, and merely link to objects in the library. This allows you to keep your elements all separate. You will appreciate the modular approach to development as your games become more complex.

Before jumping in and creating the core elements of the game, let's create the assets.

1. Create a folder where you will store the game. Create a subfolder and name it assets.
2. Create a new Flash movie and name it assets.fla.
3. Open assets.fla. The assets file will contain only the following objects:
    - Visual objects (background, the player, two enemies)
    - Sounds (start of game, end of game, collision, movement, sound track)
4. The files for assets in the game can be downloaded from the website. Each asset requires a linking ID. A linkage name can be created by right-clicking on an item in the library and choosing Properties; expand the Advanced options section; you will see a place where you can add an AS name. The AS name is a linking name. The names for the different objects you want to add are:
    - BackgroundMC
    - SmallEnemyMC
    - BigEnemyMC
    - PlayerMC
    - LoseSound
    - WinSound
    - MoveSound
    - SoundTrackSounds
5. When you have added the linked IDs to all of your sounds, you will want to save your Flash file and export the SWF into the assets folder.

At this point you have created the visual and audio assets for the game and placed them into a single folder. The next section of the game will build out the game logic but before we get into that, let's create a Class file you can use to create ActionScript variable names and links. Do this in one place so you do not need to keep linking back to the original SWF file. The advantage this gives you is that you can easily modify the Flash assets without having to rewrite all of your code.

1. Let's start by organizing the file structure. You have already created a folder that contains your game with an assets folder; now create a new subfolder from the main folder to hold the source files. Name this new folder src; add a common folder below src for all scripts and name it com. Add a subfolder to com for your custom code and name it mad, with a projects subfolder. Your structure should look like this: src\com\mad\projects\pbflyergame

2. Open your favorite ActionScript editor, such as Flash Professional, and create a new Class file named PBFlyerGame.as.

3. Add the following ActionScript to define a new class. You will see that the package name follows the same path structure as the folders you just created:

```
package com.mad.projects.pbflyergame
{
```

4. You will be adding the PushButtonLabs files in a moment, but for now let's pretend you already have, and add an import to link to the game engine and two core Flash classes:

```
import com.pblabs.engine.resource.*;
import flash.media.Sound;
import flash.sampler.Sample;
```

5. The following sets up the public classes.

```
public class PBFlyerGameResources extends ResourceBundle
{
```

6. Earlier you created an SWF file to contain all of your assets. With PBE you do not need to technically do this (you can link directly to assets such as PNG or MP3 files) but this technique will work just fine for us. This link points to the assets folder off the root of the project:

```
public static var ASSETS_SWF: String = "assets/assets.swf";
```

7. The next step is to create variable names for the linked library instance objects. Here are new variable names for the objects you created:

```
public static var MOVIE_CLIP_OBSTACLE_PLAYER: String =
"PlayerMC";
public static var MOVIE_CLIP_OBSTACLE_BIGENEMY: String =
"BigEnemyMC";
public static var MOVIE_CLIP_OBSTACLE_SMALLENEMY:
String = "SmallEnemyMC";
public static var MOVIE_CLIP_BACKGROUND_GAME_SCREEN:
String = "BackgroundMC";
[Embed(source='../../../../../assets/assets.swf',
symbol='BackgroundMC')]
public static var MOVIE_CLIP_BACKGROUND_INTRO_SCREEN:
Class;
```

8. The next step is to create variable names for the sounds you will use. The following is the sound that will be played as you move the main game player across the screen. The sound is created by linking to the assets.swf file and linking the "MoveSound" symbol with the new public variable name "MOVE_PLAYER_SOUND". This process is repeated for each of the sounds you will use.

```
[Embed(source='../../../../../assets/assets.swf',
symbol='MoveSound')]
   private static var MOVE_PLAYER_SOUND_CLASS : Class;
   public static var MOVE_PLAYER_SOUND: Sound = new MOVE_
PLAYER_SOUND_CLASS ();
```

9. The following sound will be used as the background track for the game:

```
[Embed(source='../../../../../assets/assets.swf',
symbol='SoundTrackSound')]
   private static var SOUNDTRACK_SOUND_CLASS : Class;
   public static var SOUNDTRACK_SOUND: Sound = new
SOUNDTRACK_SOUND_CLASS ();
```

10. The following sound is used when you win.

```
[Embed(source='../../../../../assets/assets.swf',
symbol='SoundTrackSound')]
   private static var SOUNDTRACK_SOUND_CLASS : Class;
   public static var SOUNDTRACK_SOUND: Sound = new
WIN_SOUND_CLASS ();
```

11. The following sound will play when you lose.

```
[Embed(source='../../../../../assets/assets.swf',
symbol='LoseSound')]
   private static var LOSE_SOUND_CLASS : Class;
   public static var LOSE_SOUND: Sound = new LOSE_SOUND_
CLASS ();}
   }
```

12. Now you will want to save your new Class file as PBFlyerGame.as.

At this point you have all the visual and audio elements for the game. The next bit is the fun part: creating custom Class files to extend PushButtonEngine.

Creating the Custom Class Files for the Game

As mentioned earlier, this is not a complete game, just enough to provide you with what you need to get started in your own development. With that said, there is a lot of code you can use.

In creating the assets Class file you also created a number of folders. The PBLabs files should be placed in the COM folder.

The Project folder contains the Class files for your game project. You have already created the resources Class file. Later, you are going to string everything together with a Game Class file. There are two main groups of Class files you will step through:

- Game Screens
- Game Play Mechanics

The structure for these files is often similar. For this reason, I will not go through all the files in great depth. The files, along with additional comments, can be downloaded from the website.

There are two screens in the game: introduction screen and game screen. They are separated into two Class files in a sub-folder called screens. Let's start with the introduction screen:

1. Using a text editor, create a new Class file and name it IntroScreen.as.

2. Declare the package and import the core classes:

```
package com.mad.projects.flashgame.screens
{
import com.pblabs.screens.BaseScreen;
import com.pblabs.screens.ScreenManager;
import com.mad.projects.flashgame.flashgameResources;
import flash.events.MouseEvent;
import flash.text.TextField;
public class IntroScreen extends BaseScreen
public function IntroScreen ()
```

3. You are going to use a simple mouse event instead of a Tap event. Both achieve the same results, but this allows you to reuse the code for traditional desktop solutions.

```
{
super ();
addEventListener(MouseEvent.MOUSE_DOWN, _onMouseDown);
}
```

4. The following adds the introduction screen background image:

```
override public function onShow () : void
{
addChild(new flashgameResources.MOVIE_CLIP_BACKGROUND_
INTRO_SCREEN ());
```

5. A text field is displayed on the screen, giving the player instructions on what to do:

```
var textField : TextField = new TextField ();
textField.width = 500;
textField.height = 400;
textField.multiline = true;
textField.wordWrap = true;
textField.htmlText = "<P ALIGN='CENTER'><FONT
SIZE='50'>Click Anywhere to Play</FONT></P>";
textField.selectable = false;
textField.x = 400 - textField.width/2;
textField.y = 300;
addChild(textField);
}
```

6. Finally, when the player taps the screen you will want the screen to change to the main game screen:

```
private function _onMouseDown (aEvent : MouseEvent) : void
{
ScreenManager.instance.goto("game_screen");
```

```
        }
      }
    }
```

7. Save your file. This completes the work for the introduction game screen.

8. Create the main game play screen. Create a new Class file in the screens folder and name it GameScreen.as. This screen does very little except load the main game screen Class files:

```
package com.mad.projects.flashgame.screens
{
import com.pblabs.engine.PBE;
import com.pblabs.screens.BaseScreen;
import com.mad.projects.flashgame.flashgame;
public class GameScreen extends BaseScreen
{
public function GameScreen ()
{
super ();
}
override public function onShow () : void
{
(PBE.mainClass as flashgame).restartGame();
}
override public function onHide () : void
{
}
}
}
```

At this point you have both screens developed. The next step is to add the Class files that extend the game. The additional Class files you will create are:

- CollisionDetectComponent
- FaceForwardComponent
- GameOverComponent
- MoveHorizontallyComponent
- ScreenTrapComponent
- ScreenWrapComponent

Each of these classes are placed in a subfolder of flashgame called components. Let's step through each of these classes.

1. Create a new Class file called CollisionDetectComponent.as in the components folder.

2. Add the following classes you will be importing:

```
package com.mad.projects.flashgame.components
{
import com.pblabs.box2D.CollisionEvent;
import com.pblabs.engine.components.TickedComponent;
import com.pblabs.engine.core.ITickedObject;
```

3. Most of the work for collision is managed through PBE but this class adds some extensions. The following declares that you are extending the ITickedObject class.

```
    public class CollisionDetectComponent extends
TickedComponent implements ITickedObject
    {
    public static const NAME : String =
"CollisionDetectComponent";
    private function get _gameOverComponent () :
GameOverComponent { return owner.lookupComponentByType
(GameOverComponent) as GameOverComponent; }
```

4. You will want to extend the Collision class so you can link to your own custom events, such as which end of game screen you want to go to:

```
    public function CollisionDetectComponent ()
    {
    super ();
    }
    protected override function onAdd() : void
    {
    super.onAdd();
    owner.eventDispatcher.addEventListener(CollisionEvent.
COLLISION_EVENT, onCollisionEvent);
    }
    protected override function onRemove() : void
    {
    super.onRemove();
    owner.eventDispatcher.removeEventListener(CollisionEvent.
COLLISION_EVENT, onCollisionEvent);
    }
    private function onCollisionEvent(aEvent:CollisionEvent) :
void
    {
    _gameOverComponent.doLoss();
    }
    }
    }
```

5. Save your file.
6. The next step is controlling the facing of the visual objects on the screen. Again, most of this work is accomplished with PBE but can be extended for custom properties.
7. Create a new Class file and name it FaceForwardComponent. as.
8. Add references to the FaceForwardComponent to Class files you want to use and extend:

```
    package com.mad.projects.flashgame.components
    {
```

```
import com.pblabs.engine.components.TickedComponent;
import com.pblabs.engine.core.ITickedObject;
import com.pblabs.engine.entity.PropertyReference;
import com.mad.utils.pbe.FlyerGameHelper;
import flash.geom.Point;
```

9. You will need to know the positions of the objects on the screen. To do this you will need to declare public constants for the names of the objects:

```
public class FaceForwardComponent extends
TickedComponent implements ITickedObject
    {
    public static const NAME : String =
"FaceForwardComponent";
    public var _position_propertyreference:PropertyReference;
    public var _rotation_propertyreference:PropertyReference;
    private var _positionPrevious_point : Point;
    private var _positionCurrent_point : Point;
    private var _rotationCurrent_num: Number;
    public function FaceForwardComponent ()
```

10. The following forces the player that you control to face up at the start of the game:

```
    {
    super ();
    _position_propertyreference = new PropertyReference
(PlayerGameHelper.SPATIAL_POSITION);
    _rotation_propertyreference = new PropertyReference
(PlayerGameHelper.SPATIAL_ROTATION);
    _positionPrevious_point = new Point (0,1000);
    }
```

11. The next step is to update the screens as you move the player:

```
override public function onTick (aDeltaTime_num :
Number) :void
    {
    _positionCurrent_point = owner.getProperty(_position_
propertyreference);
    _rotationCurrent_num = owner.getProperty(_rotation_
propertyreference);
    var positionDeltaX_num : Number = _positionCurrent_
point.x - _positionPrevious_point.x;
    var positionDeltaY_num : Number = _positionCurrent_
point.y - _positionPrevious_point.y;
    if (positionDeltaX_num < 0) {
```

12. This controls your player position as you move left on the screen:

```
_rotationCurrent_num = -90;
} else if (positionDeltaX_num > 0) {
```

13. This controls the player as you move right:

```
_rotationCurrent_num = 90;
}
if (positionDeltaY_num < 0) {
```

14. This updates as you move up the screen:

```
_rotationCurrent_num = 0;
} else if (positionDeltaY_num > 0) {
```

15. This controls movement down the screen:

```
_rotationCurrent_num = 180;
}
owner.setProperty(_rotation_propertyreference, _
rotationCurrent_num);
_positionPrevious_point = _positionCurrent_point;
}
}
}
```

16. You have now extended the code for the main player game piece to always face the correct direction.

17. The next class controls what is done when the game is over. Essentially, at this time, the only thing that happens is that the sound clips change. Of course you can extend this yourself with your own functionality.

18. Create a new Class file and name it GameOverComponent.as.

19. Add the classes you need to import into this class:

```
package com.mad.projects.flashgame.components
{
import com.pblabs.engine.PBE;
import com.pblabs.engine.components.TickedComponent;
import com.pblabs.engine.core.ITickedObject;
import com.pblabs.engine.entity.PropertyReference;
import com.mad.projects.flashgame.flashgame;
import com.mad.projects.flashgame.flashgameResources;
import com.mad.utils.pbe.FlyerGameHelper;
import flash.geom.Point;
public class GameOverComponent extends TickedComponent
implements ITickedObject
```

20. Next, identify the properties you want to control with this class. In this case, the game is over by identifying the position of the main game player control. If you are able to move the

game controller to the top of the screen then you have won. To understand that you have reached the top of the screen you need to know the position of the game player control:

```
{
public static const NAME : String =
"GameOverComponent";
public var _position_propertyreference:PropertyReferen
ce;
private var _size_propertyreference :
PropertyReference;
private var _position_point : Point;
private var _size_point : Point;
public function GameOverComponent ()
{
super ();
_position_propertyreference = new PropertyReference
(FlyerGameHelper.SPATIAL_POSITION);
_size_propertyreference = new PropertyReference
(FlyerGameHelper.SPATIAL_SIZE);
}
```

21. The next steps are to declare what happens when the game is won:

```
public function doWin () : void
{
PBE.soundManager.stopCategorySounds("sfx");
PBE.soundManager.play(flashgameResources.WIN_SOUND);
_doEndGame();
}
```

22. What if you lose? The following method controls this action:

```
public function doLoss () : void
{
PBE.soundManager.stopCategorySounds("sfx");
PBE.soundManager.play(flashgameResources.LOSE_SOUND);
_doEndGame();
}
```

23. Finally, the events used to activate the methods:

```
protected override function onAdd() : void
{
super.onAdd();
}
protected override function onRemove() : void
{
super.onRemove();
}
override public function onTick (aDeltaTime_num :
Number) :void
{
```

```
    _position_point = owner.getProperty (_position_
propertyreference);
    _size_point = owner.getProperty (_size_propertyreference);
    if (_position_point.y < 60) {
    doWin();
    }
    }
    }
    }
```

24. At this point, you can save your file. As you can see, each class is very similar in structure: you import Class objects you want to modify, you declare what you will modify, and then you extend what you modify with custom methods, properties, and events.

25. Following is a breakdown of the Move Horizontally Component.as class:

```
    {
    import com.pblabs.engine.components.ThinkingComponent;
    import com.pblabs.engine.components.TickedComponent;
    import com.pblabs.engine.entity.PropertyReference;
    import com.mad.utils.pbe.FlyerGameHelper;
    import flash.geom.Point;
    public class MoveHorizontallyComponent extends
TickedComponent
    {
    public static const NAME : String =
"MoveHorizontallyComponent";
    public var _position_propertyreference:PropertyReference;
    public var _rotation_propertyreference:PropertyReference;
    private var _position_point:Point;
    public var horizontalDirection_int:int = 1;
    public var horizontalSpeed_num:int = 3;
    public function MoveHorizontallyComponent () : void
    {
    super ();
    _position_propertyreference = new PropertyReference
(FlyerGameHelper.SPATIAL_POSITION);
    }
    override public function onTick (aDeltaTime_num :
Number) :void
    {
    _position_point = owner.getProperty(_position_
propertyreference);
    var r : * = owner.getProperty(_rotation_
propertyreference);
    _position_point.x += horizontalDirection_int *
horizontalSpeed_num/2;
```

```
            owner.setProperty(_position_propertyreference, _
        position_point);
            }
          }
        }
```

26. The following is the ActionScript class for an enemy trapping the player control:

```
        package com.mad.projects.flashgame.components
        {
        import com.pblabs.engine.PBE;
        import com.pblabs.engine.components.TickedComponent;
        import com.pblabs.engine.core.ITickedObject;
        import com.pblabs.engine.entity.PropertyReference;
        import com.mad.utils.pbe.FlyerGameHelper;
        import flash.geom.Point;
        public class ScreenTrapComponent extends
        TickedComponent implements ITickedObject
            {
            public static const NAME : String =
        "ScreenTrapComponent";
            private var _position_propertyreference :
        PropertyReference;
            private var _size_propertyreference :
        PropertyReference;
            private var _position_point : Point;
            private var _size_point : Point;
            public function ScreenTrapComponent ()
            {
            super ();
            _position_propertyreference = new PropertyReference
        (FlyerGameHelper.SPATIAL_POSITION);
            _size_propertyreference = new PropertyReference
        (FlyerGameHelper.SPATIAL_SIZE);
            }
            override public function onTick (aDeltaTime_num :
        Number) : void
            {
            _position_point = owner.getProperty(_position_
        propertyreference);
            _size_point = owner.getProperty(_size_
        propertyreference);
            if (_position_point.x + _size_point.x /2 > PBE.scene.
        sceneViewBounds.right) {
            _position_point.x = PBE.scene.sceneViewBounds.right -
        _size_point.x / 2;
            } else if (_position_point.x - _size_point.x /2 < PBE.
        scene.sceneViewBounds.left) {
            _position_point.x = PBE.scene.sceneViewBounds.left +
        _size_point.x / 2;
            }
```

```
    if (_position_point.y + _size_point.y /2 > PBE.scene.
sceneViewBounds.bottom) {
    _position_point.y = PBE.scene.sceneViewBounds.bottom -
_size_point.y / 2;
    } else if (_position_point.y - _size_point.y /2 < PBE.
scene.sceneViewBounds.top) {
    _position_point.y = PBE.scene.sceneViewBounds.top +
_size_point.y / 2;
    }
    owner.setProperty(_position_propertyreference,
_position_point);
    }
    }
    }
```

At this point you have the files need for the core components of the game. The final Class file strings all of these files together.

Linking Game Code Class Files Together in the FlashGame Class

The FlashGame folder contains an additional class called FlashGame.as that links all classes together. The structure, as with the previous classes, should now be familiar to you. Essentially, what you are doing is using the FlashGame class as the glue that binds everything together.

1. Let's step through the FlashGame class. Open the file in a text editor. The first section of code should be familiar: the classes you need to import. What is different with this import list is you are now importing *all* classes you have created and will need in the game. It is quite long.

```
    package com.mad.projects.flashgame
    {
    import com.pblabs.box2D.Box2DManagerComponent;
    import com.pblabs.engine.PBE;
    import com.pblabs.engine.debug.Logger;
    import com.pblabs.engine.entity.IEntity;
    import com.pblabs.engine.entity.PropertyReference;
    import com.pblabs.rendering2D.AnimationController;
    import com.pblabs.rendering2D.AnimationControllerInfo;
    import com.pblabs.rendering2D.SpriteSheetRenderer;
    import com.pblabs.rendering2D.spritesheet.
SWFSpriteSheetComponent;
    import com.pblabs.rendering2D.ui.SceneView;
    import com.mad.projects.flashgame.components.
CollisionDetectComponent;
    import com.mad.projects.flashgame.components.
FaceForwardComponent;
    import com.mad.projects.flashgame.components.
GameOverComponent;
```

```
    import com.mad.projects.flashgame.components.
MoveHorizontallyComponent;
    import com.mad.projects.flashgame.components.
ScreenTrapComponent;
    import com.mad.projects.flashgame.components.
ScreenWrapComponent;
    import com.mad.projects.flashgame.screens.GameScreen;
    import com.mad.projects.flashgame.screens.IntroScreen;
    import com.mad.utils.pbe.FlyerGameHelper;
    import flash.display.Sprite;
    import flash.geom.Point;
```

2. **Define the size of the game screen area. This game is being designed for the Android Nexus One screen size:**

```
    [SWF(width="800", height="480", frameRate="20")]
    public class FlashGame extends Sprite
    {
    public static var WIDTH : Number = 800;
    public static var HEIGHT: Number = 480;
```

3. **Next, you will want to load the core elements that allow the game to start:**

```
    public function flashgame ()
    {
    super ();
    PBE.startup(this);
    PBE.processManager.timeScale = 0.8;
    PBE.addResources(new flashgameResources());
    PBE.screenManager.registerScreen("intro_screen",
new IntroScreen());
    PBE.screenManager.registerScreen("game_screen",
new GameScreen());
    PBE.screenManager.goto("intro_screen");
    }
```

4. **Declare the methods you will use. The first group contains the sounds that will play:**

```
    public function restartGame ( ) : void
    {
    PBE.soundManager.play(flashgameResources.SOUNDTRACK_
SOUND,"sfx",1,9999);
    _clearEverything ();
    _createScene();
    _createBackgroundEntity();
    _createObstacleEntities();
    _createPlayerEntity();
    }
```

5. **You will want the screen to be clear of any enemies at the start of the game. Notice how you are using PushButtonEngine for most of your work.**

```
private function _clearEverything ( ) : void
{
PBE.rootGroup.destroy();
PBE.rootGroup.clear();
}
```

6. Now you will want to create the default new scene setup.

```
private function _createScene ( ) : void
{
var sceneView : SceneView = new SceneView();
sceneView.width = WIDTH;
sceneView.height = HEIGHT;
PBE.initializeScene(sceneView, FlyerGameHelper.SCENE,
null, Box2DManagerComponent);
PBE.scene.setWorldCenter(new Point (-WIDTH, -HEIGHT));
(PBE.spatialManager as Box2DManagerComponent).gravity =
new Point (0,0);
}
```

7. The following adds the main player to the screen:

```
private function _createPlayerEntity ( ) : void
{
var position_point: Point = new Point
(WIDTH*.65,HEIGHT-50);
var size_point: Point = new Point (.1,.1);
var zIndex_uint: uint = 10;
var Player_entity:IEntity = PBE.allocateEntity();
PlayerGameHelper.createSpatialEntity (Player_entity,
position_point, size_point);
var collisionType_str : String= "Player";
var collidesWithCollisionTypes_array : Array =
["Obstacle"];
PlayerGameHelper.enableCollisionDetection (Player_
entity, collisionType_str,
collidesWithCollisionTypes_array, true);
```

8. Using the assets.swf file created earlier, you can now load all
   the visual assets for the game:

```
var swfSpriteSheetComponent : SWFSpriteSheetComponent =
new SWFSpriteSheetComponent();
FlyerGameHelper.loadMovieClipAsset
(swfSpriteSheetComponent,
flashgameResources.ASSETS_SWF,
flashgameResources.MOVIE_CLIP_OBSTACLE_PLAYER);
var spriteSheetRenderer:SpriteSheetRenderer = new
SpriteSheetRenderer();
FlyerGameHelper.setupSpriteSheetRenderer
(spriteSheetRenderer,
swfSpriteSheetComponent,
0,
zIndex_uint);
```

9. Each enemy and the player have animation loops. The following are two animation loops you can use to control enemies and players:

```
var idle_animationControllerInfo:AnimationController
Info = new AnimationControllerInfo();
    idle_animationControllerInfo.loop = false;
    idle_animationControllerInfo.frameRate = 1;
    idle_animationControllerInfo.spriteSheet =
swfSpriteSheetComponent;
```

10. Animation loop 2:

```
var move_animationControllerInfo:AnimationController
Info = new AnimationControllerInfo();
    move_animationControllerInfo.loop = true;
    move_animationControllerInfo.frameRate = 1;
    move_animationControllerInfo.maxFrameDelay = 250;
    move_animationControllerInfo.spriteSheet =
swfSpriteSheetComponent;
```

11. The following saves the animation loops for later reuse:

```
var animationController : AnimationController = new
AnimationController ();
    animationController.spriteSheetReference = new
PropertyReference (PlayerGameHelper.RENDER_SPRITE_SHEET);
    animationController.currentFrameReference = new
PropertyReference (PlayerGameHelper.RENDER_SPRITE_INDEX);
    animationController.animations[PlayerGameHelper.
ANIMATION_IDLE] = idle_animationControllerInfo;
    animationController.animations[PlayerGameHelper.
ANIMATION_MOVE] = move_animationControllerInfo;
    animationController.defaultAnimation =
PlayerGameHelper.ANIMATION_IDLE;
    animationController.currentAnimationName=
PlayerGameHelper.ANIMATION_IDLE
    animationController.changeAnimationEvent=
PlayerGameHelper.ANIMATION_CHANGE_EVENT;
    animationController.currentAnimationReference= new
PropertyReference (PlayerGameHelper.CURRENT_ANIMATION_
REFERENCE);
    Player_entity.addComponent(animationController,
PlayerGameHelper.ANIMATION_CONTROLLER);
    Player_entity.addComponent(spriteSheetRenderer,
PlayerGameHelper.RENDER);
```

12. Now add the ActionScript to allow for the correct facing of the enemies:

```
var faceForwardComponent : FaceForwardComponent = new
FaceForwardComponent();
    Player_entity.addComponent (faceForwardComponent,
FaceForwardComponent.NAME);
```

13. Collision detection between the player and enemy objects can be detected with the following:

```
    var collisionDetectComponent : CollisionDetectComponent =
new CollisionDetectComponent();
    Player_entity.addComponent (collisionDetectComponent,
CollisionDetectComponent.NAME);
```

14. And you need code to initialize the whole thing:

```
    Player_entity.initialize("Player_entity");
    }
```

15. The following extends PushButtonEngine and renders the game elements on the screen:

```
    private function _createObstacleEntities ( ) : void
    {
    _createObstacleEntity (flashgameResources.MOVIE_CLIP_
OBSTACLE_SMALLENEMY, new Point (WIDTH*.0,HEIGHT*0.20), 1, 1, 30);
    _createObstacleEntity (flashgameResources.MOVIE_CLIP_
OBSTACLE_BIGENEMY, new Point (WIDTH*.20,HEIGHT*0.40), 2,
-1, 25);
    _createObstacleEntity (flashgameResources.MOVIE_CLIP_
OBSTACLE_SMALLENEMY, new Point (WIDTH*.35,HEIGHT*0.55), 3,
1, 15);
    _createObstacleEntity (flashgameResources.MOVIE_CLIP_
OBSTACLE_BIGENEMY, new Point (WIDTH*.50,HEIGHT*0.70), 4, -1, 35);
    }
    private function _createObstacleEntity (aMovieClipName_
str : String,
    aPosition_point : Point,
    aZIndex_uint: uint,
    aHorizontalDirection_int: int,
    aHorizontalSpeed_num : Number) : void
```

16. The following is used to extend collision detection:

```
    {
    var obstacle_entity:IEntity = PBE.allocateEntity();
    PlayerGameHelper.createSpatialEntity (obstacle_entity,
aPosition_point);
    var collisionType_str : String= "Obstacle";
    var collidesWithCollisionTypes_array : Array =
["Player"];
    PlayerGameHelper.enableCollisionDetection (obstacle_
entity, collisionType_str, collidesWithCollisionTypes_
array, false);
```

17. This identifies the Sprites you will load from the linked SWF asset library:

```
    var swfSpriteSheetComponent : SWFSpriteSheetComponent =
new SWFSpriteSheetComponent();
```

```
    PlayerGameHelper.loadMovieClipAsset
(swfSpriteSheetComponent, flashgameResources.ASSETS_SWF,
aMovieClipName_str);
    var spriteSheetRenderer:SpriteSheetRenderer = new
SpriteSheetRenderer();
    PlayerGameHelper.setupSpriteSheetRenderer
(spriteSheetRenderer, swfSpriteSheetComponent, 0, aZIndex_
uint);
    obstacle_entity.addComponent(spriteSheetRenderer,
PlayerGameHelper.RENDER);
```

18. Horizontal movement is initialized:

```
    var moveHorizontallyComponent:MoveHorizontallyComponent
= new MoveHorizontallyComponent();
    moveHorizontallyComponent.horizontalDirection_int =
aHorizontalDirection_int;
    moveHorizontallyComponent.horizontalSpeed_num =
aHorizontalSpeed_num;
    obstacle_entity.addComponent (
moveHorizontallyComponent, MoveHorizontallyComponent.NAME);
    var screenWrapComponent : ScreenWrapComponent = new
ScreenWrapComponent();
    obstacle_entity.addComponent (screenWrapComponent,
ScreenWrapComponent.NAME);
```

19. Correcting facing of the moving objects is initialized:

```
    var faceForwardComponent : FaceForwardComponent = new
FaceForwardComponent();
    obstacle_entity.addComponent (faceForwardComponent,
FaceForwardComponent.NAME);
    obstacle_entity.initialize("obstacle_entity" + aZIndex_
uint);
    }
    private function _createBackgroundEntity ( ) : void
    {
    var position_point: Point = new Point (0,0);
    var zIndex_uint: uint = 1;
    var background_entity:IEntity = PBE.allocateEntity();
    background_entity.initialize("background_entity");
    PlayerGameHelper.createSpatialEntity (background_
entity, position_point);
    var swfSpriteSheetComponent : SWFSpriteSheetComponent =
new SWFSpriteSheetComponent();
    PlayerGameHelper.loadMovieClipAsset
(swfSpriteSheetComponent, flashgameResources.ASSETS_SWF,
flashgameResources.MOVIE_CLIP_BACKGROUND_GAME_SCREEN);
    var spriteSheetRenderer:SpriteSheetRenderer = new
SpriteSheetRenderer();
    PlayerGameHelper.setupSpriteSheetRenderer
(spriteSheetRenderer, swfSpriteSheetComponent, 0, zIndex_
uint);
```

```
    background_entity.addComponent(spriteSheetRenderer,
PlayerGameHelper.RENDER);
    }
    }
    }
```

20. Now save your file.

21. The final step is to create an empty Flash file that will link to the Class files for the game. Create a new Flash FLA file at the root of your folder. Name the file FlashGameFrogger. fla. Set the publish properties to AIR for Android and create a Class file in the Properties. Edit the Class file to simply extend the FlashGame class you just created, as shown here:

```
package {
import com.mad.projects.flashgame.FlashGame;
public class FlashGameFrogger extends FlashGame {
public function PBFlyerGameDocumentClass() {
super();
}
}
}
```

At this point you can save your work and publish your prototype game. As mentioned before, this is not a fully functional game, but it does give you access to how you can extend PushButtonEngine for your own platform games.

Creating Isometric Worlds with TheoWorlds

Isometric is a term used to describe games such as the original SimCity and The Sims. It looks 3D (you move around a board) but it is really just 2D.

TheoWorlds is very good game environment you can use to develop your Isometric game. The Software Developers Kit from TheoWorlds includes:

- TheoChat, for online chat
- TheoMap Editor, so you can create your own worlds
- Documentation and source code

 You can check it all out at *www.theoworlds.com/*.

Zero Game Development Skills Needed for Platogo

Excited to get your own games developed but do not have the time to learn all the libraries listed in this chapter? Check out Platogo. Platogo is a place where you can go to play Flash games. It also has a great tool you can use to create your own games without needing to learn ActionScript. Platogo has an excellent designer that allows you to build simple, functional games.

Right now it does not fully support mobile platforms but you can fake the games by publishing the SWF and then loading the SWF into your Android games. This method will not work for iPhone (yet).

You can play with Platogo at *www.platogo.com/*.

Developing Your Game

You can have a lot of fun developing games for your mobile device. There are some caveats you need to keep in mind: An Android phone or iOS device is simply not as powerful as a desktop computer. Test, test, and retest your game code on your target devices to ensure that the frame rate and response time is meeting your needs.

With that said, game development is a lot of fun; the inception phase, through the design and develop phases, and even through the QA phases can be very rewarding. It seems that Flash is maturing as one of the world's more important game development environments. Time for you to get your game on! Get it? "Game on"? No? OK, I will leave the pathetic puns alone.

PROJECT: BUILDING A MOBILE GAME

Often the most complex type of app you will build for your mobile device will be a game. There are lots of good reasons for this: games use data, interaction, sound, video, pictures, and more to provide a complex experience. To the person playing the game, the work should just come together. When you play a game you should not be thinking, "Wow, this game must have been very hard to build." All you should be thinking is, "How do I kill this enemy and get to the next level?"

The goal of the project in this chapter (Figure 5.1Proj) is to give you an idea of what is needed to build a game and the types of decisions you need to make for the game to work effectively on a mobile device.

Figure 5.1Proj This project will create a space-shooting game where you blow up meteors.

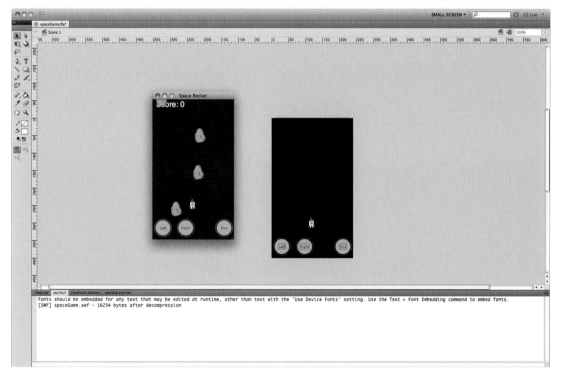

The discipline of game development is changing rapidly on mobile platforms. The type of work you can do today will seem simple in the future. There are two good reasons for this: the first is the processing power of mobile systems. Today's devices are good, but future phones will be even better. The CPU/GPU power of a phone is growing faster than Moore's Law, and a time when phones run close to the same speed as desktop PCs is not far off. The second advancement is coming directly from Adobe: the Flash Player and AIR are being optimized to leverage GPU acceleration in desktop and mobile devices. Future games will be able to run complex, 3D worlds.

Playing Space Rocket

The game you'll be developing is called Space Rocket. In the game you control a rocket that fires missiles and blows up falling rocks. Each exploding rock gives you a score of 5 points.

So, let's see what is going on in this app:

- Controls let you move left and right
- A third control allows you to fire a missile
- Rocks fall randomly down the screen
- A random space background is constantly changing
- The score is calculated as you blow up each rock
- At the end of the game you go to a screen that tells you the game is over and lists your score
- You can tap the end of game screen to replay

As you can see, there is a lot happening. To keep things simple, I have not included any sound or 3D. You can build on top of this project and make it more complicated.

Getting Started

The first step in the project is to create a new Flash movie. This movie will have a lot of action. Rocks, rockets, and background animation are all going at once.

A challenge you have in the mobile world is the speed of the processor running your game. If you have a lot happening on the screen at once then the game play will be slow. So how do you create the illusion of fast animation on a mobile device?

A method you can use to speed up animation is to reduce the size of the screen. When you do this, there are fewer pixels to move. This is the method you will use in the AIR app for Space Rocket.

1. Start Flash and create a new AIR Android app. The principles you use in the AIR Android app will also work for the BlackBerry PlayBook and iOS.
2. The default screen setting is 480 × 800. Change the size of the screen by 50%. This will make the screen 240 × 400 (Figure 5.2Proj). You still want your app to play full screen when it is loaded in Android.
3. A second modification you can make is the frame rate of the game. The default is 24fps. Change it to 15fps. Overall, you will not see much change in the graphic display, but there will be fewer frames allowing the device to keep up with your animation.
4. Open the Android Settings (Figure 5.3Proj) and, from the General tab, select the checkbox for full screen. Now your app will play full screen on any Android device.
5. While you have the Android Settings window open, change the name of the APK file to spaceRocket.apk, and the name of the app as it will appear on the Android device to Space Rocket.
6. Save your Flash project as Space Rocket.

At this point you have the basic structure for you app. Next step is to import graphics.

Figure 5.2Proj The screen resolution has been reduced to reduce the number of pixels that need to be moved on the screen.

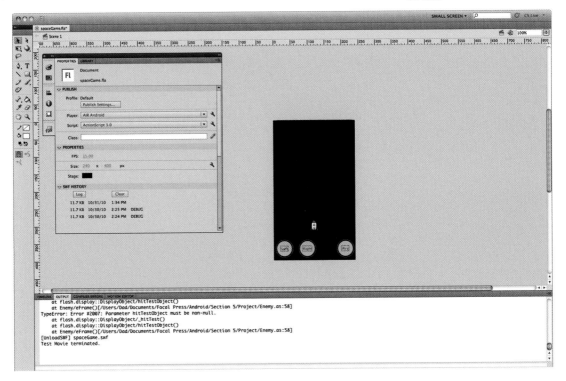

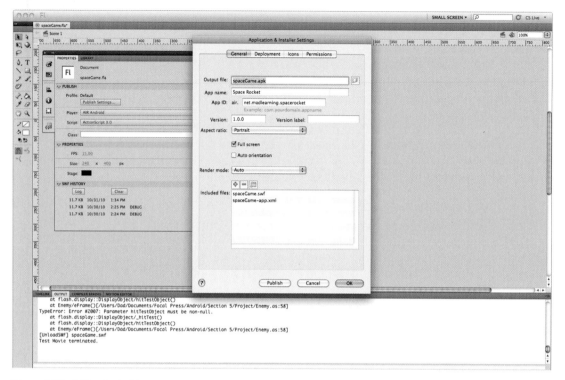

Figure 5.3Proj The Android Settings.

Game Assets and Default Layer Structure

There are three game assets you will use: a rocket, rock, and missile. Each file is included in the library of the game on the website for this book. Download the files from *www.visualizetheweb.com/ flashmobile*.

In the library, notice that there are two elements that have ActionScript Linkage names:

- Bullet
- Enemy

The files themselves reference two additional Class files you will create to control how the missile and enemies react when they collide with objects.

You will see that the default Flash file has a timeline with two frames. The first frame contains the game and the second frame contains the end of the game.

The app is also broken up into the following elements:

Frame 1:

- Left button (mcLeft)
- Right button (mcRight)
- Fire button (mcFire)
- Rocket (mcMain)
- Dynamic white text area at the top of the screen (txtScore)

Frame 2:
- Dynamic white text areas on the screen (txtFinalScore)
- Static text block stating the game is over

All three of the text areas use the default _Sans font.

These are the only assets you need for the game to work. Next, it is time to code.

Adding the Code to the Game

The code for this project is split into three distinct areas:
- Core game code
- Bullet interaction
- Enemy interaction

Let's start with the core game code. In your game, open the Timeline panel and create a new layer called Actions. This is where you will add our ActionScript for the core game code.

1. Open the Actions panel. The first action you will want to add is a stop() action preventing the movie from playing in a loop between the first and second frame. Add the following code:

   ```
   stop();
   ```

2. The second line of code will add a control that lets Flash know that you are going to be using Multitouch controls. No keyboards here:

   ```
   Multitouch.inputMode = MultitouchInputMode.TOUCH_POINT;
   ```

3. You will want to control two main buttons, the left and right buttons. These two buttons will move the rocket left and right. The following two Boolean variables see whether or not the buttons have been pressed.

   ```
   var leftMovement:Boolean = false;
   var rightMovement:Boolean = false;
   ```

4. The mainSpeed integer controls how fast the elements move on the screen. This is again another place where you can control the hardware of your device by keeping the speed low:

   ```
   var mainSpeed:int = 5;
   ```

5. The following integer controls the time, in milliseconds, you want to allow between missile shots:

   ```
   var bulletTime:int = 250;
   ```

6. The bulletTime integer controls the life of the missile. The following setting is 12 frames. In future versions of this game you control the bulletTime speed to be more or less. For instance, a harder game will have the missile dying after four frames.

   ```
   var bulletLimit:int = 12;
   ```

7. The following Boolean looks to see if a missile can be fired. Again, in a future version of this game, you may want to set up a rule such as: if you hit three rocks in a row, you cannot fire your missile for 2 seconds.

```
var shootAllow:Boolean = true;
```

8. The enemyTime integer controls how often a new enemy is made. The value is in milliseconds. Keep the number high to reduce the number of objects simultaneously on the screen.

```
var enemyTime:int = 1000;
```

9. The following specifies the time it takes to create an enemy. The lower the number, the more enemies you have on the screen.

```
var enemyLimit:int = 20;
```

10. The "score" integer holds the value of the score in the game. The default is zero.

```
var score:int = 0;
```

11. The following section of code controls all the interactions of the missile on the screen. We will come back to this later in the chapter.

```
var bulletContainer:MovieClip = new MovieClip();
addChild(bulletContainer);
```

12. Is the game over or not? The gameOver Boolean value can store the state of the game.

```
var gameOver:Boolean = false;
```

13. The following section of ActionScript controls the movements of the rocket. In the code the rocket has the name mcRocket.

```
mcRocket.addEventListener(Event.ENTER_FRAME, moveChar);
function moveChar(event:Event):void{
```

14. The following ActionScript checks that the Booleans are true and adjusts the movement of the rocket.

```
if(leftMovement){
mcRocket.x -= mainSpeed;
}
if(rightMovement){
mcRocket.x += mainSpeed;
}
```

15. The following ensures that the rocket stays on the screen.

```
if(mcRocket.x <= 0){
mcRocket.x += mainSpeed;
}
```

```
if(mcRocket.y <= 0){
mcRocket.y += mainSpeed;
}
if(mcRocket.x >= stage.stageWidth - mcRocket.width){
mcRocket.x -= mainSpeed;
}
if(mcRocket.y >= stage.stageHeight - mcRocket.height){
mcRocket.y -= mainSpeed;
}
```

16. The next section starts the control over the missiles. The first step is to check if you have reached your limit of missiles that can be fired at the same time.

```
if(bulletTime < bulletLimit){
bulletTime ++;
} else {
shootAllow = true;
```

17. When you are done firing missiles you will need to reset the bulletTime.

```
bulletTime = 0;
}
```

18. Now you will want to add rocks falling onto the screen. The first check you need to do is to see how many rocks are on the screen. What is your limit?

```
if(enemyTime < enemyLimit){
```

19. If everything is OK then add a new rock. The ++ adds just one rock. Again, this is a point where you can experiment with the code by stating if you want to add more than one new rock at a time.

```
enemyTime ++;
} else {
```

20. The following is a variable that holds the information needed for a new rock:

```
var newEnemy = new Enemy();
```

21. You do not want the rock to be created on the stage, otherwise it will look like it is blinking into existence. You want to create the illusion that the rock is coming from space. The following code ensures that the enemy is created off the stage.

```
newEnemy.y = -1 * newEnemy.height;
```

22. The following will randomly place the falling rock along the X axis.

```
newEnemy.x = int(Math.random()*(stage.stageWidth -
newEnemy.width));
```

23. Now you can add the new falling rock to the stage.

```
addChild(newEnemy);
```

24. The cacheAsBitmap is an optimization feature for mobile apps. This changes the image into a bitmap. The bitmap file format is managed more efficiently on mobile devices.

```
newEnemy.cacheAsBitmap=true;
enemyTime = 0;
}
```

25. The next section of the game controls the actions when you press the mcFire movie clip. You will be using a single Tap touch event to control the button. To activate the button, the player will need to keep tapping.

```
mcFire.addEventListener(TouchEvent.TOUCH_TAP, fl_
TapHandler);
function fl_TapHandler(event:TouchEvent):void
{
shootAllow = false;
```

26. The first action is to create a new bullet.

```
var newBullet:Bullet = new Bullet();
```

27. You have control over the position of the rocket on the screen. The following will look for the current position of the rocket and move the bullet to that position. In addition, the bullet will divide the width of the rocket by 2 to ensure the bullet fires from the center.

```
newBullet.x = mcRocket.x + mcRocket.width/2 -
newBullet.width/2;
newBullet.y = mcRocket.y;
```

28. The following adds the bullet to the Stage.

```
bulletContainer.addChild(newBullet);
}
var fl_PressTimer:Timer = new Timer(100);
fl_PressTimer.addEventListener(TimerEvent.TIMER, fl_
PressTimerHandler);
function fl_PressTimerHandler(event:TimerEvent):void
{
```

29. Now you want to add code that will control the left and right buttons. Unlike the fire button where a user will be tapping on the screen, you will find that most users will hold down the left or right button. You can emulate a long tap in Flash that, while you hold down the button, the rocket will move.

```
leftMovement = true;
}
```

30. The first step is to add the event listeners.

```
    mcLeft.addEventListener(TouchEvent.TOUCH_BEGIN, fl_
PressBeginHandler);
    mcLeft.addEventListener(TouchEvent.TOUCH_END, fl_
PressEndHandler);
    mcLeft.addEventListener(TouchEvent.TOUCH_OUT, fl_
PressEndHandler);
    mcLeft.addEventListener(TouchEvent.TOUCH_ROLL_OUT, fl_
PressEndHandler);
    function fl_PressBeginHandler(event:TouchEvent):void
    {
```

31. You will be using a timer to control when to start a long tap event.

```
    fl_PressTimer.start();
    }
    function fl_PressEndHandler(event:TouchEvent):void
    {
    fl_PressTimer.stop();
    leftMovement = false;
    }
```

32. The following sets the variable that will hold the value for when to start the long tap. The value is set to 1/10 of a second, or 100 milliseconds.

```
    var RightBtn_PressTimer:Timer = new Timer(100);
    RightBtn_PressTimer.addEventListener(TimerEvent.TIMER,
RightBtn_PressTimerHandler);
    function RightBtn_PressTimerHandler(event:TimerEvent):void
    {
    rightMovement = true;
    }
```

33. You can add the long tap event listeners for the right button.

```
    mcRight.addEventListener(TouchEvent.TOUCH_BEGIN,
rightBtn_PressBeginHandler);
    mcRight.addEventListener(TouchEvent.TOUCH_END,
rightBtn_PressEndHandler);
    mcRight.addEventListener(TouchEvent.TOUCH_OUT,
rightBtn_PressEndHandler);
    mcRight.addEventListener(TouchEvent.TOUCH_ROLL_OUT,
rightBtn_PressEndHandler);
    function rightBtn_PressBeginHandler(event:TouchEvent):void
```

34. As with the left button, a timer is used to control when to start the long tap event.

```
    {
    RightBtn_PressTimer.start();
    }
```

```
      function rightBtn_PressEndHandler(event:TouchEvent):vo
id
      {
      RightBtn_PressTimer.stop();
      rightMovement = false;
      }
```

35. The final piece of code creates the random particles on the stage background.

```
      stage.addEventListener(Event.ENTER_FRAME,
generateParticles);
```

36. The first action is to see if there is already a particle on the stage.

```
      if(particleContainer == null){
```

37. The following movie clip object will hold a new value for a particle object.

```
      var particleContainer:MovieClip = new MovieClip();
      addChild(particleContainer);
      }
      function generateParticles(event:Event):void{
```

38. You do not want hundreds of particles being created all the time. The following will randomly generate how often the particles are created.

```
      if(Math.random()*25 < 2){
```

39. You also do not want all the particles the same shape. Why not have them randomly created from 1 to 5 pixels?

```
      var mcParticle:Shape = new Shape();
      var dimensions:int = int(Math.random()*5)+1;
```

40. Now add color to your shape. Again, these are options you can modify in your own version of the game.

```
      mcParticle.graphics.beginFill(0x999999,1);
      mcParticle.graphics.drawRect(dimensions,dimensions,dime
nsions,dimensions);
```

41. As with the falling rocks, you do not want your particles all appearing at the same point. The following code randomly positions the particles on the screen.

```
      mcParticle.x = int(Math.random()*stage.stageWidth);
      mcParticle.y = -10;
      particleContainer.addChild(mcParticle);
      mcParticle.cacheAsBitmap=true;
      }
```

42. You will want to have your particles fall down the stage using the following ActionScript.

```
for(var i:int=0;i<particleContainer.numChildren;i++){
var theParticle:DisplayObject = particleContainer.
getChildAt(i);
theParticle.y += mainSpeed*.5;
```

43. The following ActionScript looks to see where on the screen the particle is. If it has reached 400 px on the Y axis, the particle will be off the bottom of the screen. ActionScript can now remove the particle and reduce your memory usage.

```
if(theParticle.y >= 400){
particleContainer.removeChild(theParticle);
```

44. The final piece of code is used to update the score.

```
txtScore.text = 'Score: '+score;
}
}
}
}
```

At this point you are very close to being done. You have two final Class files you need to create to control the missiles you fire and the rocks you hit.

Controlling the Missiles

Up to this point in the book you have added Class files mainly to the root Flash movie. Here you are going to see how you can add Class files to movie clips in the library (Figure 5.4Proj). As you would expect, the structure of a Class object on a movie clip is just the same as any Class object.

1. Let's start in Flash Professional. Open the library. Right-click on the Bullet movie clip and choose Properties.

2. The Properties window will open. Expand the Advanced Settings so you see all options. You will see an option called Class (Figure 5.5Proj).

3. Add the class name "Bullet" and select the "Edit Class Definition." An empty class will open.

```
package{
```

4. The first action is to import the objects you will use in this class.

```
import flash.display.MovieClip;
import flash.events.*;
```

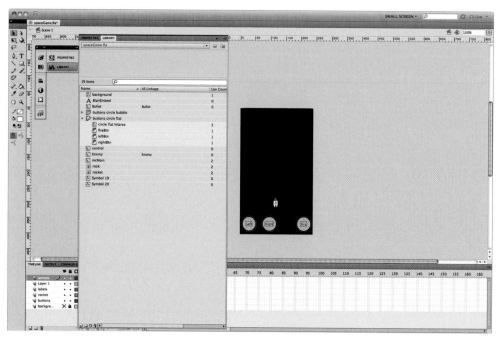

Figure 5.4Proj Class definitions
can be added to movie clips.

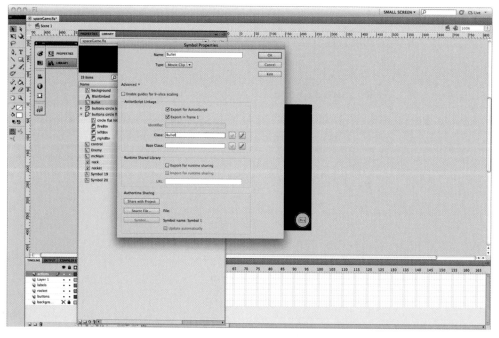

Figure 5.5Proj The class name
can be added in the Symbol
Properties window.

5. The following will force the bullet to act as a movie clip.

```
public class Bullet extends MovieClip{
```

6. The _root variable allows you to target objects on the main stage.

```
private var _root:Object;
```

7. The following variable controls the speed at which the bullet moves.

```
private var speed:int = 10;
```

8. The following function is used every time a missile is on the stage.

```
public function Bullet(){
addEventListener(Event.ADDED, beginClass);
```

9. The following event controls the missile when it is on the screen.

```
addEventListener(Event.ENTER_FRAME, eFrame);
}
private function beginClass(event:Event):void{
_root = MovieClip(root);
}
private function eFrame(event:Event):void{
```

10. The following will move the missile up the screen.

```
y -= speed;
```

11. When the missile hits –1 px on the Y axis it will be removed from the stage.

```
if(this.y < -1 * this.height){
removeEventListener(Event.ENTER_FRAME, eFrame);
_root.bulletContainer.removeChild(this);
}
if(_root.gameOver){
removeEventListener(Event.ENTER_FRAME, eFrame);
this.parent.removeChild(this);
}
}
public function removeListeners():void{
removeEventListener(Event.ENTER_FRAME, eFrame);
}
}
}
```

12. Save your Class file.
You have the first of your two custom Class files.

Controlling the Falling Rocks

The objective of the Falling Rock class is to control how the rocks interact with the missile and the space ship.

1. Right-click on the movie clip in the library called Enemy movie clip and choose properties.
2. The Properties window will open. Expand the settings so you see all options. You will see an option called Class. Add the class name Enemy and select the Edit Class Definition. An empty class will open.

   ```
   package{
   ```

3. Import the Class objects you will be using.

   ```
   import flash.display.MovieClip;
   import flash.events.*;
   ```

4. Now set the Rock to behave like a movie clip.

   ```
   public class Enemy extends MovieClip{
   ```

5. The following variables allow the rock to interact with objects on the main timeline and the speed of the falling rocks.

   ```
   private var _root:Object;
   private var speed:int = 5;
   ```

6. The following function will run every time a rock is added to the screen.

   ```
   public function Enemy(){
   addEventListener(Event.ADDED, beginClass);
   addEventListener(Event.ENTER_FRAME, eFrame);
   }
   private function beginClass(event:Event):void{
   _root = MovieClip(root);
   }
   private function eFrame(event:Event):void{
   ```

7. The following checks to see if the missile collides with a falling rock.

   ```
   for(var i:int = 0;i<_root.bulletContainer.
   numChildren;i++){
   var bulletTarget:MovieClip = _root.bulletContainer.
   getChildAt(i);
   ```

8. Using hitTest, you can do something when objects collide. In this case, if a missile hits the rock, the rock is removed from the screen.

   ```
   if(hitTestObject(bulletTarget)){
   removeEventListener(Event.ENTER_FRAME, eFrame);
   _root.removeChild(this);
   _root.bulletContainer.removeChild(bulletTarget);
   bulletTarget.removeListeners();
   ```

9. When a missile hits a rock, the score is increased by 5.

```
_root.score += 5;
  }
}
```

10. What happens if the rock hits your rocket? Dude, you lose. The following hitTest advances the game to the final screen.

```
if(hitTestObject(_root.mcRocket)){
_root.gameOver = true;
_root.gotoAndStop(2);
}
if(_root.gameOver){
removeEventListener(Event.ENTER_FRAME, eFrame);
this.parent.removeChild(this);
}
}
public function removeListeners():void{
this.removeEventListener(Event.ENTER_FRAME, eFrame);
}
}
}
```

11. Save your file.

At this point you are ready to play your game. Connect your Android device to your computer and publish your app. You will see that by controlling the screen size, the number of objects on the screen, and by forcing objects into bitmaps you have created a fast-paced arcade game.

There is a lot you can do with this game by modifying variables. Play around and have fun.

DEPLOYING MOBILE APPS WITH FLASH CS5

You've done it. You have your app ready to go into the wild and make some money; but you are not quite there yet. In this final chapter you will see what you need to do to get your app online and ready for people to purchase. You will cover the following:

- Building your app for deployment using iTunes Connect
- Building your app for deployment on the Android Market
- Building for iPad devices
- Building for Android tablets and Google TV
- Adding advertising to your apps
- Tracking your app's success
- Marketing your app

This may sound contrary, but I often find that making your application available to the world is the most painful part of selling your app—particularly when it comes to Apple's iTunes. So, without much ado, let's start with the most painful process you will ever endure: submitting an app to iTunes.

Deploying Your Apps to Apple's iTunes

Apple's iTunes Store is an amazing success story: 250,000+ apps and 6 billion downloads is nothing to sneeze at. There are many success stories of groups making millions from Apple. But, before you can get any money, you need to have your app ready for deployment.

Let's step through what you need to do to package an app for iTunes App Store.

1. You will first need to go to the Provisioning section of the iOS Developer Program Portal (Figure 6.1; *https://developer.apple.com/ios/manage/overview/index.action*).
2. Select the Distribution tab.

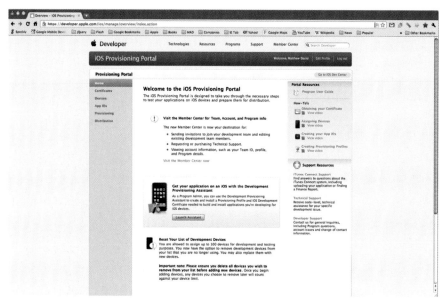

Figure 6.1 Apple's iOS Provisioning Portal; you will need to start here with every app you create for the iPhone.

3. Choose the New Profile button (Figure 6.2).
4. Choose App Store as the Distribution Method.
5. Provide a name for your app.

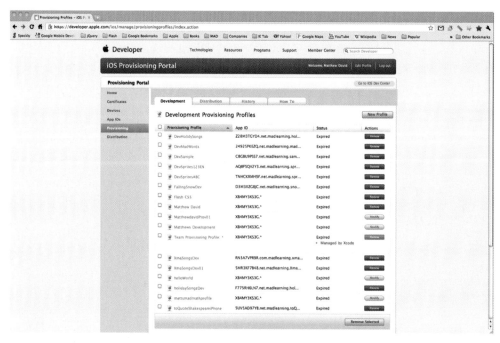

Figure 6.2 Create a new Profile for your app.

6. Select the App ID from the drop-down list that matches the app you are going to deploy (Figure 6.3).
7. Select the Submit button. You will be taken to the main Distribution Provisioning Profile page. Your new profile will take about 30 seconds to generate.
8. Select the Download button to save the new App Store profile to your desktop.
9. Open Flash and locate the Flash movie you have been working on.
10. Open the Properties panel.
11. Expand the Publish settings so you can see the different publishing profiles.
12. Select the iPhone Profile Edit button. The iPhone settings window will open (Figure 6.4).
13. Select the Deployment tab. At this time you will want to change the provisioning profile to the App Store Distribution Profile you downloaded (Figure 6.5).
14. Change the certificate to a published certificate P12 file (Figure 6.6).
15. Select Deployment > App Store from iPhone Deployment Type.

Figure 6.3 Selecting the different options for your app profile.

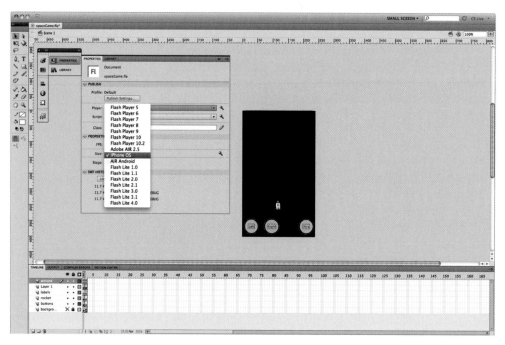

Figure 6.4 Setting iOS as the
default build type.

Figure 6.5 iOS Properties you
can modify in Flash.

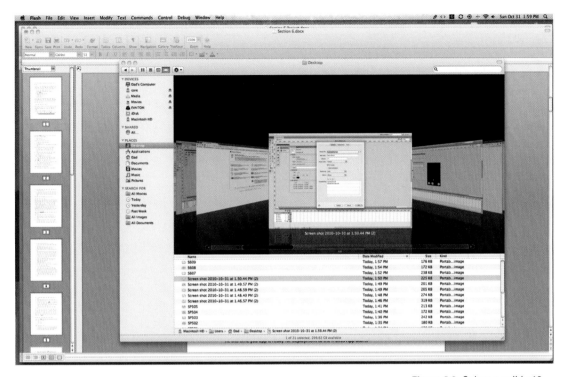

Figure 6.6 Select a valid p12 certificate.

16. Press the Publish button. It will take 6 to 10 minutes for your app to be created.
17. A new iPhone IPA file will be created in the same folder as your Flash files when the process has been completed.
18. Locate the IPA file. You will need to change the extension of the file from IPA to ZIP. Both file formats are container formats. That is, they contain all the files needed for the app to run; however, iTunes Connect will accept files only in ZIP format.

At this time your app is ready for deployment to the iTunes App Store.

Using iTunes Connect to Publish Your App

You are now very close to having an app available on the iTunes store. Can't you feel the rush! You could be selling thousands of apps in a matter of a few days. The gap between you and riches is just Apple's iTunes Connect publishing tool. You are very close now.

You will be using a new website to upload your final iPhone apps. The site is called iTunes Connect (Figure 6.7; *https:// itunesconnect.apple.com/*). In every sense, iTunes Connect is your business relationship with Apple. The site allows you to

Figure 6.7 Apple's iTunes Connect is the place where you will manage your applications.

set up your contracts, tax records, banking information, review sales trends, download financial reports, and manage your In App Purchases. You will need to complete these sections in order to sell your app in iTunes. This section is going to focus on the important part of iTunes Connect: managing your applications.

There are some tasks you can complete before you upload your app. They are:

1. Create your iPhone app in Flash Professional and compress the IPA into a ZIP.
2. Convert the 512 × 512 PNG pixel image into a JPG image. Label the new file 512.jpg.
3. You will need at least one screen shot of your app as it appears in your iPhone. Fortunately there is a very easy way to do that. At any time when your app is playing on your iPhone press the Home and Sleep buttons at the same time. The screen will flash and a screen shot will be taken of your app. The image is stored in your Camera Roll and is exactly the same size Apple needs.
4. When you have completed these three tasks you will need to go to *https://itunesconnect.apple.com*. Use your Apple Developer ID and password to log into the site.
5. Select Manage Your App from iTunes Connect. You will be taken to a screen where you can add new apps and review apps you are selling.

6. Select the Add New App button to start the process of creating a new iTunes app.

7. For the most part, the content you enter on the summary screen can be edited after your app has been submitted. There are two sections that cannot change: Application Name and Keywords. Ensure that you select a name that accurately describes what you are selling. You are allowed up to 100 characters of keywords. Use your Search Engine Optimization experience to add keywords that categorize your app. These two sections are very important.

8. The remaining fields allow you to add a description, submit the app to main categories, add copyright, version number (start with 1.0), SKU number, application/support URL, and support e-mail.

9. Upload a 512.jpg for the large icon.

10. Upload a 480 × 320 jpg image for the primary screenshot.

11. Add one to four 480 × 320 jpg images for the additional screenshots. You will get a green check mark for each successfully loaded image.

12. Select Continue to go to the Pricing and Availability screen.

13. You do not get to select a specific price for your app. Instead, Apple lists a number of tiers from which you can choose. At first glance this may seem frustrating but what Apple has done is to remove the pain of selling with different currencies. A Tier 2 app will be $0.99 in the United States, 59 pence in England, and AU$1.29 in Australia. There are over 70 different currencies that Apple manages for you. You can also choose to have screens that show the app going on sale in different countries.

14. Select the Continue button when you have completed the page. Submit the screen.

15. You will need to be on a Mac and use Apple's Application Loader to upload your packaged app to the iTunes App Store.

16. Using the Application Loader app, upload your ZIPed IPA file. The upload will take about 20 minutes. The upload is checking for some basic settings such as including the correct profile. If everything is OK then you will get an e-mail letting you know that the file has been uploaded successfully.

17. The availability option allows your app to go on sale at a specific time in the future.

18. At this point you get to review all of your content and press the Submit button.

Apple has done a lot to improve the review process for new apps. Today it takes only 5 to 7 business days for an app to be approved by Apple and appear in iTunes. I have had personal experience where an app can get rejected because the description text is not 100% correct. It can get frustrating, but once you are in the App Store you can expect exposure to 100+ million iOS devices.

Deploying Your Apps to Google's Android Market

In contrast to Apple's *uber* complex process, Google's Android Market is very easy to use. Essentially, you need three things:

- A Google account
- An APK app ready to go
- $25

Let's step through what you need to do:

1. Before going to the Android Market you will need to create an APK file that can be uploaded to the store. An APK file is the package format Google uses for Android apps. No need to compress your app into a ZIP folder.

2. Open Flash and go to your Android app. Open the Android settings and select Deployment. As this now is going to be a real app, you need to create a valid certificate. Make sure the certificate has a life of 25 years (it is the default, but double check).

3. Choose Device as the deployment mechanism. Select Publish and an APK file will be created. Now you are ready for the Android Market (Figure 6.9).

4. Start by going to *http://market.android.com*. This is the place where you will upload your apps.

Figure 6.8 As you can see, the app is the same as the iOS app, but Flash allows you to quickly change the app to an Android version.

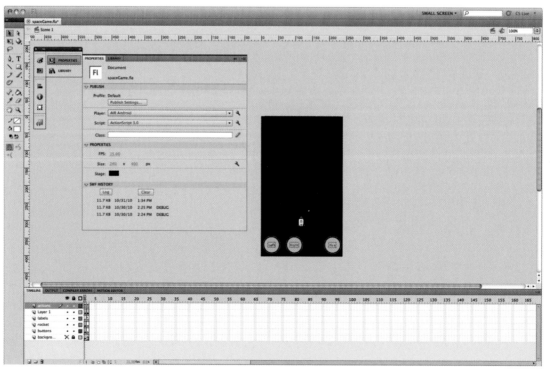

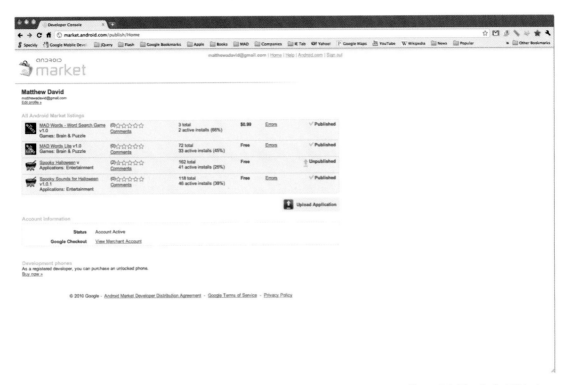

Figure 6.9 The Android Market.

5. In the bottom left-hand corner of the page is a developer's link. If you blink, you might miss it. Click on the link to start the process to become a developer. You can also write in the following URL: *http://market.android.com/publish/Home*

6. You will be asked to log in with your Google Gmail account. It has to be a Google account and not a Google Apps account.

7. You will have to pay $25.

8. When you have gone through all this, you will land on a page that will list all of your Android apps.

9. Before adding your first app, select the Merchant Account link. Selecting this link will allow people to purchase apps and, more importantly, allow you to get paid. The pay scale is 70:30—you get 70% and the carrier gets 30%.

10. Unlike Apple's complex submission process, you only need to complete five sections of content all on one page. They are: Upload Assets, Listing Details, Publishing Options, Contact Information, and Consent.

11. The Upload Assets section allows you to upload your APK file created from Flash, two screen shots, and one promotional image.

12. The Listing Details allow you to name your application and provide a description. You can choose any name you like.

13. The important part of the process is price. You can choose either free or U.S. dollars. A free app can never be converted into a paid app. The U.S. dollars option also allows you to name any price, from $0.01 to as high as you want to go. The ability to price your apps is a big difference between Apple and Google.

14. The final three sections are merely paperwork saying that you have approved the app for sale.

15. Hit Save at the bottom of the screen and you are live. There is no process check. You app is immediately live.

As you can see, the process for deploying to the Android Market is much easier than Apple iTunes Store. Both Apple and Google continue to tweak the way the market stores works for them.

Building for iPad Devices

There are over 120 million iOS devices on the market. Interestingly, the iPad accounts for 10% of the market. What is more interesting is that many analysts expect the iPad to eventually outsell handheld devices. There has never been a product launch as successful as the iPad—including the DVD player, the iPod, and the iPhone. Good thing Flash lets you build for the iPad.

As you might expect, developing for the iPad is almost identical to the iPhone in Flash Professional. After all, you are still using the same Flash, the same ActionScript, and the same process to build your API files.

But there are some differences. The main difference is the overall screen size. The iPad has a screen resolution of 1024 × 768 pixels. This gives you dramatically more room to work with than the iPhone screen. The current iPad supports 132 ppi images, but it is fully expected that the next version will also support the super high-density 320 ppi images used in the iPhone 4 Retina display. With that said, you can use some gorgeous images on the iPad.

The overall speed of the iPad is very good. The iPad was the first device from Apple to support the A4 System-on-Chip design that later appeared on the iPhone 4 and iPod Touch. The iPad has less RAM than the iPhone 4. This can be a problem when creating apps that use a lot of data. For instance, you may have an app with two or more video screens going at once. You will see a frame rate drop if you do that.

Memory management is something you need to be conscious of when you develop for the iPad. The main issue you are presented with is the large screen. A larger screen means more pixels. Even with a faster chip than the iPhone 3GS, you will still see dropped frame rates if you have large animation sequences.

Finally, when you are packaging your iPad app there are two additional steps you need to take. The first is to ensure that you use a large Default.png screen image. The screen size is 1024 × 768 pixels. The second is that you will want to add a new launch icon that will show up on the iPad. The icon will need to be 72 × 72 pixels.

With this all in mind, the development and submission process for the iPad is almost identical.

Building for Tablets and TV

It is likely that 2011 will be known as the year the tablets went to war. In 2010 Apple released the iPad to massive success. Other hardware companies, such as Dell and Samsung, are pushing out their own tablets running a slew of different technologies, the most popular being Android.

The problem is that Google has already stated that Android 2.2 is *not* the tablet version of Android. The tablets Dell and others are pushing out are, in many respects, big phones. Google is pushing for Android 3.5 to support tablets. Expect that in early 2011. As with the iPad, expect each Android Tablet to have its quirks. Will Adobe be there to support your work? Well, it is there already.

But there are other tablets on the market. BlackBerry's PlayBook tablet is a real tablet; to create apps on the device you have to use AIR. A third operating system that hardware companies are looking to use for tablet form factors is Microsoft's Windows 7. AIR has been supported on Windows 7 for two years.

Today, Flash Professional gives you the tools to target all the popular tablets on the market. Watch the tablet wars take shape in 2011—mark my words, this is the next "big deal."

So what about the news around Smart TVs? There is Google TV, Apple TV 2 (running iOS), and many other smaller companies. What about these groups?

Over the last two decades many companies have tried to convert the way we consume TV. Frankly, no one has succeeded. The core problem is that watching TV is a passive experience done within a group. When you are sitting down watching a show, doesn't it drive you nuts when someone else in the room has the remote control and insists on channel surfing? Imagine what it will be like when that same person has a keyboard and, in the middle of your favorite show, decides to update their Facebook page?

It will likely be 2012 or even 2013 before anything happens with apps on the TV. Of course, Flash is already there. Google TV is built on Android and Apple's TV is built on iOS. Both are not

Publishing Universal Apps

 Flash does give you the ability to build apps that will publish to both the iPhone and iPad. These are called Universal Apps. You will need to experiment with this process to get it right. My personal experience is that some apps port well as Universal Apps and others simply do not. Try it out.

accepting third-party apps yet. But both have the potential, and Google has already said they want apps.

You may want to take this progression in developing your first apps: develop for handheld devices, then tablets, and wait to see what happens with Smart TVs.

Adding Advertising to Your Apps

You hear it all the time: how can I make money from my apps? This is not an easy question to answer.

The current implementation of app development in Flash really only allows for you to either sell or give your apps away for free. Currently, Adobe does not easily support advertising or in-app purchases in your apps. But, expect this to change as the ability to add advertising and in-app purchases comes to mobile AIR.

Both ad and in-app supported models are based on a business model called Freemium. The concept is this: Give away your apps and eliminate the purchase barrier but then make money later.

The advertising model is an easy model to understand. Two groups are emerging as the leaders for mobile ad revenue: AdMob (owned by Google) and Apple's iAds.

In-app purchasing is a model where you give away your game but to add additional levels or buy virtual goods you allow a user to purchase these features on the game. This is the approach Zynga uses for its wildly popular FarmVille—need more virtual currency, then buy it with real cash.

There are real benefits to the Freemium model. Experiment with selling and giving apps away for free. You will be surprised how many downloads you get when you give away your app. The difference can be a 100:1.

Of course, the Freemium model requires that Adobe provide a vehicle for developers to use it. It will be surprising if they do not.

Tracking Your App's Success

You have built your app, you have made money from sales, and you need to go to the next stage: building version 2.0. How do you go about that? Often, when you are building an app, it is difficult to tell how well your customers are receiving it. What is the most popular level of a game? Is feature XYZ being used in the app? How often is the app played each day and in which country?

In other words, how do you track your app's success? A tool used by many website owners to track user activity on a website is Google Analytics. Fortunately, there is a version of Google Analytics you can use for your Flash apps.

To get started you will need to go to the following web address: *http://code.google.com/apis/analytics/docs/tracking/flash TrackingIntro.html*

From here, Google provides ways you can add Google Analytics tracking to your applications. This applied to all Flash applications, not just apps. We will get into the details of using the tracking in the project after this chapter.

To use Analytics you will need to have a registered Analytics account. You can do that at the following web address: *www. google.com/analytics/*. The sign-up process is very easy. For your work, you will get a Google Analytics ID. It will look something like this: UA-XXXXXXXXX. Once you have the UA ID then you will be able to successfully add analytics to your apps.

The Google Analytics website is always expanding and offering new features and services. Check out the following YouTube channels for more information on Google Mobile and Google Analytics:

- *www.youtube.com/user/GoogleMobile*
- *www.youtube.com/user/GoogleWebmasterHelp*

These tools will give you additional knowledge to make more informed decisions about how to expand your apps.

Marketing Your Apps

The final step you need to take with your apps is to market them. At the end of the day this really comes down to two things: (1) writing a lot about your apps to increase interest in them and (2) buying ad space. There is no holy grail solution when it comes to marketing. Yes, there are some companies who have had runaway success without spending a single dime on advertising, but they are the exception, not the rule.

Check out how Chase is marketing its apps: it uses conventional TV ads. Other companies, such as Zynga, make frequent posts to their blogs and take advantage of viral advertising on websites such as Facebook. And yet other companies (such as the makers of Doodle Jump—one of my personal favorite games) use Twitter as the main tool for advertising.

What I am saying is this: There are no clear and defined paths for marketing your apps. What you need to do is experiment with all of them to see which models get the best response. It will be a lot of hard work but the result will be worth it.

Summary

It seems like a contrary thing to say, but creating your app is the easy task for a developer: selling your app is hard work. First you need to choose which market store you will be selling your app through and then you need to track the sales process to see how well your app is doing. There will be times when you take an iOS app and port it to another platform. When you do this make sure you update your Google Analytics tracking so you keep track of the sales for each platform.

Finally, you need to tell the world that they must buy your app. Reach in and channel your inner sales skills. It may take a village to raise a child; it certainly takes a team to sell an app. But get your apps out there. Mobile devices are the next wave of technology; time to jump onto a new train to find out where it takes you.

PROJECT: PUBLISHING YOUR APPS INTO THE MANY DIFFERENT APP STORES

The focus of this project is not the creation of an iOS or Android app: It is the publication process. If I have said it once, I have said it a thousand times: Creating your app is the easy task. Publishing is a pain in the....

By the time you finish this project you will be able to successfully submit your app to the iTunes App Store and Google's Android Market.

Choosing Where to Sell Your Application

Why is publishing an app so difficult? Well, it depends on where you are publishing. All online app stores are not created equal. Are you just targeting the iPhone crowd? Do you want your app on Android devices? What about BlackBerry?

Currently, Flash Professional will build apps that you can submit to the following:

- Apple's iTunes App Store
- Google's Android Market (Figure 6.1Proj)

The list is increasing regularly. The challenge you have is to understand all the different requirements each store has.

Did I mention that the list of stores is growing? Here are more stores coming during 2011:

- Verizon and T-Mobile Market Stores
- Amazon Market Store
- BlackBerry PlayBook Market Store
- Android App Store
  In addition, Adobe will also likely support stores such as:
- Windows Phone 7
- Direct-to-TV devices, such as Sony Blu-ray App Store
- Nokia's Symbian and MeeGo App Stores

The goal for Adobe is developing an application that can run anywhere on any device on any screen size. This makes it a challenge for you as the developer to understand where to place your focus.

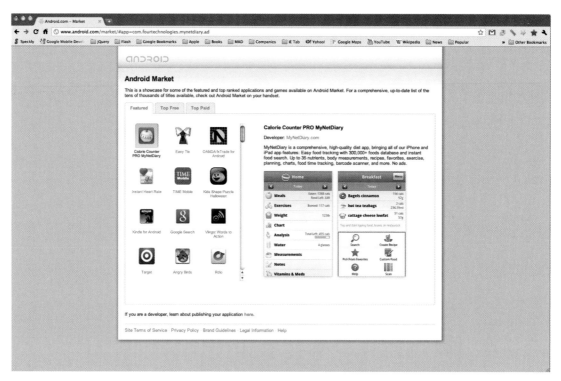

Figure 6.1Proj The Android Market.

For now, the two leaders are Apple and Google. Apple services hundreds of millions of customers with its App Store and Google is catching up fast. No doubt a third company will follow suit.

To demonstrate the different steps you need to take, you can use the Space Rocket game you created in the previous project as the app you will be submitting to different app stores.

Publishing Android Apps in Your Own Store

Let's start with the easiest app submission process: deploying an Android app directly from your own website.

1. Start by opening the Space Rocket game you created earlier.
2. Open the Android settings.
3. Select the second tab, Deployment, and change the Deployment Type to Device Release.
4. Publish your app.
5. You now have an APK file. To publish this app from your website, all you have to do is upload the APK to your website and link to it. When a customer comes to your website using their Android phone and selects the link, the APK file will install on their Android phone.

How about that? Super easy, wasn't it?

Now, let's take it up a notch and head over to Google's Android Market.

Deploying to the Android Market

As with publishing an app to your website, the Android Market will require an APK file. There are some additional steps you need to take to make sure your app can be accepted.

1. Open the Space Rocket Flash movie.
2. From the Properties panel select the Android settings and open the Application & Installer Settings window.
3. You have four taps you can control: General, Deployment, Icons, and Permissions (Figure 6.2Proj).
4. Select the General tab.
5. In the previous chapter you gave your app a name. Now you must give your app an ID, a unique identifier for your app. The convention is this: com.websitename.appname. So, if your website is *www.focalpress.com* and you have an app called SpaceRocket, then you would write com.focalpress.spacerocket.
6. Select the Deployment tab.
7. From Deployment Type, choose Device Release.

Figure 6.2Proj Publish settings for Android deployment.

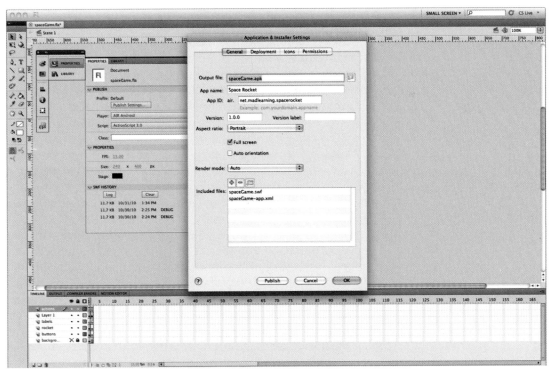

8. In the certificate section, press the New button. You will need to create a 25-year certificate for your app. After 25 years the customer will need to update the app (but what they should really do is replace their phone—can you imagine how out of date a 25-year mobile is?).

9. Select the Icons tab.

10. You do not need to have icons when you submit your app to the Android Market Store, but it really helps. There are three different icon sizes you need: 36 × 36, 48 × 48, and 72 × 72. Unlike Apple iTunes App Store icon requirements, you can have icons with a transparent background. This is easily done using Adobe's Fireworks.

11. Finally, select the Permissions tab. Select the hardware features used in the app. If you have a link to a web page, you must select the INTERNET option.

12. Now you can publish your APK file.

13. Once you have your APK file, head over to the Google Android Market at *http://market.android.com.*

14. If you have not already done so, register as an Android developer. This will set you back $25 but will give you access to a global market. I think it is a fair deal.

15. Google's submission process places a focus on simplicity. You have most of the files you need to submit to the Android Market Store. You will add a couple more in a moment.

16. To get started loading a new app, go to the following URL after you have been accepted into the program: *http://market .android.com/publish/Home.*

17. This page is your landing app management page. It allows you to see at a glance all the apps you are selling, how many have been sold, any errors that have been reported, and, most importantly, a button to upload a new app.

18. Select the Upload Application button; you will be taken to a single page where Google is going to ask you for a few details. Nothing too crazy, you just need to provide a title for your app, a description (you only get 325 characters, so make it good), a promotional description (even fewer characters, 80, so think Twitter text), and you can choose which type of app you are uploading. (Figure 6.3Proj)

19. In addition, pick out whether the app is free or has a price. If you make the app free, then you can never charge a price for it in the future. Bummer. If you do add a price, then the price will be U.S. dollars. All transactions for new apps is managed by Google Checkout. Using Google Checkout means that when someone buys something from you, you receive the payment in 48 hours.

20. The most important part of the Upload an Application screen is the first section of the screen: Uploading Assets.

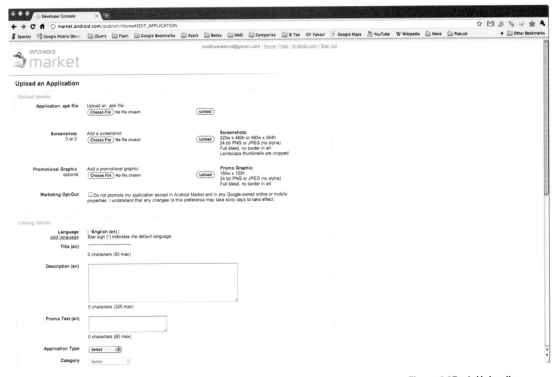

Figure 6.3Proj Uploading a new app to the Android Market.

21. Choose and upload the APK file you created.
22. You will also need to develop two screen shot images. Take screen shots of the app from your phone. There are several apps you can get that will help you with this (such as Edward Kim's Screenshot It). The two images you need to create should be either 20w × 480h or 480w × 854h.
23. You also have the option of creating a small Promo Image (180 × 120). I would create one. You never know when Google will use your app for a promotion.
24. Complete the rest of the Upload page (checking boxes, mostly) and select Publish. Your app is now immediately available for sale to all countries the Android Market services.

That's it. The Google app submission process is very easy. The hard process comes next: Apple's iTunes App Store.

Running the Gauntlet That Is Apple's iTunes App Store Submission Process

The third part of this project is to successfully submit an app to Apple's iTunes App Store. This is not an easy accomplishment. Typically, I put aside one to two hours to step through the

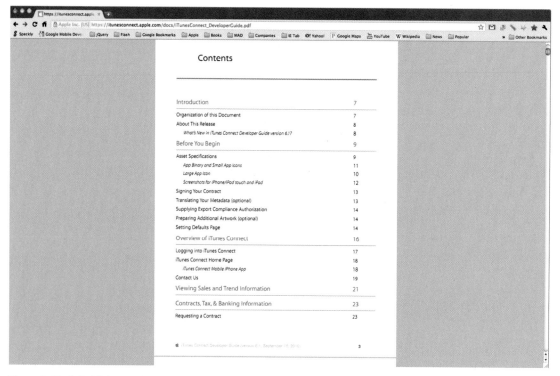

Figure 6.4Proj Publish settings for Android deployment.

process. Apple has made the process so complicated that you need to download a submission guide. The document can be found at *https://itunesconnect.apple.com/docs/iTunesConnect_ DeveloperGuide.pdf.* (Figure 6.4Proj).

Amazingly, Apple's submission guide is over 170 pages. In addition, Apple changes its rules and process regularly. For instance, in February 2010 you could submit apps created with Flash to the App Store, then in March you could not, then in September Apple once again changed its mind. During this time the screens you use to submit your apps also changed three times.

With that said, the following steps are guidelines. I fully expect that some of these steps will have changed by the time you come to read this book. Just send me an e-mail if you have any questions.

So, before we jump into the process, why do we need to submit apps to Apple's App Store? The answer is numbers: 120 million iOS devices. The market for Apple's iOS is huge. It includes phones (iPhone), portable game systems (iPod Touch), Tablets (iPad), and soon, the Apple TV (it runs iOS, too). These are all systems running today. A simply huge market.

So, without further ado, let's jump in.

1. As with Google Android Market, there are two steps you need to go through in creating an iPhone App: building the IPA file and the submission process. Start by opening the Space Rocket game you created earlier. In File Settings, change the publish type to iOS.

2. Open the iOS Settings. You will see you have three tabs: General, Deployment, and Icons. (Figure 6.5Proj)

3. The General tab allows you to name the app as it appears on the screen in iOS; choose the target device and select where you are saving your final IPA file. Something to note is that the IPA file you create is an iOS 3 app, not iOS 4.

4. Select the Deployment tab. This is one of two hard sections. Adobe has a helper file you can view at *http://help.adobe.com/ en_US/as3/iphone/index.html*, which walks you through adding a Developer/Release certificate. You will be creating an IPA for submission to the iTunes App Store. You will want to use your Release iOS Certificate.

5. In addition, you will need to download a Deployment Provisioning Profile from the iTunes App Store. Again, Adobe covers the details, but it essentially requires that you go to Apple's Developer site (*http://developer.apple.com/ios*), register your app, and create a deployment profile.

Figure 6.5Proj Publish settings for iOS deployment.

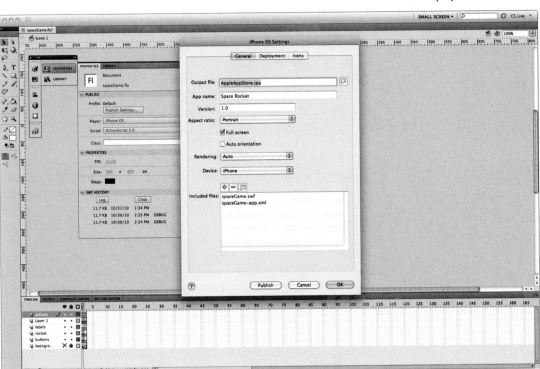

6. The AppID is the name you give the application on Apple's Developer site.

7. The final step is to create the icons for your app. There are five different icons you need to create: 29 × 29, 48 × 48 (for iPad), 57 × 57, 72 × 72 (for iPad), 512 × 512.

8. Select OK and build your app. Cross your fingers you got it all right. Don't get too frustrated if you have to review Adobe's documents a few times the first time you try this process (or the seventh or twentieth), because you have to remember a lot of different things for the application build to work correctly.

9. Now you have an IPA file that works correctly. When you are developing your app, use a Developer version of the Provisioning Profile to load the app, via iTunes, onto your iPhone. Capture screen shots of your app by pressing the Home and Close buttons together. There will be a screen shutter sound and an image of your screen will be saved to the Camera Roll. Take a few of these, you will need them in the submission process.

10. You will need to compress your IPA file into a ZIP file. The iTunes App Store will only accept applications in ZIP format from Flash Professional.

11. Applications for the iTunes App Store are all managed through Apple's iTunes Connect website: *http://itunesconnect.apple.com.*

12. Apple provides you with a lot of different tools and services at this site, but for now, the focus is on uploading a new application.

13. Select the Manage Your Applications button. You will see a list of all the applications you have written.

14. Select Add New App.

15. The first screen will ask you to give your app a name and a SKU (Figure 6.6Proj). These can be anything you want.

16. The third option requires that you associate your new app with a named app from the iOS Developers site. Select Continue when you have these options selected.

17. The next screen requires that you add metadata about your app (Figure 6.7Proj). This includes Keywords, Description (6500-character limit, so get as descriptive as possible), and the primary and secondary category for the app.

18. You will also need to upload screen shots of the app and a 512 × 512 image. This is where you use the screen shots you took earlier on your iPhone.

19. Save your settings. You will be taken to a summary screen of your settings. Select the View Details button. When you go to the metadata summary screen you will see a blue button named Ready to Upload App. Select the button.

20. You will be asked if the application has encryption. Do not use encryption for your first app to keep things easy. Say "no" on this screen.

Figure 6.6Proj Uploading a new app to iTunes Connect.

Figure 6.7Proj Adding metadata to your application.

21. The next screen lets you know that now is the time to upload your app—BEWARE: MAC ONLY AREA. Sorry folks, by the time you get to this screen you will see that you need to download an OS X app to upload your app. There is no Windows love on the Apple iTunes Store.

22. Download and install the Application Loader app.

23. Open the Application Loader. The first thing it will ask you is for your iTunes Connect ID and Password. Enter both. A list of the new apps waiting to be submitted will appear in a drop-down. Select the app you want to upload from the drop-down. The next screen will ask you to find the ZIP file containing the app.

24. Click the next screen to upload the app.

25. You will receive an e-mail letting you know that your app has been submitted to the iTunes App Store.

26. Now you need to wait. It could be a week or two before your app is reviewed. The review also does not mean your app will be accepted. My personal experience for the 24 iTunes apps I have submitted has been a 1:4 rejection ratio. So far, not one rejection has been due to the app not working. It is typically for more weird and obscure reasons. You will no doubt have fun finding these out.

At this point, you have submitted your app to the iTunes App Store and you are ready to start making money.

During this project you did not create anything tangible, such as a game, but you covered what I think is the hardest and most rewarding element of creating applications: submitting to online stores.

Adobe is working on ways in which you can submit to many online stores more easily. Watch what they are doing carefully as the online market stores will continue to increase due to a simple reason: they work. Both the iTunes App Store and Android Market provide evidence that customers like having all their apps in one place. Get used to submitting your apps to many stores.

INDEX

Note: Page numbers followed by *b* indicate boxes, *f* indicate figures and *t* indicate tables.